This book belongs to:

Table of Contents

Table of Contents

I Can Checklist:

Number Sense

Read, represent, compose, and decompose whole numbers up to and including 1000, using a variety of tools and strategies, and describe various ways they are used in everyday life. For example,

- ***I can*** *say and write numbers all the way to 1000.*
- ***I can*** *break up numbers into parts and put them together again.*
- ***I can*** *use numbers in real life, like counting my steps to walk 500 steps.*

Compare and order whole numbers up to and including 1000, in various contexts. For example,

- ***I can*** *tell which number is bigger or smaller when I see two numbers.*
- ***I can*** *line up numbers from the smallest to the biggest and vice versa.*

Round whole numbers to the nearest ten or hundred, in various contexts. For example,

- ***I can*** *round numbers to the nearest ten.*
- ***I can*** *round numbers to the nearest hundred.*

Count to 1000, including by 50s, 100s, and 200s, using a variety of tools and strategies. For example,

- ***I can*** *count all the way to 1000.*
- ***I can*** *count by 50s, 100s, and 200s, like saying 200, 400, 600, until I reach 1000.*

Use place value when describing and representing multi-digit numbers in a variety of ways, including with base-ten materials. For example,

- ***I can*** *tell what each digit in a number means.*
- ***I can*** *show a number using items like blocks or beads.*

Counting Practice

1. Count forward by **2s**. Fill in the missing numbers.

763							

2. Count forward by **5s**. Fill in the missing numbers.

660							

3. Count forward by **10s**. Fill in the missing numbers.

305							

4. Count forward by **25s**. Fill in the missing numbers.

375							

5. Count backward by **10s**. Fill in the missing numbers.

855							

6. Count backward by **100s**. Fill in the missing numbers.

935							

7. Count backward by **20s**. Fill in the missing numbers.

140							

8. Counting backward by 5s from 425, which three numbers should come next?

a. **420, 415, 410** b. **435, 430, 425** c. **415, 405, 395**

Ordering Numbers

Numbers can be ordered from least to greatest, or from greatest to least.

least to greatest	greatest to least
620, 627, 632	**632, 627, 620**

1 Circle the greatest number in each pair.

a 744 or 767 b 215 or 155 c 541 or 554 d 101 or 98

2 Circle the least number in each pair.

a 899 or 980 b 442 or 439 c 199 or 299 d 801 or 789

3 Order the numbers from least to greatest.

a 25, 15, 75, 90, 35 ______, ______, ______, ______, ______

b 196, 89, 202, 178, 95 ______, ______, ______, ______, ______

4 Order the numbers from greatest to least.

a 560, 506, 416, 656, 516 ______, ______, ______, ______, ______

b 67, 75, 83, 61, 74 ______, ______, ______, ______, ______

5 Manuel's lemonade stand sold the following amounts in June:

$54, $38, $67, $51, $49, $54

Sort the amounts from greatest to least.

________, ________, ________, ________, ________, ________

I can order numbers.

Greater Than, Less Than, and Equal

Compare numbers using one of these math symbols:

>	<	=
greater than	less than	equal to
85 > 40	**14 < 21**	**204 = 204**

1 Compare the numbers using the math symbols >, <, or =.

a. 564 ☐ 543

b. 200 ☐ 200

c. 14 ☐ 78

d. 772 ☐ 758

e. 211 ☐ 601

f. 820 ☐ 920

g. 199 ☐ 199

h. 401 ☐ 372

i. 943 ☐ 934

j. 519 ☐ 519

2 Choose the symbol that correctly compares the numbers: **960 ____ 690**

a. =   b. <   c. >

I can compare numbers.

Representing Numbers in Written Form

1 one	2 two	3 three	4 four	5 five	6 six	7 seven
8 eight	9 nine	10 ten	11 eleven	12 twelve	13 thirteen	14 fourteen
15 fifteen	16 sixteen	17 seventeen	18 eighteen	19 nineteen	20 twenty	30 thirty
40 forty	50 fifty	60 sixty	70 seventy	80 eighty	90 ninety	100 hundred

1. Write the number in **written form**.

a) 44 ______________________ b) 21 ______________________

c) 98 ______________________ d) 76 ______________________

e) 455 ____

f) 194 ____

g) 302 ____

2. The CN Tower is 553 m tall. Write the height in **written form**.

____

3. The distance between Montreal and Ottawa is 198 km.
Write the distance in **written form**.

____

I can represent numbers in written form.

Representing Numbers in Different Ways

5237 is a **four-digit** number written in **Standard Form.**

The **digit 5** stands for **5000.**
The **digit 2** stands for **200.**
The **digit 3** stands for **30.**
The **digit 7** stands for **7.**

Place Value Chart

thousands	hundreds	tens	ones
5	2	3	7

Express **5237** in different ways:

- **Expanded Form**: 5000 + 200 + 30 + 7
- **Written Form**: five thousand two hundred thirty-seven

1. Fill in the chart.

Standard Form	Expanded Form	Written Form
1708		
	600 + 30 + 7	
		eight hundred ninety-three

2. The Buccaneer restaurant sold four hundred sixty-eight orders of perch dinners in the month of July. What is this number in **expanded form**?

____

3. What is the biggest number using the digits **2 4 9**? _______________

4. What is the digit in the tens place in **871** in words? _______________

I can represent numbers in different ways.

Number Bonds

Decompose a number by breaking down the number into hundreds, tens, and ones.

273: 200, 70, 3

1 **Decompose** the numbers.

a) 527: ◯, 20, ◯

b) 968: ◯, ◯, 8

c) 346: ◯, ◯, ◯

Compose a number by taking three lesser numbers and combining them to make a greater whole number.

400, 60, 7: 467

2 **Compose** the numbers.

a) ______
200, 80, 1

b) ______
500, 40, 3

c) ______
400, 60, 2

I can compose and decompose numbers.

Counting Hundreds, Tens, and Ones

Count the tens and ones. Write how many blocks in all.

1

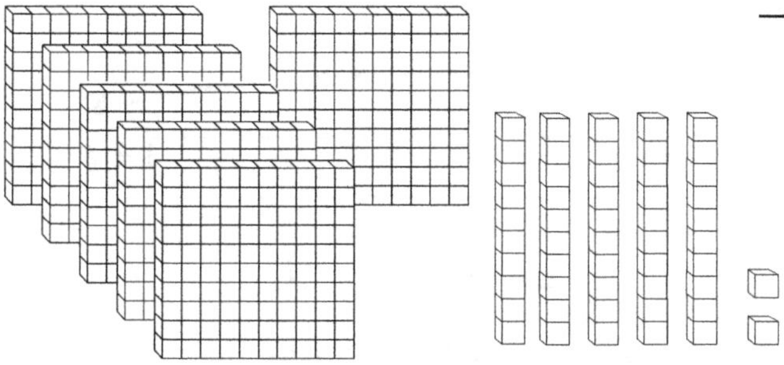

_____ hundreds _____ tens _____ ones

__________ + __________ + __________

There are _______________ blocks.

2

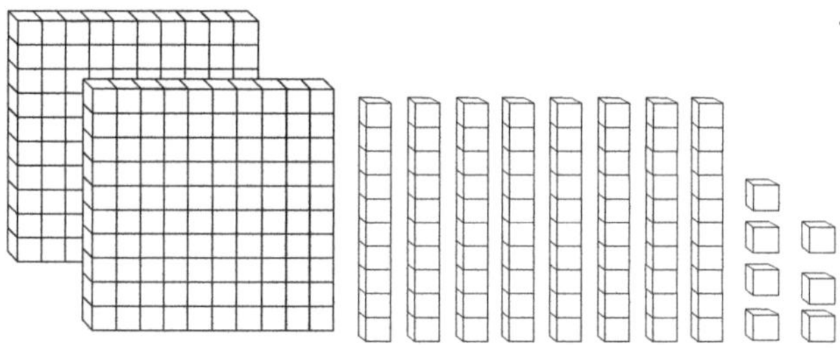

_____ hundreds _____ tens _____ ones

__________ + __________ + __________

There are _______________ blocks.

3

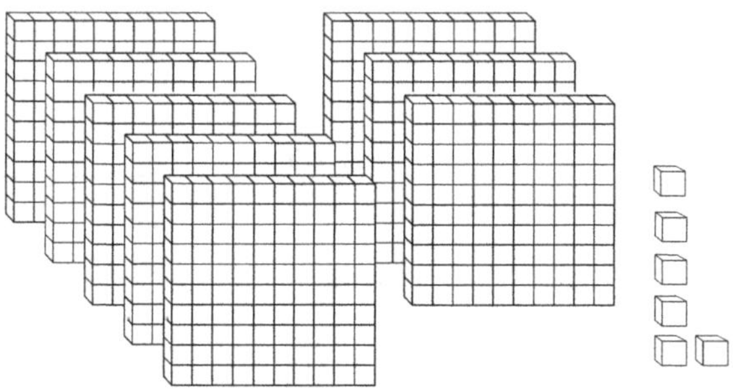

_____ hundreds _____ tens _____ ones

__________ + __________ + __________

There are _______________ blocks.

4 Represent the number 294 in two different ways.

Round Up or Round Down

Round a number by looking at the digit to the right.

Round up if the circled digit is a **5, 6, 7, 8, or 9.**

Round down if the circled digit is a **0, 1, 2, 3, or 4.**

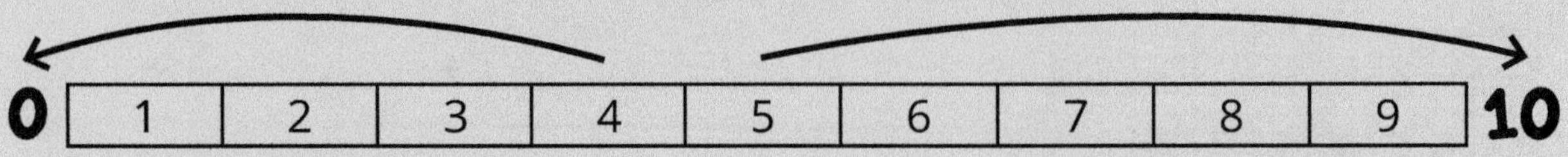

Example A:

Round **137** to the **nearest ten.**

13(7) ⟶ 140

Example B:

Round **219** to the **nearest hundred.**

2(1)9 ⟶ 200

1 Round each number to the **nearest ten**.

a 46 ____________ b 51 ____________ c 765 ____________

2 Round each number to the nearest hundred.

a 431 ____________ b 840 ____________ c 263 ____________

d 190 ____________ e 372 ____________ f 548 ____________

3 When rounded to the nearest hundred, the number of stickers in Lisa's stamp collection is 200. Which answer could be the actual number of stickers in her collection?

a 270 b 186 c 133 d 120

I can round numbers.

Rounding Numbers Using a Number Line

Round a number by looking at the digit to the right.

Round up if the circled digit is a **5, 6, 7, 8, or 9.**

Round down if the circled digit is a **0, 1, 2, 3, or 4.**

458

400 410 420 430 440 450 460 470 480 490 500

458 is **closer** to **460** on the number line when rounding to the nearest ten.

458 is **closer** to **500** on the number line when rounding to the nearest hundred.

Circle the number on the number line when rounded to the nearest ten.

1 Find and label 853 on the number line.

850 851 852 853 854 855 856 857 858 859 **860**

a Is 853 closer to 850 or to 860? ____________________

b What is 853 rounded to the nearest ten? ____________________

2 Find and label 175 on the number line.

100 110 120 130 140 150 160 170 180 190 **200**

a Is 175 closer to 170 or to 180? ____________________

b What is 175 rounded to the nearest hundred? ____________________

I can round numbers using a number line.

Show What You Know!

1 Consider the set of base-ten blocks pictured below.

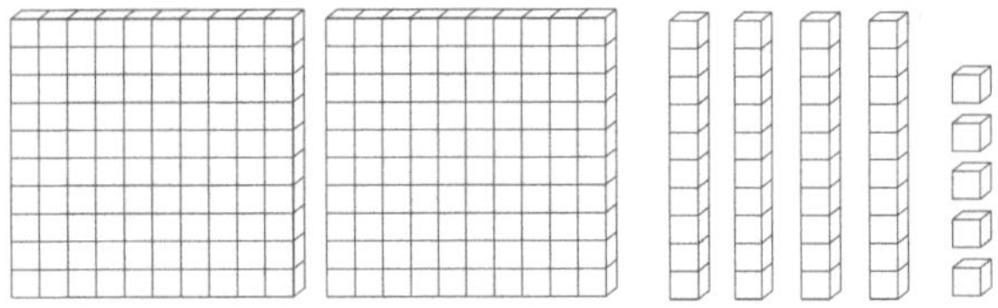

Which of the following sets of base-ten blocks combines with this set to represent 498?

a

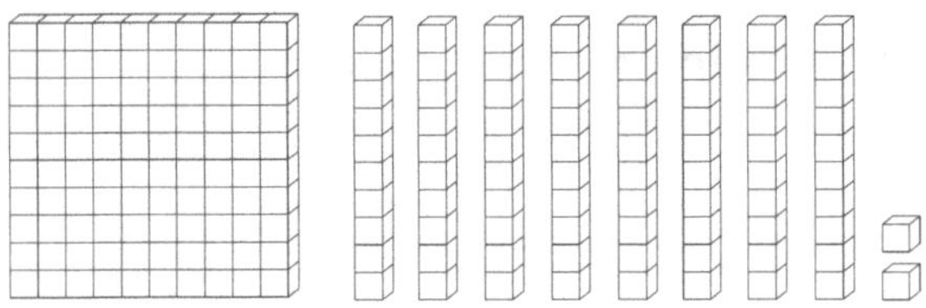

b

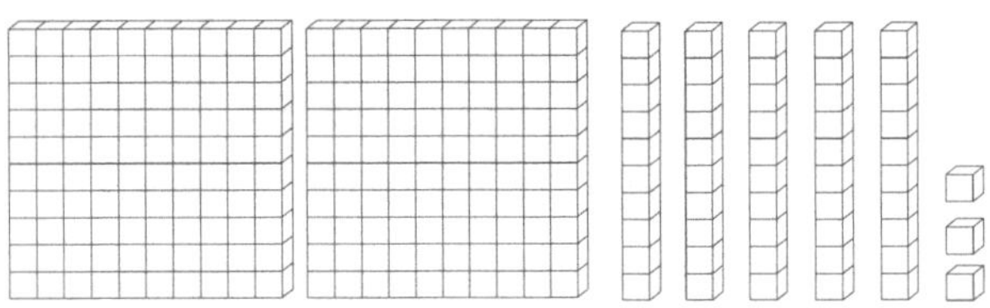

c

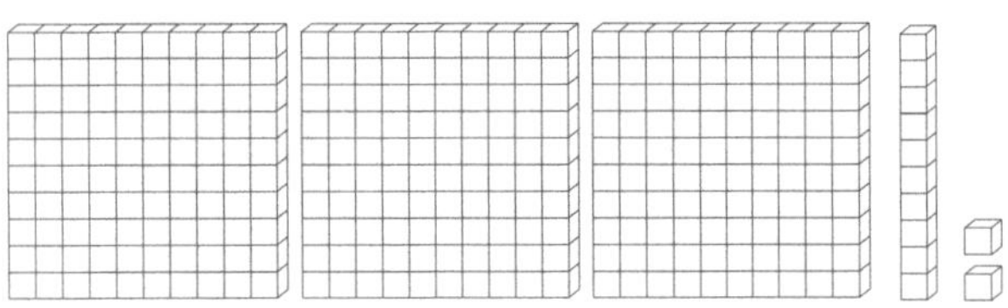

d

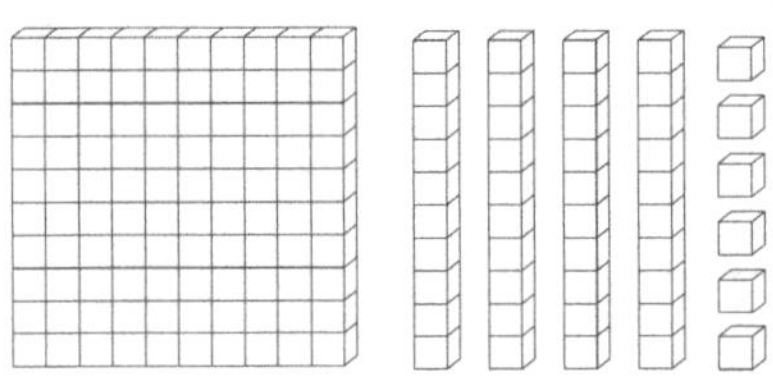

2 Which number list shows counting forward by 25?

a 100, 200, 300, 400

b 30, 35, 40, 45

c 150, 175, 200, 225

d 75, 100, 150, 200

3 Which number is equal to 8 hundreds, 12 tens, and 3 ones?

a 923 **b** 812

c 813 **d** 8123

4 What is 597 when rounded to the nearest ten?

a 590 **b** 610

c 600 **d** 500

5 What is 449 when rounded to the nearest hundred?

a 450 **b** 400

c 500 **d** 440

Show What You Know! (continued)

6. What does the digit 4 represent in the number 541?

   a. 4 ones
   b. 4 tens
   c. 40 tens
   d. 4 hundreds

7. Which set of numbers shows counting backward by 5?

   a. 650, 640, 630, 620
   b. 550, 525, 500, 475
   c. 240, 245, 250, 255
   d. 880, 875, 870, 865

8. There are 3 bins of books in a classroom. The number of books in each bin is shown in the picture below.

35	53	22

Robert takes all the books out of the bins and puts them into piles of 10. How many piles of 10 books each can Robert make with all the books?

Justify your answer.

Robert can make ________ piles of 10 books each.

I Can Checklist:
Fractions

Use drawings to represent, solve, and compare the results of fair-share problems that involve sharing up to 20 items among 2, 3, 4, 5, 6, 8, and 10 sharers, including problems that result in whole numbers, mixed numbers, and fractional amounts. For example,

- ***I can*** *draw pictures to show how to share things evenly.*
- ***I can*** *use my pictures to find answers to sharing problems.*
- ***I can*** *use my pictures to compare different sharing situations.*

Represent and solve fair-share problems that focus on determining and using equivalent fractions, including problems that involve halves, fourths, and eighths; thirds and sixths; and fifths and tenths. For example,

- ***I can*** *draw and use same-sized fractions to solve problems.*
- ***I can*** *solve problems that involve fractions like halves, fourths, thirds, and sixths.*

Fractions Show Equal Parts

A **fraction** shows equal parts of a whole.

Numerator – the number that shows the number of parts being counted.

Denominator – the number that shows the total number of equal parts in the whole.

numerator — $\frac{3}{4}$ — *denominator*

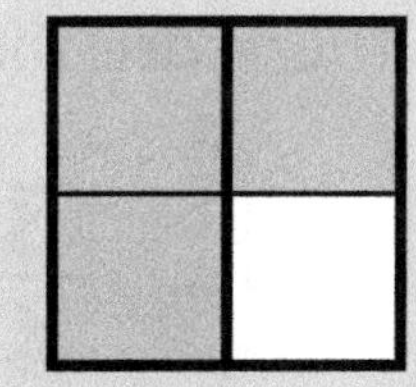

This means 3 out of 4 parts are shaded.

1 Write the correct fraction for the shaded part of the shape. Highlight the numerator in orange. Highlight the denominator in yellow.

a 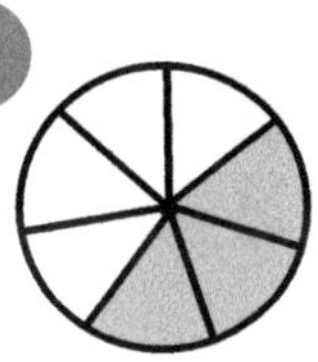 ______

b 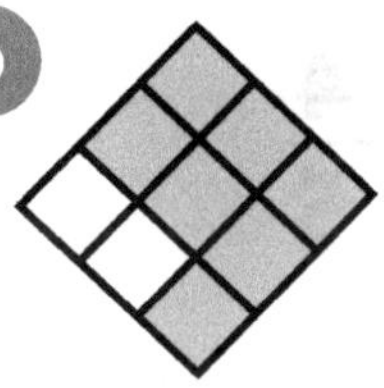 ______

c 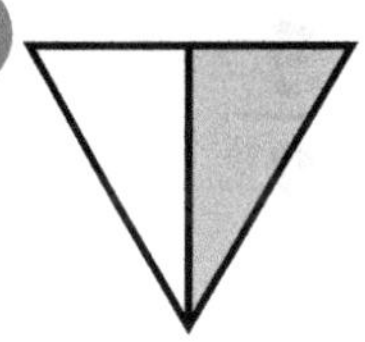 ______

d 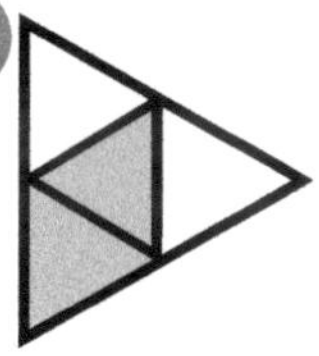 ______

e 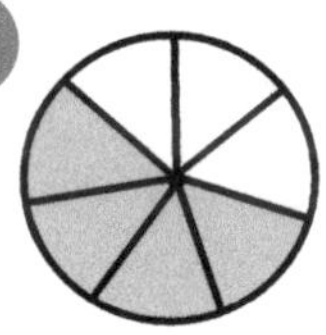 ______

f 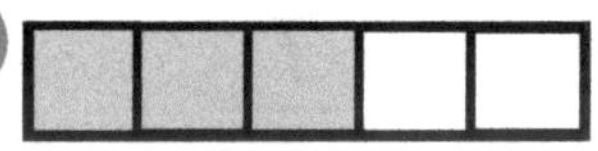 ______

2 Colour some parts of the shape. Then write the matching fraction.

a  ______

b 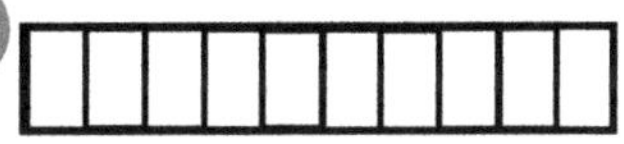 ______

c 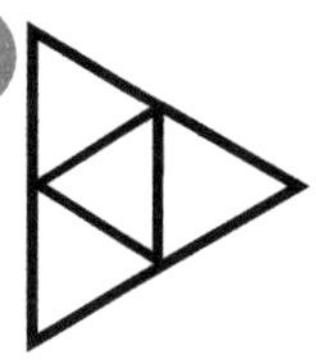 ______

d 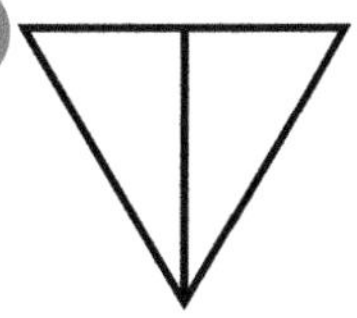 ______

e  ______

f 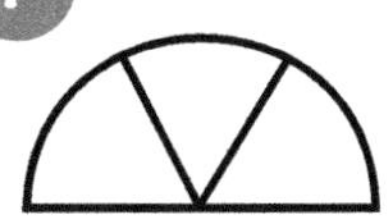 ______

Types of Fractions

There are three types of fractions:

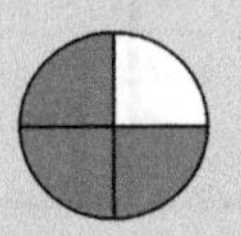 $\frac{3}{4}$

Proper fractions have a numerator that is smaller than the denominator.

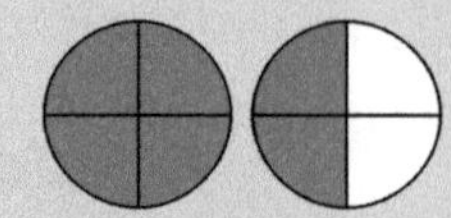 $\frac{6}{4}$

Improper fractions have a numerator that is larger than the denominator.

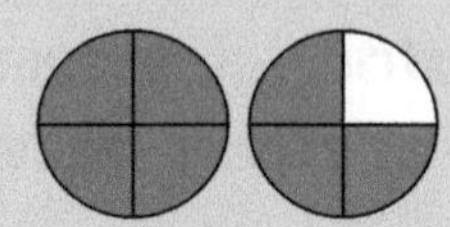 $1\frac{3}{4}$

Mixed fractions have a whole number and proper fraction.

1 Write whether the type of fraction is proper, improper, or mixed.

a) $\frac{5}{2}$ ________________

b) $\frac{4}{5}$ ________________

c) $1\frac{1}{2}$ ________________

d) $\frac{7}{8}$ ________________

e) $2\frac{2}{3}$ ________________

f) $\frac{3}{2}$ ________________

g) $4\frac{7}{10}$ ________________

h) $\frac{3}{5}$ ________________

i) $\frac{4}{3}$ ________________

2 Draw the fraction. Circle the type of fraction.

a) $\frac{8}{4}$

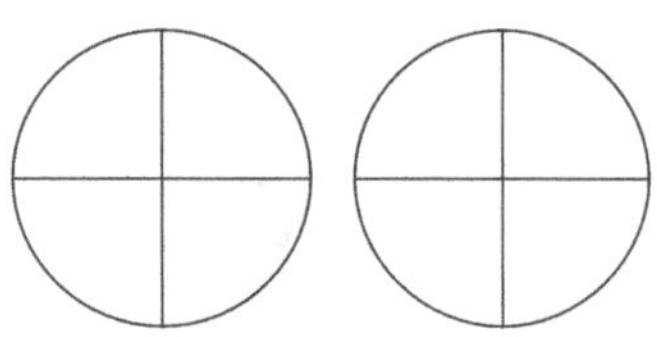

improper fraction mixed fraction

b) $1\frac{2}{3}$

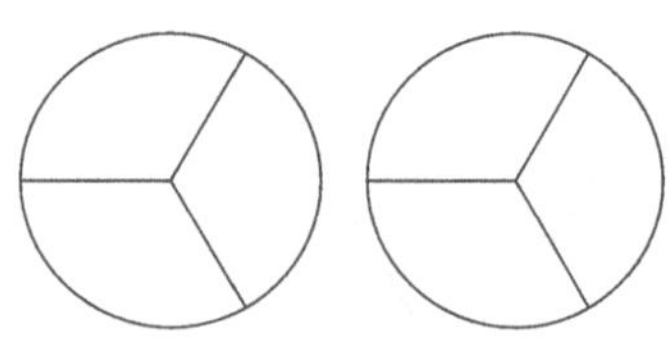

improper fraction mixed fraction

I can identify types of fractions.

Exploring Fractions

1 Read the instructions. Colour the fractions.

a Colour $\frac{1}{4}$ red.

Colour $\frac{1}{4}$ green.

Colour $\frac{1}{4}$ blue.

Colour $\frac{1}{4}$ yellow.

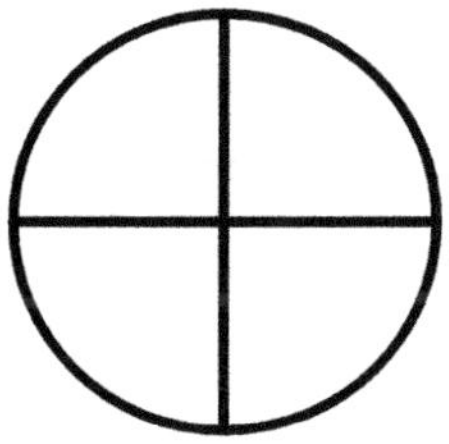

b Colour $\frac{1}{2}$ yellow.

Colour $\frac{1}{2}$ blue.

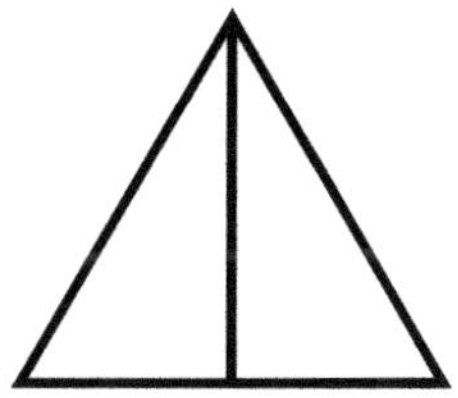

c Colour one half of the group blue.

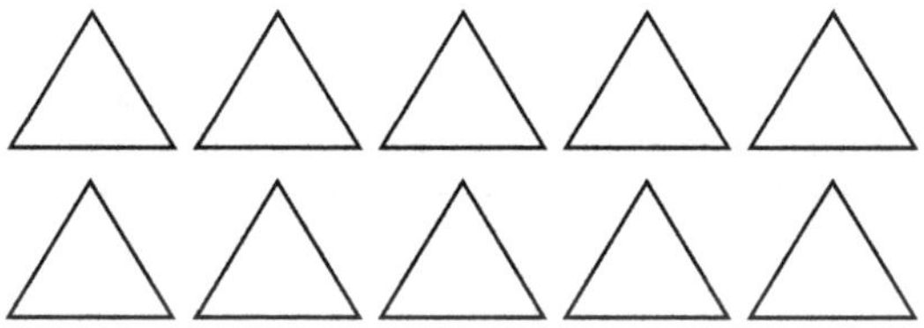

d Colour two thirds of the group yellow.

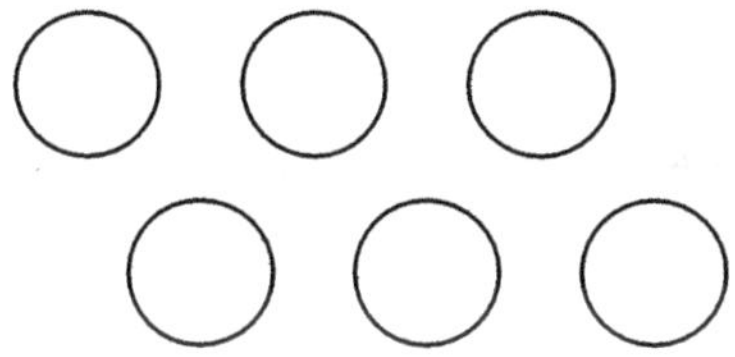

2 What fraction is shaded?

a

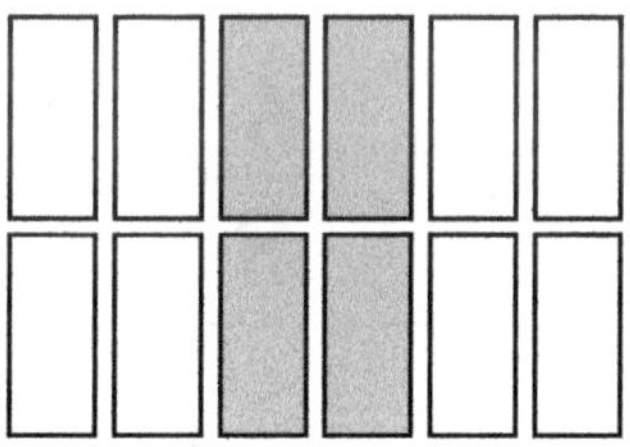

____

b

____

3 What fraction of the shapes are circles?

What fraction of the shapes are squares?

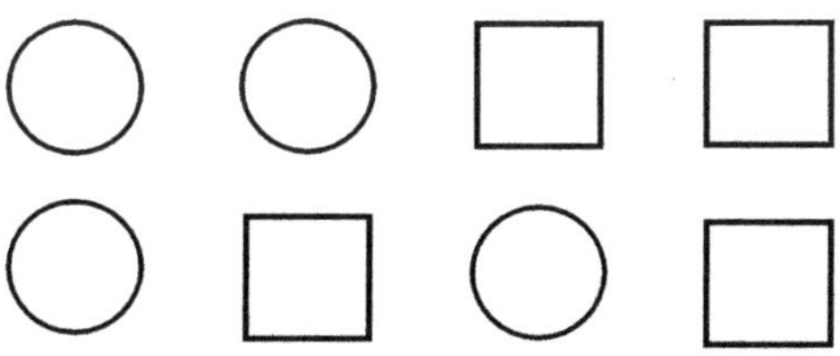

circles __________ squares __________

Exploring Fraction Bars

one whole 1

one half $\frac{1}{2}$	one half $\frac{1}{2}$

one third $\frac{1}{3}$	one third $\frac{1}{3}$	one third $\frac{1}{3}$

one quarter $\frac{1}{4}$	one quarter $\frac{1}{4}$	one quarter $\frac{1}{4}$	one quarter $\frac{1}{4}$

$\frac{1}{6}$ one sixth	$\frac{1}{6}$ one sixth	$\frac{1}{6}$ one sixth	$\frac{1}{6}$ one sixth	$\frac{1}{6}$ one sixth	$\frac{1}{6}$ one sixth

$\frac{1}{8}$ one eighth	$\frac{1}{8}$ one eighth	$\frac{1}{8}$ one eighth	$\frac{1}{8}$ one eighth	$\frac{1}{8}$ one eighth	$\frac{1}{8}$ one eighth	$\frac{1}{8}$ one eighth	$\frac{1}{8}$ one eighth

$\frac{1}{10}$ one tenth	$\frac{1}{10}$ one tenth	$\frac{1}{10}$ one tenth	$\frac{1}{10}$ one tenth	$\frac{1}{10}$ one tenth	$\frac{1}{10}$ one tenth	$\frac{1}{10}$ one tenth	$\frac{1}{10}$ one tenth	$\frac{1}{10}$ one tenth	$\frac{1}{10}$ one tenth

1. Write the equivalent fraction and colour in the fraction bars.

a $\frac{1}{2} = \frac{\square}{6}$

$\frac{1}{2}$	$\frac{1}{2}$

$\frac{1}{6}$	$\frac{1}{6}$	$\frac{1}{6}$	$\frac{1}{6}$	$\frac{1}{6}$	$\frac{1}{6}$

b $\frac{\square}{4} = \frac{6}{8}$

$\frac{1}{4}$	$\frac{1}{4}$	$\frac{1}{4}$	$\frac{1}{4}$

$\frac{1}{8}$	$\frac{1}{8}$	$\frac{1}{8}$	$\frac{1}{8}$	$\frac{1}{8}$	$\frac{1}{8}$	$\frac{1}{8}$	$\frac{1}{8}$

c $\frac{\square}{4} = \frac{1}{2}$

$\frac{1}{4}$	$\frac{1}{4}$	$\frac{1}{4}$	$\frac{1}{4}$

$\frac{1}{2}$	$\frac{1}{2}$

d $\frac{4}{8} = \frac{\square}{2}$

$\frac{1}{8}$	$\frac{1}{8}$	$\frac{1}{8}$	$\frac{1}{8}$	$\frac{1}{8}$	$\frac{1}{8}$	$\frac{1}{8}$	$\frac{1}{8}$

$\frac{1}{2}$	$\frac{1}{2}$

I can write equivalent fractions.

Exploring Fraction Bars (continued)

2 Colour each fraction on the bar. Circle if the fraction is closest to 0, $\frac{1}{2}$, or 1.

a $\frac{7}{8}$

0 $\frac{1}{2}$ 1

b $\frac{1}{6}$

0 $\frac{1}{2}$ 1

c $\frac{6}{10}$

0 $\frac{1}{2}$ 1

3 Circle the fraction that is larger.

a one whole or one third

b $\frac{1}{3}$ or $\frac{1}{4}$

c one half or one quarter

d $\frac{1}{3}$ or $\frac{1}{2}$

4 How many one quarters make one half? Draw a picture.

Exploring Equivalent Fractions

Equivalent fractions have the same value.

For example,
Ben and Jenna share 2 pies.
The first pie is cut in half.
The second pie is cut in quarters.

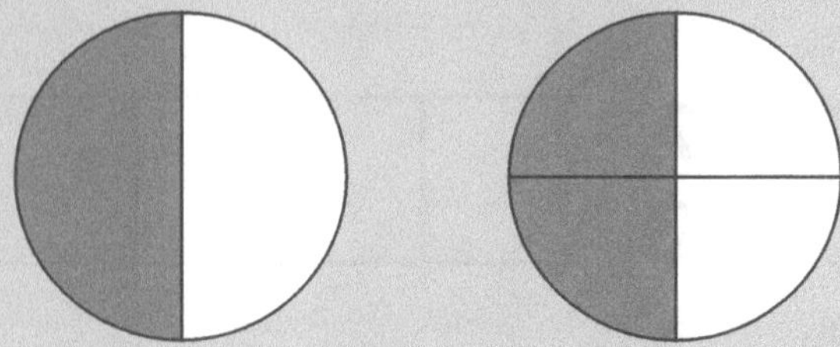

Pie 1 **Pie 2**

For Pie 1, Ben and Jenna each get $\frac{1}{2}$ pieces.

For Pie 2, Ben and Jenna each get $\frac{2}{4}$ pieces.

For both pies, Ben and Jenna get the **same amount** of pie.

Colour in the fraction for each model.

Circle if the two fractions are equivalent or not equivalent.

1 $\frac{1}{2}$ $\frac{1}{4}$

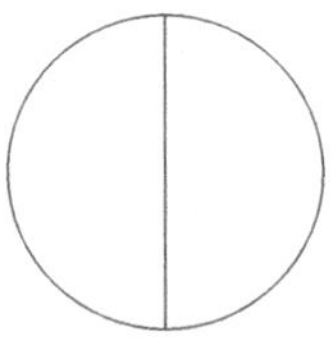

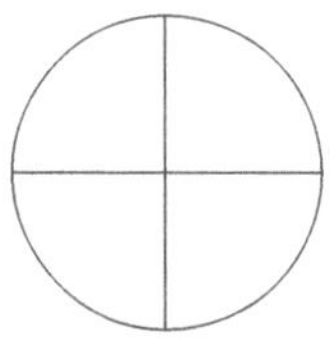

equivalent **not equivalent**

2 $\frac{2}{3}$ $\frac{4}{6}$

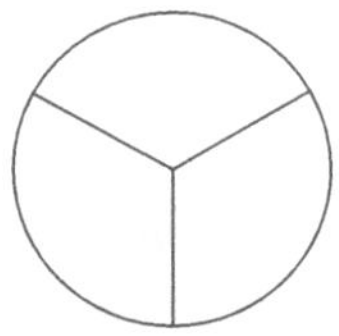

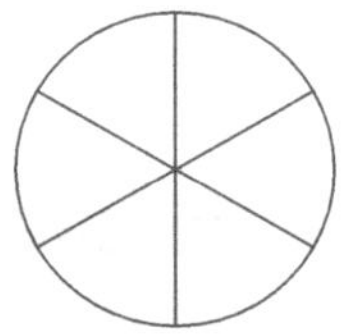

equivalent **not equivalent**

3 $\frac{3}{4}$ $\frac{6}{8}$

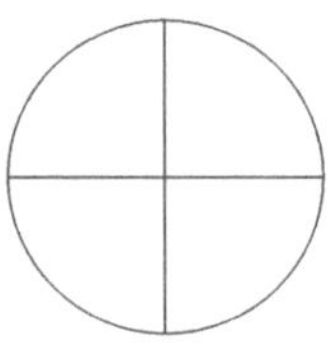

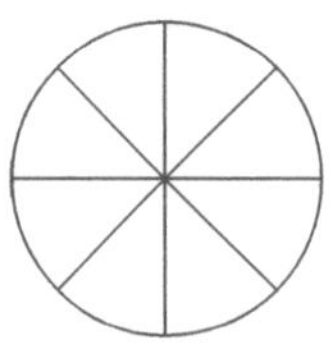

equivalent **not equivalent**

4 $\frac{2}{5}$ $\frac{3}{10}$

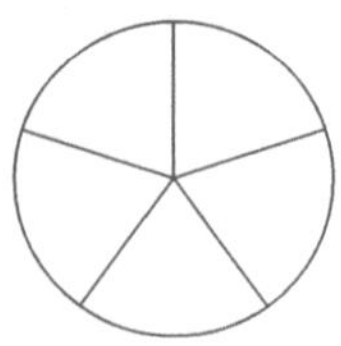

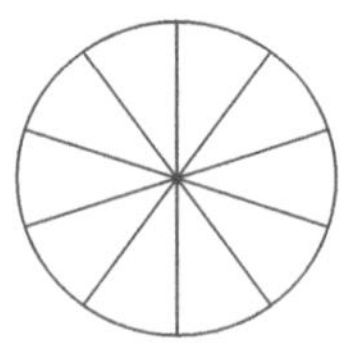

equivalent **not equivalent**

I can find equivalent fractions.

Writing Equivalent Fractions

1 Write a fraction equivalent to the given fraction.

Use the bar model to prove your answer.

a $\frac{1}{3}$ — = ___

b $\frac{2}{5}$ — = ___

c $\frac{4}{10}$ — = ___

d $\frac{4}{6}$ — = ___

2 Maria shares her pizza with 3 friends.

How much of the pizza does each person get? Show your thinking.

I can make equivalent fractions.

Comparing Fractions

1 Colour and compare the fractions using greater than >, less than <, or equal =.

a $\frac{3}{4}$ 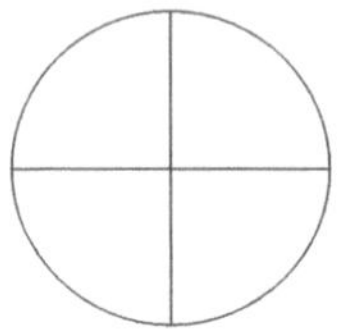 ☐ 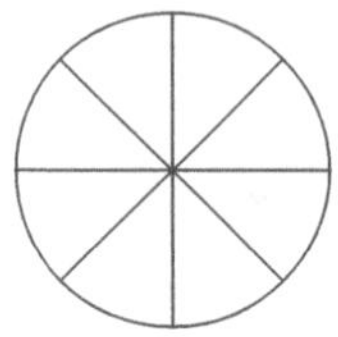 $\frac{1}{2}$

b $\frac{2}{8}$ 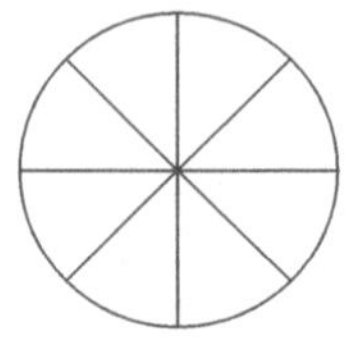 ☐ 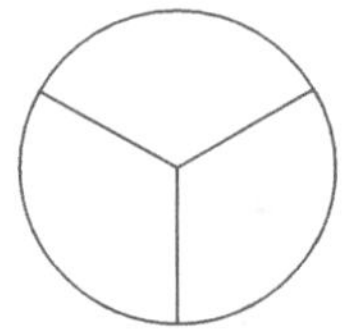 $\frac{1}{3}$

c

$\frac{1}{3}$		$\frac{1}{3}$		$\frac{1}{3}$	
$\frac{1}{6}$	$\frac{1}{6}$	$\frac{1}{6}$	$\frac{1}{6}$	$\frac{1}{6}$	$\frac{1}{6}$

$\frac{2}{3}$ ☐ $\frac{3}{6}$

d

$\frac{1}{8}$	$\frac{1}{8}$	$\frac{1}{8}$	$\frac{1}{8}$	$\frac{1}{8}$	$\frac{1}{8}$	$\frac{1}{8}$	$\frac{1}{8}$
$\frac{1}{4}$		$\frac{1}{4}$		$\frac{1}{4}$		$\frac{1}{4}$	

$\frac{4}{8}$ ☐ $\frac{3}{4}$

2 Solve.

a Thia and Max both have an orange. Thia cuts hers into 4 wedges and eats 2 wedges. Max cuts his into 8 wedges and eats 6 wedges. Who ate more of their orange?

Thia **Max**

b Barry and Alina baked brownies. Barry takes home $\frac{1}{2}$ of the brownies. Alina takes home $\frac{1}{4}$ of the brownies. Who takes home more brownies?

Barry **Alina**

3 Write the fraction.

a Greater than $\frac{4}{6}$ ____________

b Less than $\frac{1}{2}$ ____________

I can compare fractions.

Fair Shares

Fair shares are when a group of people equally share a number of objects.

Look at the objects below and answer the questions.

1

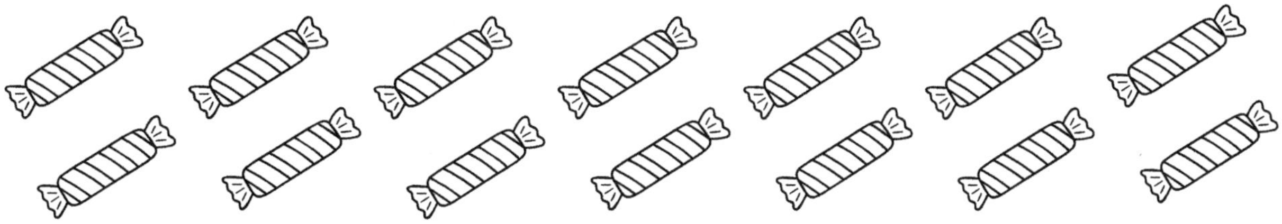

a How many candies are there? ____________________

b **Ellie** and **Mika** want to share the candies equally.
How many candies will each person get? ____________________

c **Five more** friends come along.
How many candies will each person get? ____________________

2

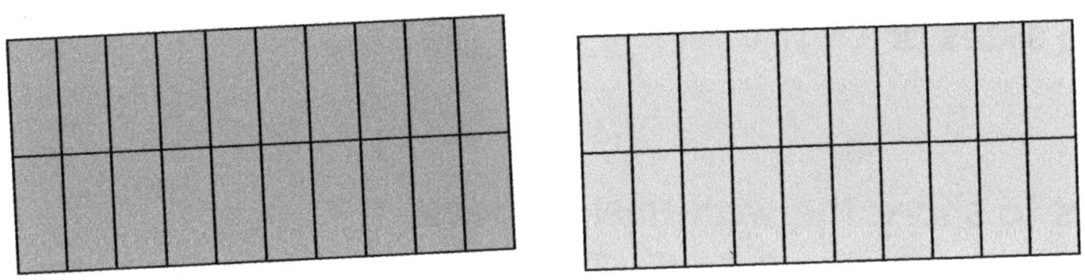

a **Danny** has **2 chocolate bars** that he wants to share with **10 people**. How many pieces will each person get? ____________________

b **Ling** is one of the people who is getting some chocolate.
What fraction of the chocolate bar is she getting? ____________________

Fair Shares with Remainders

Look at the objects below and answer the questions.

1. How many watermelon slices are there? ______________________

2. **Josh** and **Zainab** want to share the watermelon slices equally.
How many watermelon slices will they each get?

How many watermelon slices are left over? __________

3. **Hana** also wants to share the watermelon slices.
How many watermelon slices will **Josh, Zainab**, and **Hana** each get?

How many watermelon slices are left over? __________

I can fair share with remainders.

Fraction Word Problems

Solve the word problem. Draw a picture and show your thinking.

1. Caleb has 12 marbles. One half of the marbles are blue. The other half of the marbles are red. How many marbles are blue?

2. Evan has 8 apple slices for a snack. He put caramel on three quarters of the apple slices. How many apple slices have caramel on them?

3. Zoe cut a pie into 6 equal slices. She gave 2 slices to her friend Peter. What fraction of the pie does Zoe have left?

4. There are 16 players on Alex's hockey team. Half of the players wears blue uniforms. The rest of the players wear red uniforms. How many players wear red?

I can solve fair share word problems.

Show What You Know!

1

a) How many shells are there? ____________________

b) **Jessica** and **Mateo** want to share the shells equally.
How many shells will each person get? ____________

c) **Five more** friends come along.
How many shells will each person get? ____________________

d) How many shells are left over? ____________________

2 Write the correct fraction for the shaded part of the shape.
Highlight the numerator in orange. Highlight the denominator in yellow.

a) 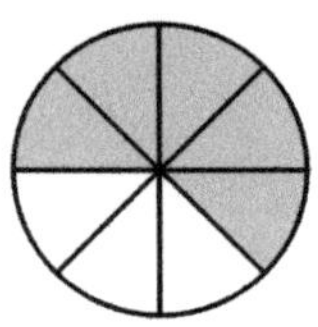 ______

b) 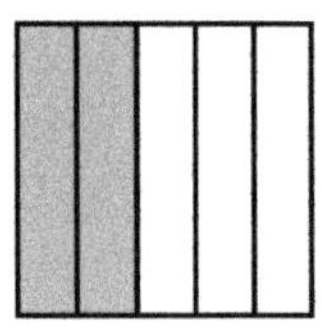 ______

c) 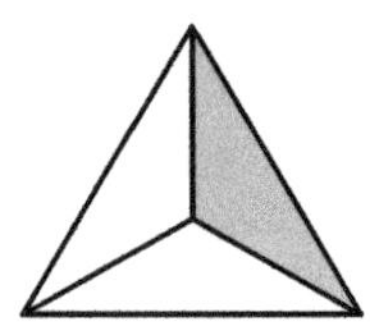 ______

3 Draw the fraction. Circle the type of fraction.

a) $\frac{3}{2}$

improper fraction   mixed fraction

b) $2\frac{3}{4}$

improper fraction   mixed fraction

Show What You Know! (continued)

4 Read the instructions. Colour the fraction.

a **Colour one fourth of the group green.**

b **Colour one half of the group blue.**

5 Colour the fraction on the bar. Circle if the fraction is closest to 0, $\frac{1}{2}$, or 1.

$\frac{3}{8}$ 0 $\frac{1}{2}$ 1

6 Write a fraction equivalent to the given fraction.
Use the bar model to prove your answer.

a $\frac{2}{4}$

b $\frac{2}{6}$

7 Solve the word problem. Draw a picture and show your thinking.

Anna cut a pizza into 8 equal slices. She gave 4 slices to her friends. What fraction of the pizza does Anna have left?

I Can Checklist:
Operations

Use the properties of operations, and the relationships between multiplication and division, to solve problems and check calculations. For example,

- ***I can*** *use tricks like "flip-flop" (commutative property) or "grouping" (associative property) to make math easier.*
- ***I can*** *use multiplication and division to solve problems and check my answers.*

Recall and demonstrate multiplication facts of 2, 5, and 10, and related division facts. For example,

- ***I can*** *remember and show times tables for 2, 5, and 10.*
- ***I can*** *use my knowledge of times tables to solve division problems.*

Use mental math strategies, including estimation, to add and subtract whole numbers that add up to no more than 1000, and explain the strategies used. For example,

- ***I can*** *use tricks in my head to add and subtract numbers.*
- ***I can*** *make good guesses (estimates) to check my answers.*

Demonstrate an understanding of algorithms for adding and subtracting whole numbers by making connections to, and describing the way, other tools and strategies are used to add and subtract. For example,

- ***I can*** *connect different tools and strategies to add and subtract.*
- ***I can*** *explain how I use tools and strategies to add and subtract numbers.*

Represent and solve problems involving the addition and subtraction of whole numbers that add up to no more than 1000, using various tools and algorithms. For example,

- ***I can*** *use tools like counters or number lines to add and subtract numbers up to 1000.*
- ***I can*** *use steps (algorithms) to add and subtract big numbers.*

Using Estimation to Add and Subtract

Estimation is a mental math strategy for addition and subtraction.

For example,
Round each number to the nearest ten, then add.

62	→	**60**
+ 28	→	**+ 30**
		90

Rounding the numbers gives the approximate total.

1 Round each number to the nearest ten, then add or subtract.

a
$$\begin{array}{r} 23 \\ +\ 56 \\ \hline \end{array} \rightarrow \begin{array}{r} \\ +\ \_\_\_\_ \end{array}$$

b
$$\begin{array}{r} 65 \\ +\ 24 \\ \hline \end{array} \rightarrow \begin{array}{r} \\ +\ \_\_\_\_ \end{array}$$

c
$$\begin{array}{r} 76 \\ -\ 18 \\ \hline \end{array} \rightarrow \begin{array}{r} \\ -\ \_\_\_\_ \end{array}$$

d
$$\begin{array}{r} 52 \\ -\ 41 \\ \hline \end{array} \rightarrow \begin{array}{r} \\ -\ \_\_\_\_ \end{array}$$

e
$$\begin{array}{r} 34 \\ +\ 92 \\ \hline \end{array} \rightarrow \begin{array}{r} \\ +\ \_\_\_\_ \end{array}$$

f
$$\begin{array}{r} 16 \\ +\ 78 \\ \hline \end{array} \rightarrow \begin{array}{r} \\ +\ \_\_\_\_ \end{array}$$

2 Round each number in the problem and use estimation to solve.

Leroy has 325 millilitres of juice in one cup. He adds 265 millilitres that he has in another cup. Approximately how many millilitres of juice does Leroy have to the nearest hundred?

I can use estimation to add and subtract.

Three-Digit Addition Without Regrouping

Line up the **ones, tens,** and **hundreds.**

Add the **ones.**

hundreds	tens	**ones**
2	2	3
+ 3	4	5
		8

Next, add the **tens.**

hundreds	**tens**	ones
2	2	3
+ 3	4	5
	6	8

Then, add the **hundreds.**

hundreds	tens	ones
2	2	3
+ 3	4	5
5	6	8

1 Use the hundreds, tens, and ones chart to add. Shade the ones column in yellow. Shade the tens column in orange. Shade the hundreds column in green.

a)

4	5	4
+ 2	3	1

b)

1	2	2
+ 5	1	5

c)

3	7	1
+ 3	2	7

d)

1	3	5
+ 7	6	2

e)

4	1	2
+ 5	5	0

f)

7	2	3
+ 2	2	5

g)

4	6	2
+ 2	2	3

h)

2	8	4
+ 3	1	1

2 There were 625 adult's tickets and 132 children's tickets sold for the movie. How many tickets were sold in total?

I can add without regrouping.

Three-Digit Addition Without Regrouping (continued)

3 Find the sums. Solve the riddle.

A	B	C	D	E	F
121 + 237	123 + 346	134 + 432	212 + 125	246 + 113	255 + 524
G	**H**	**I**	**J**	**L**	**M**
152 + 37	313 + 154	266 + 112	155 + 341	171 + 528	284 + 215
N	**O**	**P**	**Q**	**R**	**S**
516 + 181	321 + 217	524 + 432	435 + 204	112 + 352	443 + 143
T	**U**	**V**	**W**	**X**	**Y**
253 + 416	142 + 101	564 + 223	305 + 12	171 + 321	416 + 120

Why did the cookie go to the doctor?

___ ___ ___ ___ ___ ___ ___ / ___ ___ / ___ ___ ___
469 359 566 358 243 586 359   378 669   317 358 586

___ ___ ___ ___ ___ ___ ___ / ___ ___ ___ ___ ___ ___ !
779 359 359 699 378 697 189   566 464 243 499 469 536

Three-Digit Addition with Regrouping

1. **Add the ones. 5 + 7 = 12**
   Regroup 12 ones as 1 ten and 2 ones.

2. **Add the tens. 1 + 3 + 9 = 13**
   Regroup 13 tens as 1 hundred 3 tens.

3. **Add the hundreds. 1 + 3 + 2 = 6**

	hundreds	tens	ones
	1	1	
	3	3	7
+	2	9	5
	6	3	2

1 Use a hundreds, tens, and ones chart to add. Shade the ones column in yellow. Shade the tens column in orange. Shade the hundreds column in green.

a

	1	4	3
+	6	7	8

b

	7	8	4
+	1	9	6

c

	2	6	4
+	5	9	7

d

	4	9	2
+	3	4	8

e

	8	2	5
+	1	9	7

f

	2	6	2
+	3	5	8

g

	5	3	6
+	3	8	5

h

	6	7	9
+	1	5	1

2 Andrew reads 136 pages of a book in the first week, then reads 178 pages the next week. How many pages of the book did Andrew read in two weeks?

I can add with regrouping.

Three-Digit Addition with Regrouping (continued)

3 Find the sums. Solve the riddle.

A	B	C	D	E	F
153 + 554	167 + 575	277 + 281	366 + 152	788 + 164	419 + 378
G	**H**	**I**	**J**	**K**	**L**
124 + 296	194 + 572	259 + 613	170 + 555	247 + 249	181 + 88
M	**N**	**O**	**P**	**Q**	**R**
517 + 47	155 + 571	125 + 395	343 + 117	468 + 258	182 + 475
S	**T**	**U**	**V**	**W**	**Y**
291 + 182	357 + 361	496 + 460	515 + 38	179 + 617	564 + 353

What do you get when you cross a cow and a camel?

___ / ___ ___ ___ ___ ___ / ___ ___ ___ ___ ___ ___ ___ ___ ___ !

707 / 269 956 564 460 917 / 564 872 269 496 473 766 707 496 952

Addition Strategies

Plus Zero

Add 0 to a number and the number stays the same.

5 + 0 = 5

Friends of Ten

There are six sets of number pairs that equal 10.

10 + 0 = 10　7 + 3 = 10

9 + 1 = 10　6 + 4 = 10

8 + 2 = 10　5 + 5 = 10

Turn Around

Add the numbers in any order and the total stays the same.

2 + 1 = 3 or 1 + 2 = 3

Doubles Plus 1

Double the number and add one more.

3 + 4 = 3 + 3 + 1

Doubles

Add the number to itself and that number doubles.

4 + 4 = 8

Count On

Count on to add small numbers such as 1, 2, or 3.

11 + 2 = 13

Draw a Picture

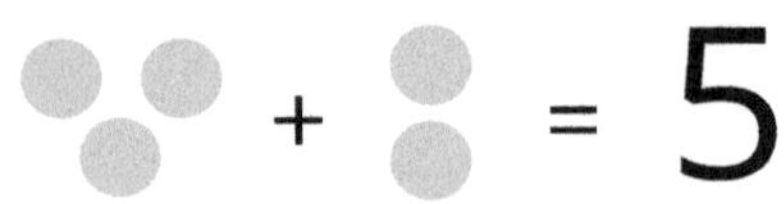

3 + 2 = 5

Subtraction Strategies

Minus Zero

Subtract 0 from a number and the number stays the same.

8 – 0 = 8

Friends of Ten

If you know the tens partner, then you know the related subtraction fact.

9 + 1 = 10 or 10 – 1 = 9

A Number Minus Itself

Subtract a number from itself and the result is 0.

7 – 7 = 0

Doubles

If you know the doubles fact, then you know the related subtraction fact.

2 + 2 = 4 or 4 – 2 = 2

Count Backward

Count back to take away small numbers such as 1, 2, or 3.

11 – 2 = 9

Use a Number Line

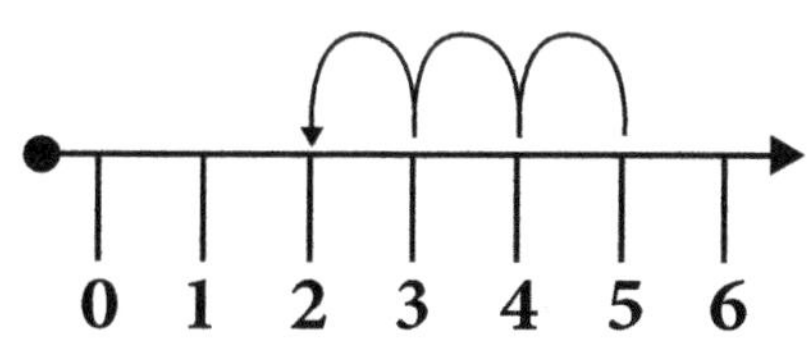

5 – 3 = ? 5 – 3 = 2

Think Addition

Every subtraction problem can be solved as an addition problem.

4 + 1 = 5 or 5 – 1 = 4

Draw a Picture

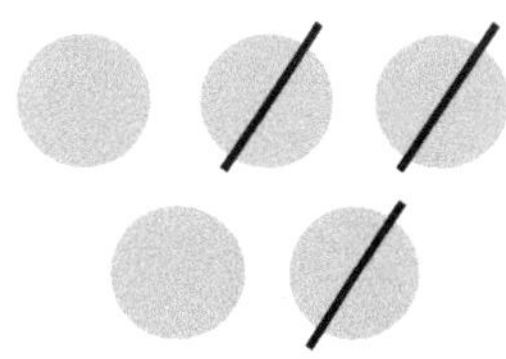

5 – 3 = 2

Three-Digit Subtraction Without Regrouping

Line up the **ones, tens,** and **hundreds.**

Subtract the **ones.**

hundreds	tens	**ones**
5	8	6
− 2	4	1
		5

Next, subtract the **tens.**

hundreds	**tens**	ones
5	8	6
− 2	4	1
	4	5

Then, subtract the **hundreds.**

hundreds	tens	ones
5	8	6
− 2	4	1
3	4	5

1. Use the hundreds, tens, and ones chart to subtract. Shade the ones column in yellow. Shade the tens column in orange. Shade the hundreds column in green.

a.

5	5	9
− 2	4	6

b.

7	8	9
− 3	4	5

c.

2	3	9
− 1	2	1

d.

6	4	2
− 4	2	0

e.

5	3	7
− 2	2	6

f.

5	7	5
− 3	2	4

g.

9	7	9
− 5	2	9

h.

2	5	8
− 1	3	2

2. There are 789 birds in a flock. 332 birds leave the flock.
How many birds are left?

I can subtract without regrouping.

Three-Digit Subtraction Without Regrouping (continued)

3. Find the differences. Solve the riddle.

A	**B**	**C**	**E**	**F**
453 - 100	552 - 421	978 - 653	667 - 127	861 - 641
G 767 - 302	**H** 444 - 202	**I** 498 - 325	**K** 346 - 223	**L** 276 - 31
O 959 - 147	**R** 214 - 113	**S** 335 - 113	**T** 716 - 405	**Y** 789 - 665

How do you know which rabbits are old?

___ ___ ___ ___ / ___ ___ ___ / ___ ___ ___
245 812 812 123 / 220 812 101 / 311 242 540

___ ___ ___ ___ / ___ ___ ___ ___ ___ !
465 101 540 124 / 242 353 101 540 222

Three-Digit Subtraction with Regrouping

Line up the **ones, tens, and hundreds.**
Subtract the ones.

Trade 1 hundred from the hundreds column for 10 tens in the tens column.
Subtract the tens.
Then subtract the hundreds.

	hundreds	**tens**	ones
	5	14	
	~~6~~	~~4~~	6
−	3	8	3
	2	6	3

You cannot take 8 from 4. So, trade 1 hundred from the hundreds column for 10 tens. Now there are 14 tens.

1 Use a hundreds, tens, and ones chart to subtract. Shade the ones column in yellow. Shade the tens column in orange. Shade the hundreds column in green.

a) 837 − 644 =

b) 509 − 341 =

c) 316 − 155 =

d) 723 − 131 =

e) 605 − 495 =

f) 719 − 182 =

g) 934 − 653 =

h) 712 − 442 =

I can subtract with regrouping.

Three-Digit Subtraction with Regrouping (continued)

2 Find the differences. Solve the riddle.

A	B	C	D	E
154 − 26	295 − 136	977 − 886	886 − 139	104 − 32
G	**H**	**I**	**J**	**K**
312 − 205	728 − 109	530 − 223	240 − 111	649 − 259
N	**R**	**S**	**T**	**W**
543 − 409	366 − 137	987 − 892	116 − 70	416 − 152

What was the spider doing on the computer?

___ ___ ___ ___ ___ ___ ___ ___ ___ /
95 72 128 229 91 619 307 134 107

___ ___ ___ / ___ ___ ___ !
46 619 72 264 72 159

Show What You Know!

1 Solve. Show your work.

a) A bakery made 874 cookies for a school event. During the event, 405 cookies were eaten. How many cookies were left after the event?

b) At the zoo, there were 389 visitors in the morning and 475 visitors in the afternoon. How many visitors in total were there that day?

c) During a school carnival, 285 tickets were sold for the roller coaster ride and 527 tickets were sold for the Ferris wheel. How many tickets were sold in total for both rides?

d) Lisa had 532 candies, but she gave 297 candies to her friends. How many candies does Lisa have left?

Show What You Know! (continued)

2 Solve. Show your work.

a Tom has 358 marbles, and his friend Jerry has 234 marbles. If they combine their marbles together, how many marbles do they have in total?

b A toy store has 832 stuffed animals in stock. During a sale, 459 of them were sold. How many stuffed animals were left in the store after the sale?

c In a school library, there are 456 fiction books and 274 non-fiction books. How many books are there in total in the library?

d There are 725 balloons at a party. During the party, 305 balloons pop. How many balloons are still filled with air at the end of the party?

I Can Checklist:
Multiplication & Division

Represent multiplication of numbers up to 10 × 10 and division up to 100 ÷ 10, using a variety of tools and drawings, including arrays. For example,

- ***I can*** *use tools and pictures to show multiplication up to 10 x 10 and division up to 100 ÷ 10.*
- ***I can*** *solve multiplication and division problems using my pictures and tools.*

Represent and solve problems involving multiplication and division, including problems that involve groups of one half, one fourth, and one third, using tools and drawings. For example,

- ***I can*** *use tools and pictures to solve problems that involve halves, fourths, and thirds.*

Represent the connection between the numerator of a fraction and the repeated addition of the unit fraction with the same denominator using various tools and drawings, and standard fractional notation. For example,

- ***I can*** *explain the connection between the top number (numerator) of a fraction and repeated addition.*

Use the ratios of 1 to 2, 1 to 5, and 1 to 10 to scale up numbers and to solve problems. For example,

- ***I can*** *use ratios to make numbers bigger.*
- ***I can*** *solve problems using ratios.*

Exploring Arrays

In the **array**, there are 2 rows with 4 blocks in each row.
Skip count by 4s to count the blocks.

The multiplication statement is 2 × 4 = 8.

factors product

1 Write a multiplication statement for the array.

a

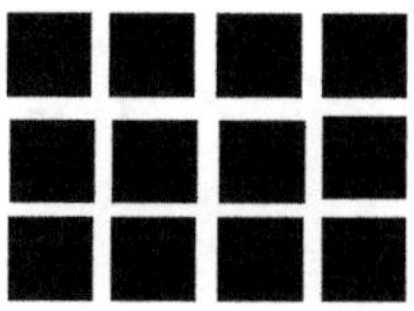

____ rows and ____ blocks in each row ________________

b

____ rows and ____ blocks in each row ________________

2 Write a multiplication statement for each array.

a

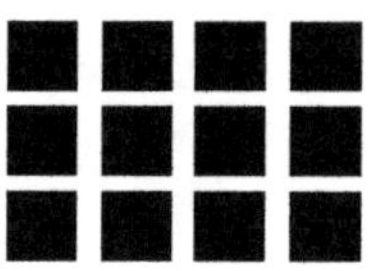

b

3 Draw an array for the multiplication statement. Write the answer.

a

8 × 3 = ________________

b

7 × 2 = ________________

Multiply by 0 and 1

The product is always the same as the greater factor when any number is multiplied by 1.

For example, 10 × 1 = 10.

The product is always 0 when any factor is multiplied by 0.

For example, 0 × 4 = 0.

1 Multiply.

a) $11 \times 1 =$ ____ b) $0 \times 6 =$ ____ c) $0 \times 2 =$ ____ d) $1 \times 1 =$ ____

e) $4 \times 1 =$ ____ f) $0 \times 7 =$ ____ g) $9 \times 1 =$ ____ h) $0 \times 3 =$ ____

i) $2 \times 1 =$ ____ j) $8 \times 1 =$ ____ k) $0 \times 12 =$ ____ l) $3 \times 1 =$ ____

m) $0 \times 8 =$ ____ n) $5 \times 1 =$ ____ o) $6 \times 1 =$ ____ p) $0 \times 5 =$ ____

q) $0 \times 9 =$ ____ r) $12 \times 1 =$ ____ s) $0 \times 1 =$ ____ t) $7 \times 1 =$ ____

I can multiply by 0 and 1.

Two Times Table

1 Solve each question to solve the riddle.

Hint: Not all of the letters are used in the answer.

A	E	I	M	N
8 × 2 = ____	5 × 2 = ____	11 × 2 = ____	0 × 2 = ____	12 × 2 = ____
O	**P**	**S**	**T**	**X**
1 × 2 = ____	4 × 2 = ____	10 × 2 = ____	2 × 2 = ____	7 × 2 = ____

What do you call a fake noodle?

___	___	/	___	___	___	___	___	___	___	!
16	24		22	0	8	16	20	4	16	

2 Find the missing factor.

a 2 × __ = 12 b __ × 2 = 2 c 2 × __ = 18 d __ × 2 = 14

e __ × 2 = 16 f 2 × __ = 22 g __ × 2 = 10 h 2 × __ = 24

3 Sally has 2 bags of cookies. Each bag contains 8 cookies.
How many cookies does Sally have in total?

I can multiply by 2.

Three Times Table

1 Solve each question to solve the riddle.

Hint: Not all of the letters are used in the answer.

E	**I**	**G**	**O**	**P**
$10 \times 3 =$ ____	$7 \times 3 =$ ____	$4 \times 3 =$ ____	$8 \times 3 =$ ____	$2 \times 3 =$ ____
R	**S**	**T**	**V**	**W**
$6 \times 3 =$ ____	$12 \times 3 =$ ____	$9 \times 3 =$ ____	$5 \times 3 =$ ____	$3 \times 3 =$ ____

Why was the broom late?

___	___	/	___	___	___	___	___	___	___	___	___	!
21	27		24	15	30	18	36	9	30	6	27	

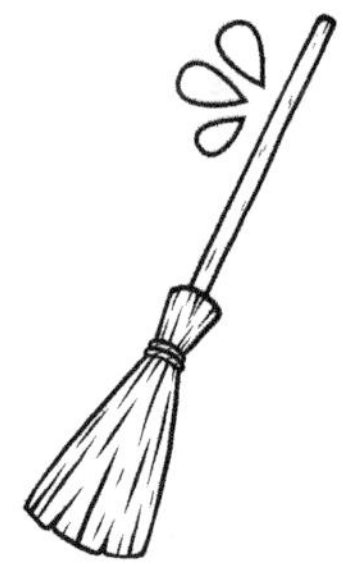

2 Find the missing factor.

a) $3 \times$ __ $= 12$ b) __ $\times 3 = 3$ c) $3 \times$ __ $= 6$ d) __ $\times 3 = 0$

e) __ $\times 3 = 24$ f) $3 \times$ __ $= 27$ g) __ $\times 3 = 21$ h) $3 \times$ __ $= 15$

3 Amy has 3 packs of crayons. Each pack contains 4 crayons.
How many crayons does Amy have in total?

I can multiply by 3.

Four Times Table

1 Solve each question to solve the riddle.

Hint: Not all of the letters are used in the answer.

A	B	C	E	G
$0 \times 4 =$ ____	$3 \times 4 =$ ____	$8 \times 4 =$ ____	$2 \times 4 =$ ____	$12 \times 4 =$ ____
K	**L**	**R**	**T**	**U**
$11 \times 4 =$ ____	$9 \times 4 =$ ____	$6 \times 4 =$ ____	$7 \times 4 =$ ____	$5 \times 4 =$ ____

What vehicle has four wheels and flies?

___ / ___ ___ ___ ___ ___ ___ ___ / ___ ___ ___ ___ ___!

0 / 48 0 24 12 0 48 8 / 28 24 20 32 44

2 Find the missing factor.

a) $4 \times$ __ $= 12$ b) __ $\times 4 = 8$ c) $4 \times$ __ $= 24$ d) __ $\times 4 = 32$

e) __ $\times 4 = 16$ f) $4 \times$ __ $= 28$ g) __ $\times 4 = 36$ h) $4 \times$ __ $= 44$

3 There are 4 children in a class. Each child has 7 pencils.
How many pencils are there in total?

I can multiply by 4.

Five Times Table

1 Solve each question to solve the riddle.

Hint: Not all of the letters are used in the answer.

A	**E**	**F**	**H**	**L**
6 × 5 = ____	7 × 5 = ____	1 × 5 = ____	4 × 5 = ____	2 × 5 = ____
M	**O**	**P**	**S**	**T**
9 × 5 = ____	3 × 5 = ____	8 × 5 = ____	0 × 5 = ____	5 × 5 = ____

How many months of the year have 28 days?

___ ___ ___ / ___ ___ / ___ ___ ___ ___!

30 10 10 / 15 5 / 25 20 35 45

2 Find the missing factor.

a 5 × __ = 15 b __ × 5 = 20 c 5 × __ = 55 d __ × 5 = 10

e __ × 5 = 45 f 5 × __ = 0 g __ × 5 = 40 h 5 × __ = 30

3 A farmer has 5 fields. Each field has 9 cows.
How many cows are there in total?

I can multiply by 5.

Six Times Table

1 Solve each question to solve the riddle.

A	B	E	H	I
3 × 6 = ____	11 × 6 = ____	8 × 6 = ____	9 × 6 = ____	5 × 6 = ____
K	**N**	**R**	**T**	**V**
2 × 6 = ____	10 × 6 = ____	6 × 6 = ____	12 × 6 = ____	4 × 6 = ____

Where do some fish keep their money?

___ ___ ___ / ___ ___ ___ ___ ___ / ___ ___ ___ ___!
72 54 48 / 36 30 24 48 36 / 66 18 60 12

2 Find the missing factor.

a) 6 × __ = 66 b) __ × 6 = 6 c) 6 × __ = 36 d) __ × 6 = 48

e) __ × 6 = 42 f) 6 × __ = 60 g) __ × 6 = 0 h) 6 × __ = 18

3 Tom has 6 toy cars. Each toy car has 4 wheels.
How many wheels are there in total?

I can multiply by 6.

Seven Times Table

1 Solve each question to solve the riddle.

Hint: Not all of the letters are used in the answer.

A	C	D	E	H
5 × 7 = ____	7 × 7 = ____	3 × 7 = ____	10 × 7 = ____	8 × 7 = ____
L	**M**	**O**	**P**	**S**
12 × 7 = ____	4 × 7 = ____	6 × 7 = ____	9 × 7 = ____	11 × 7 = ____

What kind of dog loves to have baths?

___ / ___ ___ ___ ___ ___ ___ ___ ___ ___ ___ !

35 / 77 56 35 28 63 42 42 21 84 70

2 Find the missing factor.

a 7 × __ = 14 b __ × 7 = 7 c 7 × __ = 21 d __ × 7 = 56

e __ × 7 = 70 f 7 × __ = 84 g __ × 7 = 42 h 7 × __ = 49

3 There are 7 candies in each bowl. There are 5 bowls.
How many candies are there in total?

I can multiply by 7.

Eight Times Table

1 Solve each question to solve the riddle.

Hint: Not all of the letters are used in the answer.

A	C	E	H	M
8 × 8 = ____	2 × 8 = ____	12 × 8 = ____	9 × 8 = ____	0 × 8 = ____
P	**R**	**S**	**T**	**W**
4 × 8 = ____	10 × 8 = ____	5 × 8 = ____	6 × 8 = ____	7 × 8 = ____

What do cats like to read in the morning?

___ ___ ___ / ___ ___ ___ ___ ___ ___ ___ ___ ___ !

48 72 96 / 0 96 56 40 32 64 32 96 80

2 Find the missing factor.

a) 8 × __ = 32 b) __ × 8 = 56 c) 8 × __ = 16 d) __ × 8 = 96

e) __ × 8 = 40 f) 8 × __ = 48 g) __ × 8 = 8 h) 8 × __ = 80

3 Jenny has 8 boxes of apples. Each box contains 9 apples. How many apples does Jenny have in total?

I can multiply by 8.

Nine Times Table

1. Solve each question to solve the riddle.

A	E	G	I	L
12 × 9 = ____	6 × 9 = ____	11 × 9 = ____	8 × 9 = ____	0 × 9 = ____
N	**P**	**S**	**T**	**W**
10 × 9 = ____	1 × 9 = ____	7 × 9 = ____	5 × 9 = ____	4 × 9 = ____

Why did the banana go to the doctor?

___ ___ / ___ ___ ___ ___ ' ___ / ___ ___ ___ ___ ___ ___ ___ /
72 45 / 36 108 63 90 ' 45 / 9 54 54 0 72 90 99 /

___ ___ ___ ___ !
36 54 0 0 !

2. Find the missing factor.

a) 9 × __ = 18 b) __ × 9 = 9 c) 9 × __ = 27 d) __ × 9 = 54

3. Mark has 9 bags of marbles. Each bag contains 10 marbles. How many marbles does Mark have in total?

I can multiply by 9.

Ten Times Table

1. Solve each question to solve the riddle.

E	F	G	H	I
12 × 10 = ____	4 × 10 = ____	5 × 10 = ____	10 × 10 = ____	0 × 10 = ____
K	**O**	**R**	**T**	**Y**
11 × 10 = ____	1 × 10 = ____	6 × 10 = ____	9 × 10 = ____	3 × 10 = ____

Why was the piano locked out?

___ ___ / ___ ___ ___ ___ ___ ___ / ___ ___ ___ / ___ ___ ___ !

0 90 / 40 10 60 50 10 90 / 90 100 120 / 110 120 30

2. Find the missing factor.

a) 10 × ____ = 20 b) ____ × 10 = 60 c) 10 × ____ = 110 d) ____ × 10 = 50

e) ____ × 10 = 30 f) 10 × ____ = 70 g) ____ × 10 = 0 h) 10 × ____ = 10

3. Sarah has 10 sets of crayons. Each set contains 4 crayons.
How many crayons does Sarah have in total?

I can multiply by 10.

Multiplication Division Table

1 Fill in the missing numbers.

×/÷	0	1	2	3	4	5	6	7	8	9	10
0	0	0	0	0	0		0	0	0	0	0
1	0		2	3	4	5	6	7	8		10
2	0	2	4		8	10	12	14	16	18	20
3		3	6	9	12	15	18		24	27	30
4	0	4	8	12		20	24	28	32	36	40
5	0	5		15	20	25	30	35	40		50
6		6	12	18	24	30		42	48	54	60
7	0	7	14	21	28		42	49	56	63	
8	0	8		24	32	40	48	56	64	72	80
9	0	9	18	27		45	54	63	72	81	90
10	0		20	30	40	50	60	70	80		100

Exploring Division

Division means dividing things into equal groups.

Put 6 boxes into groups of 3. 

The division statement is 6 ÷ 3 = 2.

dividend divisor quotient

Use circles to divide shapes into groups. Complete the division statement.

1 Divide 8 squares into groups of 4.

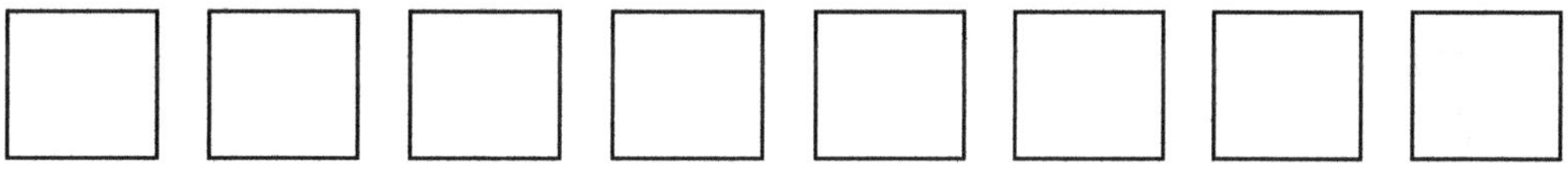

_______ groups

$8 \div 4 =$ _______

2 Divide 10 triangles into groups of 2.

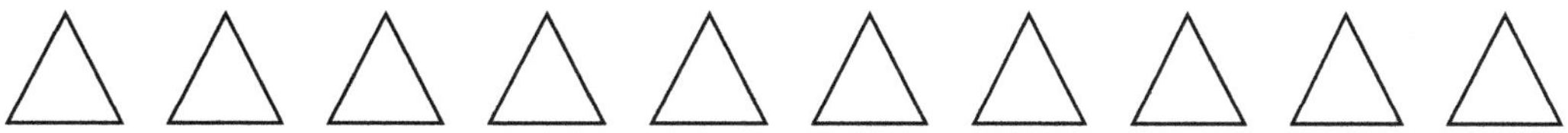

_______ groups

$10 \div 2 =$ _______

3 Divide 12 stars into groups of 3.

_______ groups

$12 \div 3 =$ _______

I can divide.

Relate Multiplication to Division

Use the array to complete the number sentence.

5 columns

2 rows 

Multiply

2 × <u>5</u> = 10

↑ 2 rows ↑ 5 columns ↑ total squares

Divide

10 ÷ 2 = <u>5</u>

↑ total squares ↑ 2 rows ↑ 5 columns

1

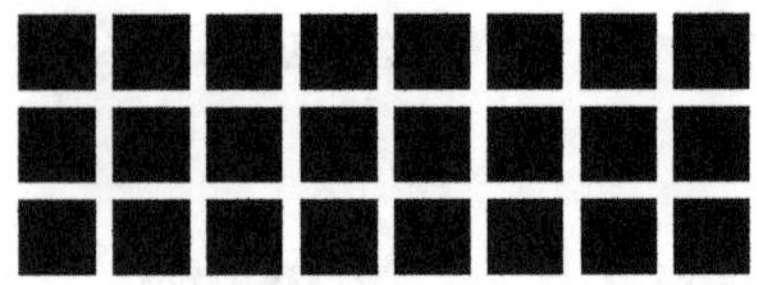

3 × _______ = 24

24 ÷ 3 = _______

2

_______ × 6 = 30

30 ÷ 6 = _______

3

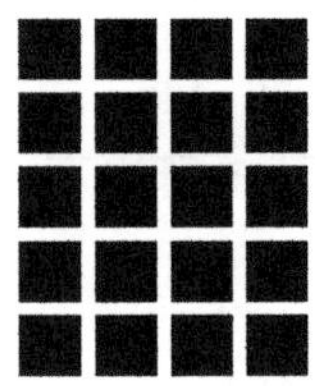

_______ × 4 = 20

20 ÷ 4 = _______

4

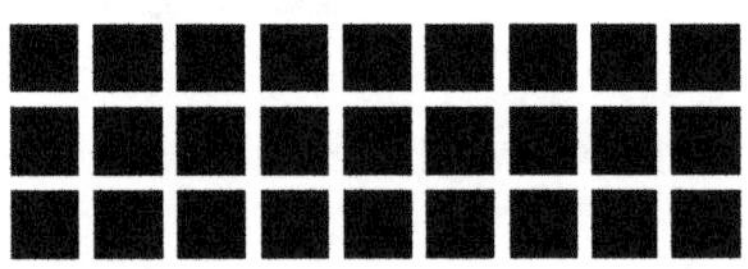

_______ × 9 = 27

27 ÷ 9 = _______

5

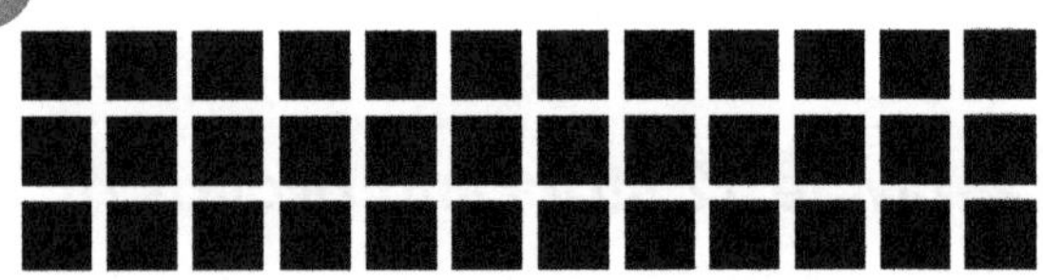

_______ × 12 = 36

36 ÷ 12 = _______

I can fill in number sentences.

Use Related Multiplication Facts
to Divide with 0 and 1

The quotient is always 1 when any number other than 0 is divided by itself. The **quotient** is the answer you get when you divide.

For example, 5 ÷ 5 = 1.

Think of a related multiplication fact. 5 × 1 = 5 so 5 ÷ 5 = 1

The quotient is always the same as the dividend when any number is divided by 1. The **dividend** is the number you start with when you divide.

For example, 8 ÷1 = 8.

Think of a related multiplication fact. 8 × 1 = 8 so 8 ÷ 1 = 8

The quotient is always 0 when 0 is divided by any number other than 0.

For example, 0 ÷ 3 = 0.

Think of a related multiplication fact. 3 × 0 = 0 so 0 ÷ 3 = 0

You cannot divide any number by 0.

Divide.

1. 11 ÷ 1 = _____
2. 5 ÷ 5 = _____
3. 0 ÷ 9 = _____
4. 8 ÷ 8 = _____
5. 0 ÷ 7 = _____
6. 7 ÷ 7 = _____
7. 0 ÷ 1 = _____
8. 0 ÷ 2 = _____
9. 6 ÷ 1 = _____
10. 0 ÷ 8 = _____
11. 9 ÷ 1 = _____
12. 4 ÷ 1 = _____

I can divide by 0 and 1.

Divide by 2

1 Solve each question to solve the riddle.

Hint: Not all of the letters are used in the answer.

A 14 ÷ 2 = ___	**E** 2 ÷ 2 = ___	**F** 10 ÷ 2 = ___	**H** 24 ÷ 2 = ___
I 6 ÷ 2 = ___	**L** 0 ÷ 2 = ___	**N** 8 ÷ 2 = ___	**O** 16 ÷ 2 = ___
S 22 ÷ 2 = ___	**T** 18 ÷ 2 = ___	**U** 12 ÷ 2 = ___	**W** 4 ÷ 2 = ___

How do you know when the moon has had enough to eat?

___ ___ ___ ___ / ___ ___ / ___ ___ / ___ ___ ___ ___ !

2 12 1 4 / 3 9 / 3 11 / 5 6 0 0

2 Find the missing dividend.

a ___ ÷ 2 = 6 **b** ___ ÷ 2 = 8 **c** ___ ÷ 2 = 12 **d** ___ ÷ 2 = 11

3 A farmer has 12 eggs. He wants to put them into cartons, with each carton holding 2 eggs. How many cartons will the farmer need?

I can divide by 2.

Divide by 3

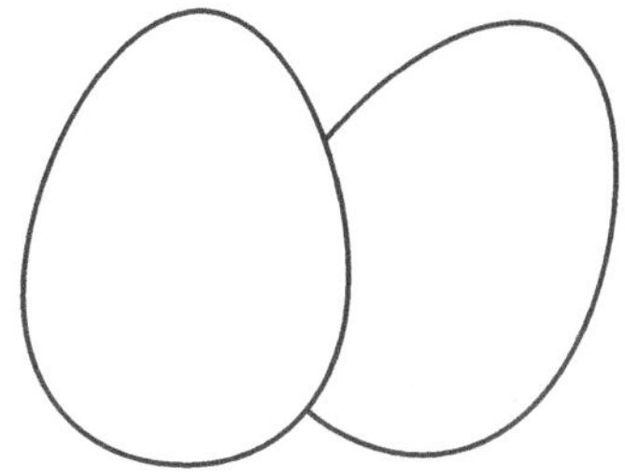

1 Solve each question to solve the riddle.

Hint: Not all of the letters are used in the answer.

A 15 ÷ 3 = ___	**C** 3 ÷ 3 = ___	**E** 24 ÷ 3 = ___	**K** 33 ÷ 3 = ___
L 6 ÷ 3 = ___	**M** 21 ÷ 3 = ___	**O** 27 ÷ 3 = ___	**P** 36 ÷ 3 = ___
R 30 ÷ 3 = ___	**S** 18 ÷ 3 = ___	**U** 12 ÷ 3 = ___	**Y** 9 ÷ 3 = ___

What did one egg say to the other egg?

___	___	___	/	___	___	___	___	___	/	___	___	/	___	___	!
3	9	4		1	10	5	1	11		7	8		4	12	

2 Find the missing dividend.

a ___ ÷ 3 = 9 **b** ___ ÷ 3 = 8 **c** ___ ÷ 3 = 7 **d** ___ ÷ 3 = 3

3 There are 21 apples in a basket. If Kaya wants to divide them equally among 3 friends, how many apples will each friend get?

Divide by 4

1 Solve each question to solve the riddle.

Hint: Not all of the letters are used in the answer.

A	D	E	I
20 ÷ 4 = ___	48 ÷ 4 = ___	8 ÷ 4 = ___	40 ÷ 4 = ___
L	**N**	**O**	**R**
16 ÷ 4 = ___	4 ÷ 4 = ___	36 ÷ 4 = ___	12 ÷ 4 = ___
S	**T**	**U**	**W**
28 ÷ 4 = ___	32 ÷ 4 = ___	44 ÷ 4 = ___	24 ÷ 4 = ___

Why did the clock get sick?

___ ___ / ___ ___ ___ / ___ ___ ___ / ___ ___ ___ ___!

10 8 / 6 5 7 / 3 11 1 / 12 9 6 1

2 Find the missing dividend.

a ___ ÷ 4 = 7 b ___ ÷ 4 = 5 c ___ ÷ 4 = 10 d ___ ÷ 4 = 1

3 A bakery baked 16 cupcakes. They want to package them in boxes, with each box holding 4 cupcakes. How many boxes will the bakery need?

I can divide by 4.

Divide by 5

1 Solve each question to solve the riddle.

Hint: Not all of the letters are used in the answer.

A 40 ÷ 5 = ___	**B** 10 ÷ 5 = ___	**E** 5 ÷ 5 = ___	**G** 45 ÷ 5 = ___
I 35 ÷ 5 = ___	**L** 25 ÷ 5 = ___	**N** 55 ÷ 5 = ___	**P** 20 ÷ 5 = ___
R 60 ÷ 5 = ___	**S** 15 ÷ 5 = ___	**T** 30 ÷ 5 = ___	**U** 50 ÷ 5 = ___

What is black, white, and red all over?

___ / ___ ___ ___ ___ ___ ___ ___ ___ / ___ ___ ___ ___ ___ ___ ___

8 / 3 10 11 2 10 12 11 6 / 4 1 11 9 10 7 11

2 Find the missing dividend.

a ___ ÷ 5 = 12 b ___ ÷ 5 = 10 c ___ ÷ 5 = 8 d ___ ÷ 5 = 3

3 Tom has 35 marbles that he wants to distribute equally into 5 bags. How many marbles will he put in each bag?

Divide by 6

1. Solve each question to solve the riddle.
   Hint: Not all of the letters are used in the answer.

A 24 ÷ 6 = ___	E 48 ÷ 6 = ___	F 12 ÷ 6 = ___	G 30 ÷ 6 = ___
H 18 ÷ 6 = ___	K 42 ÷ 6 = ___	L 6 ÷ 6 = ___	O 54 ÷ 6 = ___
R 72 ÷ 6 = ___	T 36 ÷ 6 = ___	W 60 ÷ 6 = ___	Y 66 ÷ 6 = ___

How do you make a goldfish old?

___ ___ ___ ___ / ___ ___ ___ ___ / ___ ___ ___ / ___ ___ ___ ___ ___ ___ / ___!
6 4 7 8 / 4 10 4 11 / 6 3 8 / 1 8 6 6 8 12 / 5

2. Find the missing dividend.

a) ___ ÷ 6 = 9 b) ___ ÷ 6 = 8 c) ___ ÷ 6 = 3 d) ___ ÷ 6 = 7

3. A toy store has 48 toy cars that they want to display on shelves. Each shelf can hold 6 toy cars. How many shelves will the store need?

 I can divide by 6.

Divide by 7

1 Solve each question to solve the riddle.

Hint: Not all of the letters are used in the answer.

A	C	D	E
63 ÷ 7 = ___	84 ÷ 7 = ___	42 ÷ 7 = ___	49 ÷ 7 = ___
F	**L**	**N**	**O**
14 ÷ 7 = ___	21 ÷ 7 = ___	56 ÷ 7 = ___	35 ÷ 7 = ___
R	**S**	**T**	**U**
77 ÷ 7 = ___	7 ÷ 7 = ___	28 ÷ 7 = ___	70 ÷ 7 = ___

How many tickles does it take to make an octopus to laugh?

___ ___ ___ ___ ___ ___ ___ ___ ___ /
4 7 8 4 9 12 3 7 1

___ ___ / ___ ___ ___ ___ ___ ___!
5 2 12 5 10 11 1 7

2 Find the missing dividend.

a ___ ÷ 7 = 8 **b** ___ ÷ 7 = 5 **c** ___ ÷ 7 = 6 **d** ___ ÷ 7 = 10

3 Jenny has 49 candies. She wants to divide the candies equally among her 7 friends. How many candies will each friend get?

Divide by 8

1 Solve each question to solve the riddle.

Hint: Not all of the letters are used in the answer.

A 48 ÷ 8 = ___	**B** 24 ÷ 8 = ___	**C** 40 ÷ 8 = ___	**E** 32 ÷ 8 = ___
L 56 ÷ 8 = ___	**M** 72 ÷ 8 = ___	**N** 96 ÷ 8 = ___	**O** 16 ÷ 8 = ___
P 80 ÷ 8 = ___	**R** 64 ÷ 8 = ___	**S** 8 ÷ 8 = ___	**U** 88 ÷ 8 = ___

What goes up when rain comes down?

___ ___ / ___ ___ ___ ___ ___ ___ ___ ___!
6 12 / 11 9 3 8 4 7 7 6

2 Find the missing dividend.

a ___ ÷ 8 = 3   b ___ ÷ 8 = 11   c ___ ÷ 8 = 8   d ___ ÷ 8 = 10

3 Mark has a collection of 64 stickers that he wants to put into albums. Each album can hold 8 stickers. How many albums will Mark need?

I can divide by 8.

Divide by 9

1. Solve each question to solve the riddle.

   Hint: Not all of the letters are used in the answer.

A	B	C	D
45 ÷ 9 = ___	36 ÷ 9 = ___	72 ÷ 9 = ___	99 ÷ 9 = ___
H	**I**	**O**	**R**
18 ÷ 9 = ___	81 ÷ 9 = ___	54 ÷ 9 = ___	90 ÷ 9 = ___
S	**T**	**U**	**V**
27 ÷ 9 = ___	63 ÷ 9 = ___	9 ÷ 9 = ___	108 ÷ 9 = ___

Why did the computer go to the doctor?

___ ___ / ___ ___ ___ / ___ / ___ ___ ___ ___ ___ !

9 7 / 2 5 11 / 5 / 12 9 10 1 3

2. Find the missing dividend.

a ___ ÷ 9 = 4 b ___ ÷ 9 = 8 c ___ ÷ 9 = 3 d ___ ÷ 9 = 5

3. There are 45 chocolates in a box. Sarah wants to share them equally among 9 friends. How many chocolates will each friend get?

Divide by 10

1 Solve each question to solve the riddle.

Hint: Not all of the letters are used in the answer.

A	E	G	H
40 ÷ 10 = ___	80 ÷ 10 = ___	110 ÷ 10 = ___	30 ÷ 10 = ___
I	**M**	**O**	**P**
120 ÷ 10 = ___	20 ÷ 10 = ___	60 ÷ 10 = ___	10 ÷ 10 = ___
R	**T**	**U**	**V**
90 ÷ 10 = ___	50 ÷ 10 = ___	70 ÷ 10 = ___	100 ÷ 10 = ___

Where do cows like to go on a Saturday night?

___ ___ ___ / ___ ___ ___ ___ ___ ___ ___ /
5 3 8 / 2 6 6 6 10 12 8 /

___ ___ ___ ___ ___ ___ ___!
5 3 8 4 5 9 8

2 Find the missing dividend.

a ___ ÷ 10 = 8 **b** ___ ÷ 10 = 3 **c** ___ ÷ 10 = 12 **d** ___ ÷ 10 = 7

3 A soccer team has 70 players. They want to form equal groups for practice, with each group having 10 players. How many groups will the team form?

I can divide by 10.

Repeated Addition with Fractions

Numerators are how many parts of the whole you have. → $\frac{1}{5}$

Denominators are the total number of parts in the whole. → 5

Add pieces to a whole by using repeated addition.

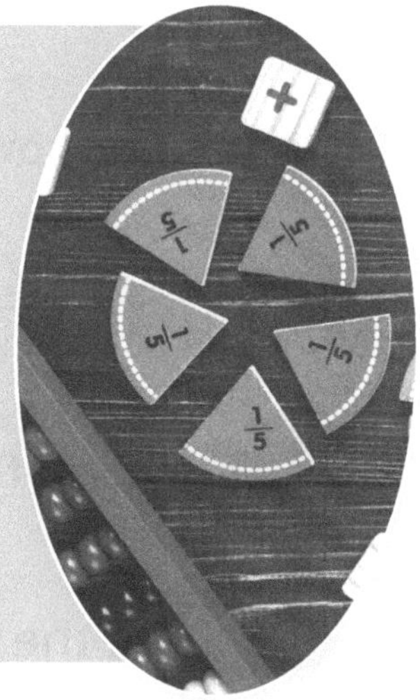

$$\frac{1}{5} + \frac{1}{5} + \frac{1}{5} + \frac{1}{5} + \frac{1}{5} = \frac{5}{5}$$

Use repeated addition to add the fraction pieces.

Colour in the fraction model and write the fraction below.

1

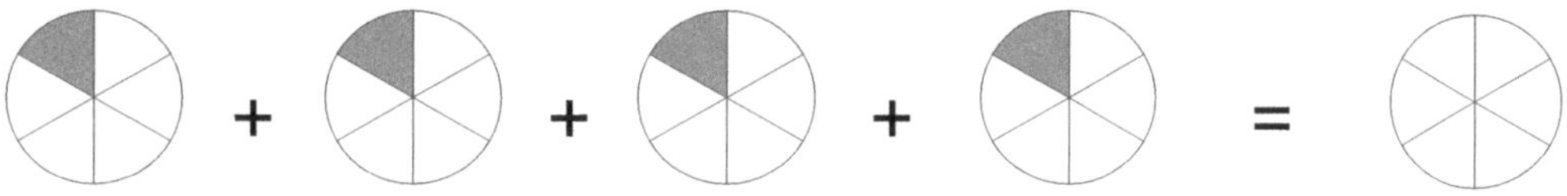

$\frac{\square}{\square} + \frac{\square}{\square} + \frac{\square}{\square} + \frac{\square}{\square} = \frac{\square}{\square}$

2

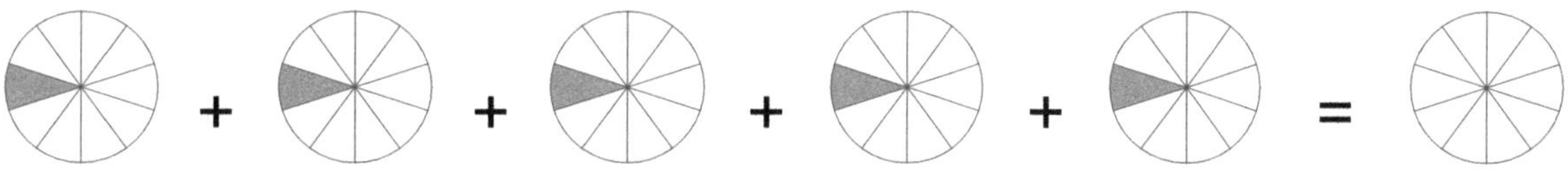

$\frac{\square}{\square} + \frac{\square}{\square} + \frac{\square}{\square} + \frac{\square}{\square} + \frac{\square}{\square} = \frac{\square}{\square}$

3

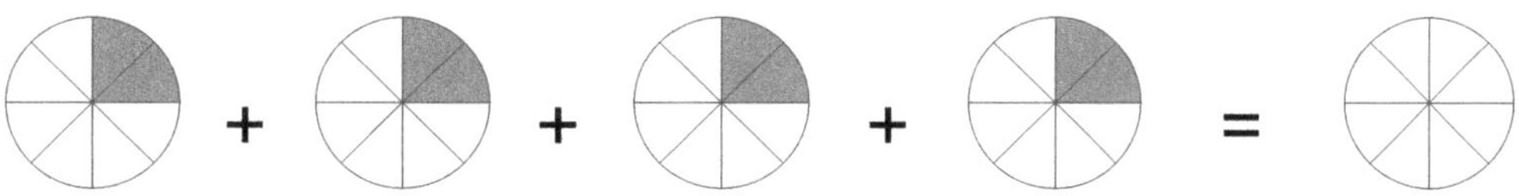

$\frac{\square}{\square} + \frac{\square}{\square} + \frac{\square}{\square} + \frac{\square}{\square} = \frac{\square}{\square}$

I can add fractions.

Stating Ratios

A **ratio** shows the relationship between two amounts.

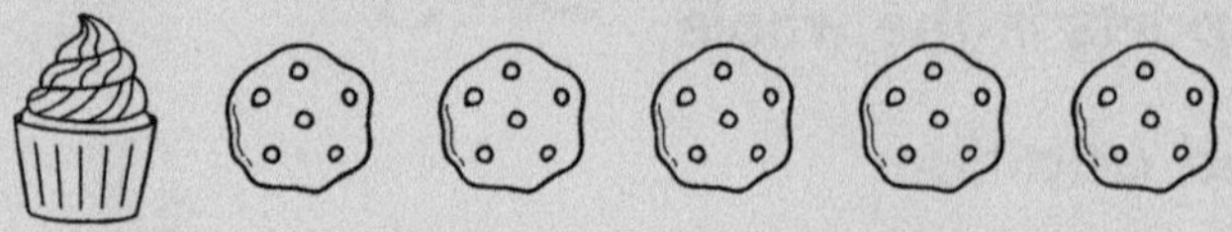

For every 1 cupcake, there are 5 cookies.

The ratio of cupcakes to cookies can be expressed as 1:5, or 1 to 5, or $\frac{1}{5}$.

1 State the ratio three ways.

a The ratio of strawberries to doughnuts is

____ : ____

____ to ____

$\frac{\_\_\_}{\_\_\_}$

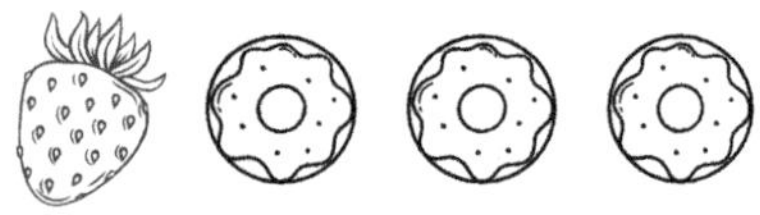

b The ratio of grapes to pineapples is

____ : ____

____ to ____

$\frac{\_\_\_}{\_\_\_}$

c The ratio of ice cream to cookies is

____ : ____

____ to ____

$\frac{\_\_\_}{\_\_\_}$

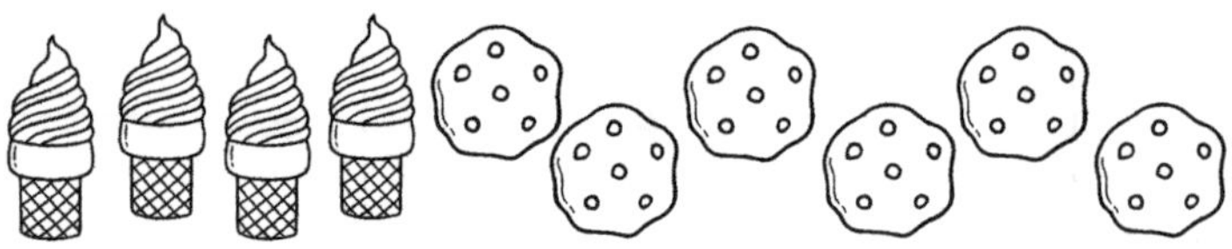

2 At the market there are 5 potatoes for every 1 tomato. What is the ratio?

I can state ratios.

Scaling Ratios

A **ratio** shows the relationship between two amounts.

The ratio of notebooks to backpacks is 2:4.

This can be scaled up to 4 notebooks for every 8 backpacks, or 4:8.

This can be scaled down to 1 notebook for every 2 backpacks, or 1:2.

State the ratio. Then state a scaled up and scaled down equivalent.

1

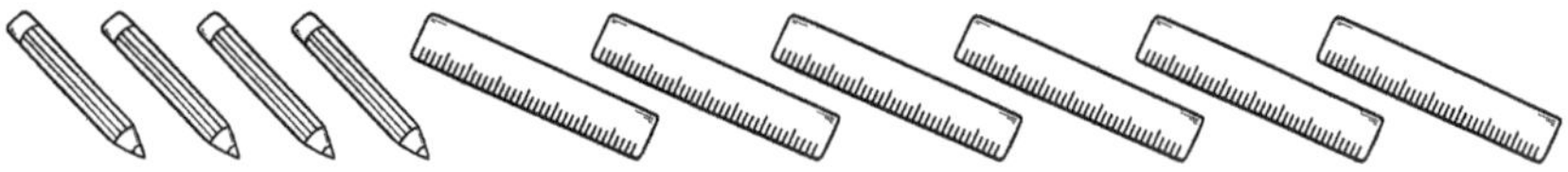

The ratio of pencils to rulers is ______ : ______.

Scaled up: ______ : ______ Scaled down: ______ : ______

2

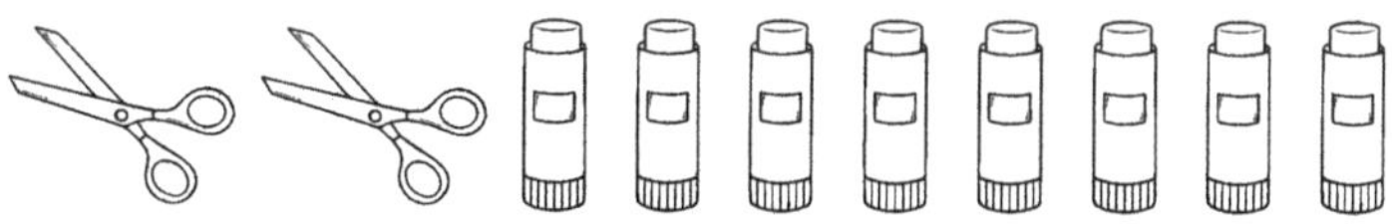

The ratio of scissors to glue sticks is ______ : ______.

Scaled up: ______ : ______ Scaled down: ______ : ______

3

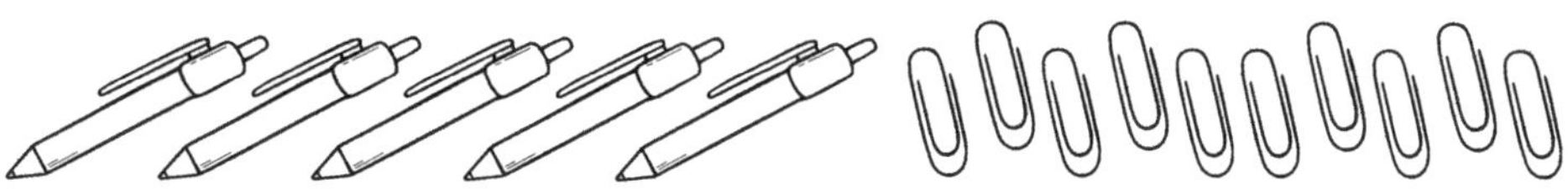

The ratio of pens to paperclips is ______ : ______.

Scaled up: ______ : ______ Scaled down: ______ : ______

I can scale ratios.

Show What You Know!

1 Choose the number sentence that describes the drawing below.

(X X X / X X X) (X X X / X X X) (X X X / X X X)

(a) 3 × 4 = 12

(b) 6 × 2 = 12

(c) 3 × 6 = 18

(d) 4 × 2 = 8

2 Pick the number to correctly complete the number sentence below.

? × 9 = 9

(a) 2 (b) 9

(c) 0 (d) 1

3 Choose which of the following does not have the same value as 6 × 3.

(a) 9 × 2 (b) 3 × 6

(c) 2 × 9 (d) 4 × 4

4 What is 24 ÷ 8?

(a) 4 (b) 16

(c) 12 (d) 3

5 Solve.

(a) 5 × ____ = 35 (b) ____ ÷ 8 = 4 (c) 6 × ____ = 42 (d) ____ ÷ 10 = 3

(e) ____ ÷ 3 = 8 (f) 9 × ____ = 45 (g) 4 × ____ = 12 (h) 64 ÷ ____ = 8

(i) 2 × ____ = 20 (j) ____ ÷ 1 = 7 (k) ____ ÷ 4 = 6 (l) ____ × 7 = 63

Show What You Know! (continued)

6 Use repeated addition to add the fraction pieces.

Colour in the fraction model and write the fraction below.

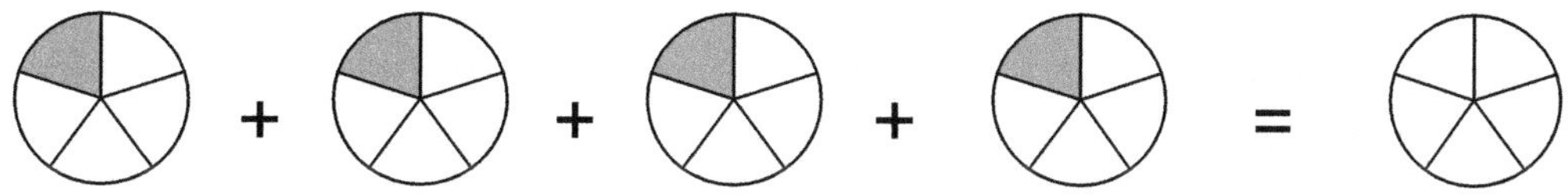

___ + ___ + ___ + ___ = ___

7 State the ratio three ways.

a **The ratio of lanterns to mugs is**

_______ : _______

_______ to _______

___

b **The ratio of pencils to glue is**

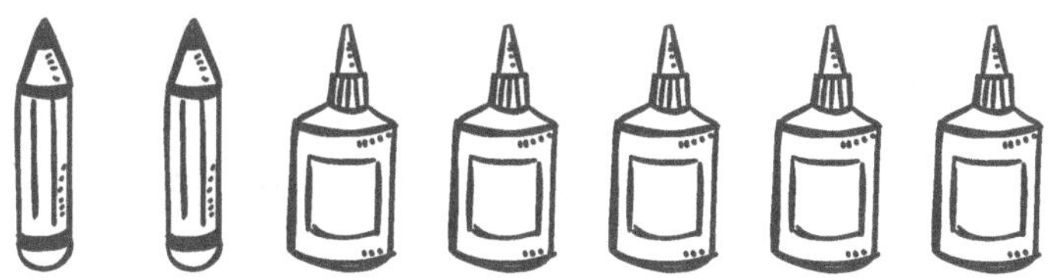

_______ : _______

_______ to _______

___

8 State the ratio. Then state a scaled up and scaled down equivalent.

The ratio of drinks to sandwiches is _______ : _______ .

Scaled up: _______ : _______ **Scaled down: _______ : _______**

I Can Checklist:

Patterning

Identify and describe repeating elements and operations in a variety of patterns, including patterns found in real-life contexts. For example,

- ***I can** find and talk about parts that repeat in different patterns, like a colour pattern in my sock drawer.*
- ***I can** spot patterns in real-life things, like the days of the week repeating every seven days.*
- ***I can** point out operations (add, subtract, multiply, divide) that repeat in a pattern.*

Create and translate patterns that have repeating elements, movements, or operations using various representations, including shapes, numbers, and tables of values. For example,

- ***I can** make patterns with shapes, numbers, or tables.*
- ***I can** change patterns into different forms.*

Determine pattern rules and use them to extend patterns, make and justify predictions, and identify missing elements in patterns that have repeating elements, movements, or operations. For example,

- ***I can** figure out the rule of a pattern and use it to make the pattern longer.*
- ***I can** use pattern rules to guess what will happen next and find missing parts in patterns.*

Create and describe patterns to illustrate relationships among whole numbers up to 1000. For example,

- ***I can** make and talk about number patterns up to 1000.*
- ***I can** use patterns to show connections between numbers.*

Exploring Patterns

A **pattern** repeats. The **core** of the pattern repeats over and over.

□ ○ □ ○ □ ○ □ ○ □ ○ □ ○ □ ○ □ ○

1. Circle the core of the repeating pattern.

a. 5 5 8 8 5 5 8 8 5 5 8 8 5 5

b. △ ▽ △ ▽ △ ▽ △ ▽ △ ▽ △ ▽ △ ▽ △

c. ★ ○ ■ ★ ○ ■ ★ ○ ■ ★ ○ ■ ★

A **term** is a single piece of a pattern.

10 20 30 40 50 60

Pattern rule: Start at 10. Add 10 each time.

2. Write the first 5 terms for each pattern rule.

a. Pattern rule: Start at 5. Add 3 each time.

b. Pattern rule: Add 20 each time, starting at 40.

c. Pattern rule: Begin at 100 and add 50 each time.

I can identify the core and terms of patterns.

Extending Patterns

Extending a pattern adds the next terms to the pattern based on the pattern rule.

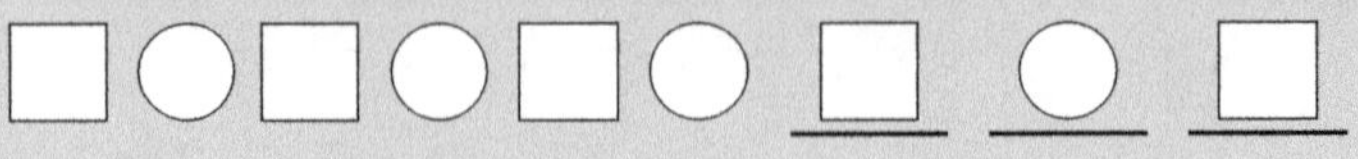

Extend the pattern by its next two terms.

1. 3 4 5 3 4 5 3 4 5 _____ _____

2.  _____ _____

3. 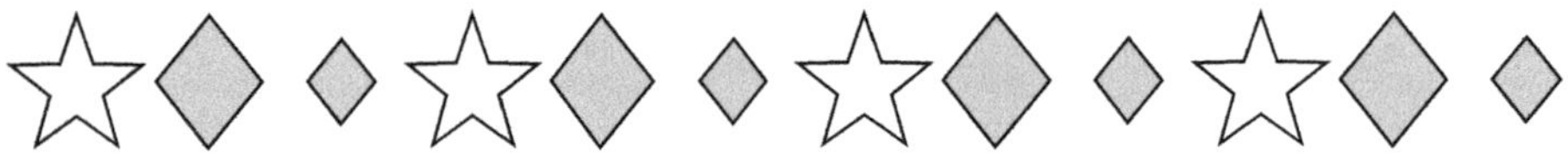 _____ _____

4. 25 50 75 25 50 75 25 _____ _____

5. 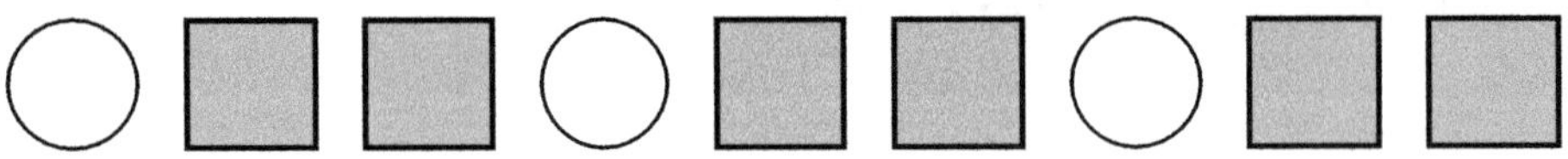 _____ _____

6. 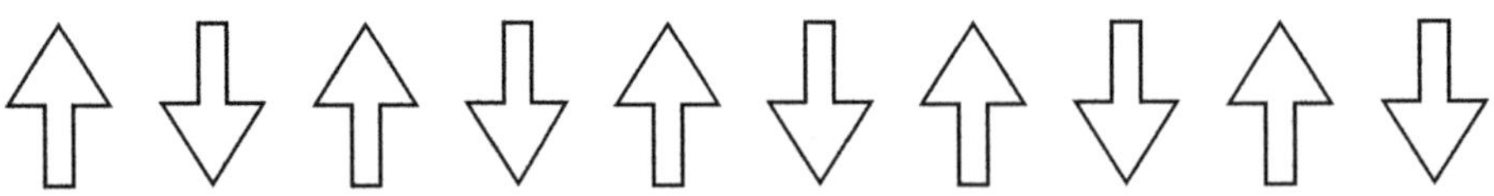 _____ _____

7. 20 10 30 20 10 30 20 _____ _____

I can extend patterns.

Translating Patterns

Translating a pattern means changing each term of a pattern into another term while keeping the pattern rule the same. Here is the same pattern in different forms.

Shapes	Sounds	Letters
	clap, quack, clap, quack, clap	A B A B A

Translate each pattern into two different forms.

1. 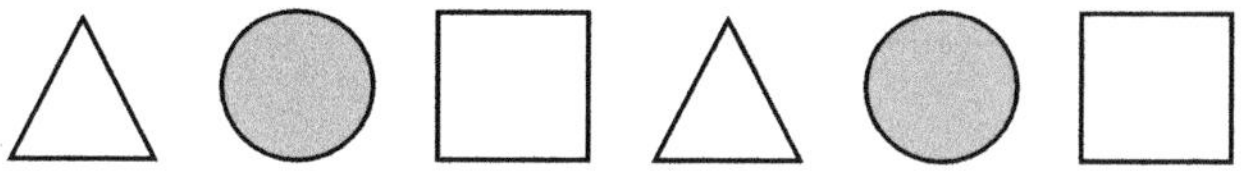

2. 50 50 100 50 50 100

3. 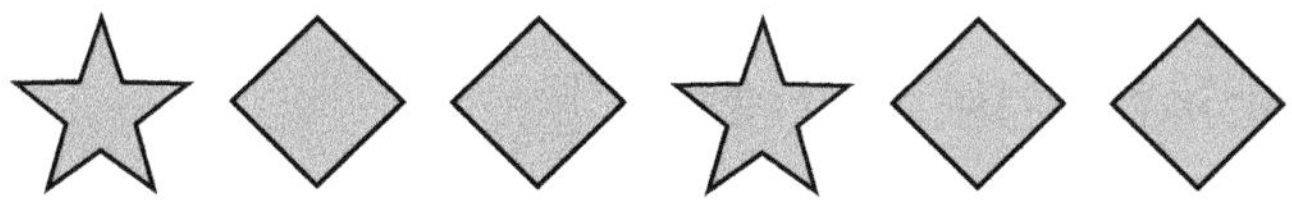

4. 

I can translate patterns.

Exploring Increasing Number Patterns

In an **increasing number pattern,** the number increases by the same amount each time.

2 (+2) 4 (+2) 6 (+2) 8 (+2) 10 (+2) 12 (+2) 14 (+2) 16 (+2) 18 (+2) 20

Pattern rule: Start at 2. Add 2 each time.

1. Extend the increasing number pattern.

   a. 5, 10, 15, ______, ______, ______, ______

   Pattern rule: ____________________

   b. 7, 17, 27, ______, ______, ______, ______

   Pattern rule: ____________________

   c. 235, 240, 245, ______, ______, ______, ______

   Pattern rule: ____________________

2. Fill in the missing number to complete the pattern.

   a. 22, ______, 26, 28, 30, 32

   b. 106, 109, 112, ______, 118

3. Create your own increasing number pattern.

   ______, ______, ______, ______, ______

   Pattern rule: ____________________

I can increase number patterns.

Exploring Decreasing Number Patterns

In a **decreasing number pattern**, the number decreases by the same amount each time.

20 (−2) 18 (−2) 16 (−2) 14 (−2) 12 (−2) 10 (−2) 8 (−2) 6 (−2) 4 (−2) 2

Pattern rule: Start at 20. Subtract 2 each time.

1 Extend the decreasing number pattern.

a 700, 600, 500, ______, ______, ______, ______

Pattern rule: ____

b 94, 84, 74, ______, ______, ______, ______

Pattern rule: ____

c 300, 275, 250, ______, ______, ______, ______

Pattern rule: ____

2 Fill in the missing number to complete the pattern.

a 72, 63, 54, ______, 36

b 895, 795, ______, 595, 495

3 Create your own decreasing number pattern.

______, ______, ______, ______, ______

Pattern rule: ____

I can decrease number patterns.

Exploring Growing Patterns

1. Continue the growing pattern.

a 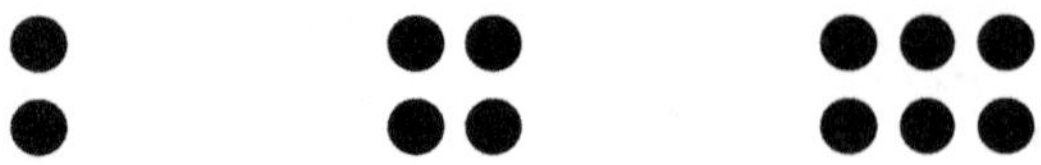 ____________ ____________

b **Create a growing pattern using a geometric shape. Describe your pattern rule.**

Pattern rule: ____

2. Jerry created a pattern for art class using geometric shapes. Draw the next part of the pattern.

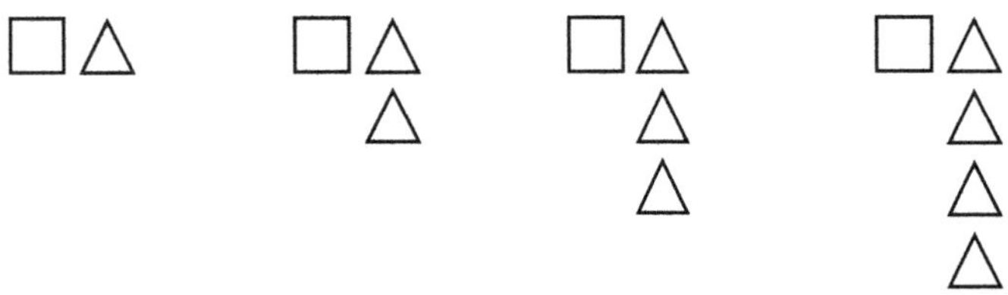

____

3. Milly drew a growing pattern. Draw the next part of the pattern.

____

I can continue growing patterns.

Exploring Shrinking Patterns

1. Continue the shrinking pattern.

a.

______ ______

b. **Create a shrinking pattern using a geometric shape. Describe your pattern rule.**

Pattern rule: ______________________

2. A pattern is made by removing 2 blocks each time.
How many blocks will the next two terms have? Show your work.

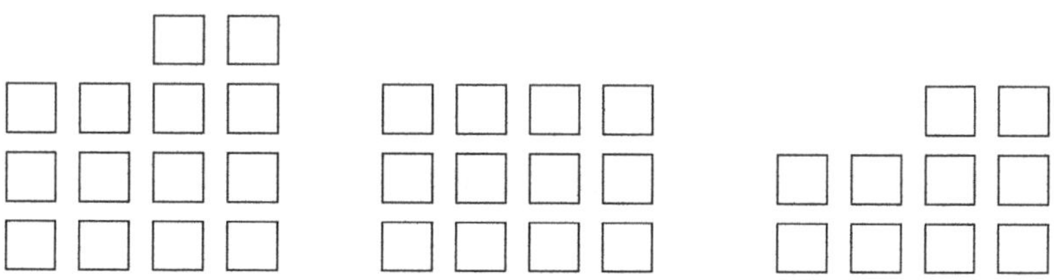

______ ______

Term 1 Term 2 Term 3 Term 4 Term 5

I can continue shrinking patterns.

Exploring Pattern Attributes

An **attribute** of a pattern is a characteristic that is used to describe the pattern, like the size, colour, or orientation.

Size

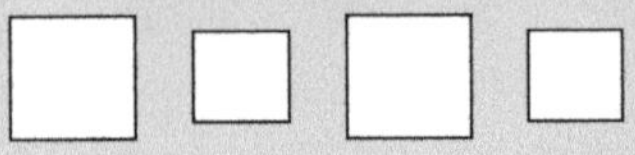

Colour

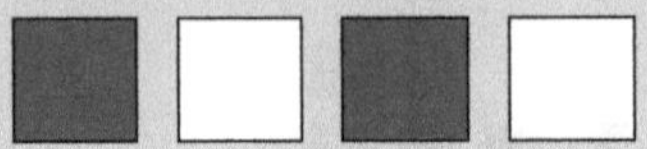

Orientation

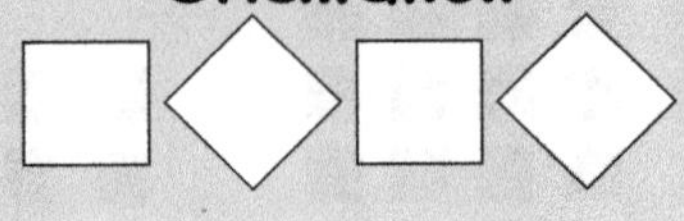

1 Patterns can have more than one attribute. How does the pattern change? Circle the attributes. Describe the pattern rule to a partner.

a 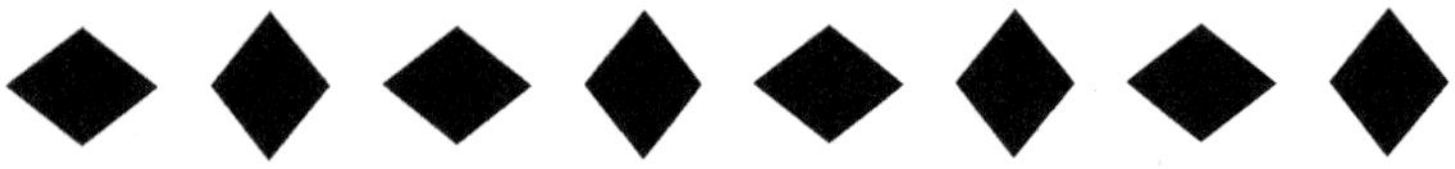 size colour orientation

b 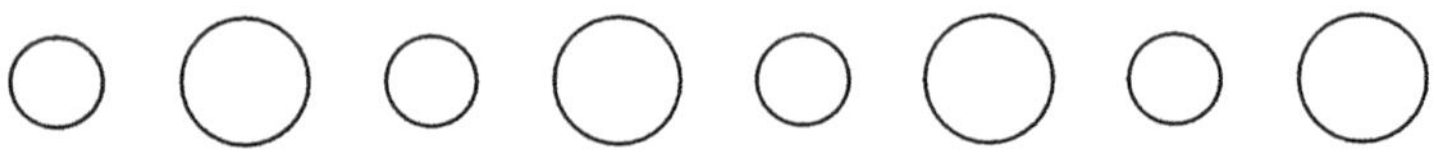 size colour orientation

c 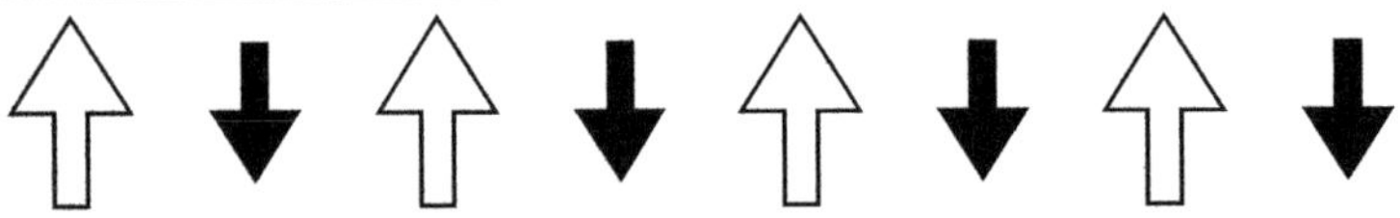 size colour orientation

2 Create a repeating pattern that changes **shape and orientation**.

3 Create a repeating pattern that changes **colour and size**.

4 Create a repeating pattern that changes **colour and orientation**.

I can identify pattern attributes.

Input Output Tables

Input output tables show patterns using a table of values.
The input is the number that is being changed.
The output is the number after the change.

Pattern rule: Input + 1 = Output

Input	Output
1	2
2	3
3	4

1. Complete the input/output table using the given pattern rule.

a) Rule: Add 50

Input	Output
1	
2	
3	
4	

b) Rule: Multiply by 2

Input	Output
1	
2	
3	
4	

c) Rule: Multiply by 5

Input	Output
1	
2	
3	
4	

d) Rule: Add 100

Input	Output
1	
2	
3	
4	

2. Mrs. Banh gives 4 papers to each of her students. Complete the table.

Students	1	2	3	4	5	6	7	8
Papers								

I can fill in input/output tables.

Solving Pattern Problems

1 Madison has a book with 11 chapters. She reads chapter 1 on the first day of September. Three days later, she reads chapter 2.

September						
S	M	T	W	Th	F	S
	1 Chapter 1	2	3	4	5	6
7	8	9	10	11	12	13
14	15	16	17	18	19	20
21	22	23	24	25	26	27
28	29	30				

Will Madison finish the book by September 30 if she continues to read one chapter every three days?

Circle one: **Yes** **No**

Explain your answer.

I can solve pattern problems.

Solving Pattern Problems (continued)

2. Mrs. Bell has 8 full boxes of crayons and 6 loose crayons. She starts by counting the 6 loose crayons, then adds in each full crayon box like this:

   6, 16, 26, 36, . . .

   How many crayons does she have in total?

Show your work.

Mrs. Bell has ____________ crayons.

3. Lee wants to collect 98 marbles.
   He already has 17 marbles and buys 9 more each week.
   How many weeks will it take for Lee to have a total of 98 marbles?

Show your work.

It takes ___________ weeks for Lee to have 98 marbles.

I can solve pattern problems.

Show What You Know!

1. Circle the core of the repeating pattern.

6 7 8 6 7 8 6 7 8 6 7 8

2. Draw the figure that comes next in the pattern.

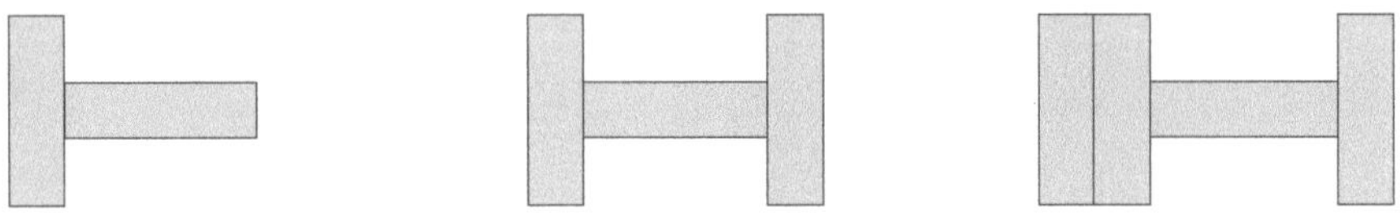

____

3. Extend the number pattern.

a. **100, 125, 150, _______, _______, _______, _______**

Pattern rule: ____

b. **90, 88, 86, _______, _______, _______, _______**

Pattern rule: ____

4. Translate the pattern into two different forms.

9 9 4 4 9 9 4 4 9 9 4 4

Show What You Know! (continued)

5 Niall makes the shrinking pattern below.

a Fill in the blanks with the next 3 numbers in Niall's pattern.

81, 77, 73, 69, ____, ____, ____

b Describe Niall's pattern rule.

c Use Niall's pattern rule to fill in the missing numbers in the pattern below.

_____, 36, _____, _____, 24, _____

6 Create a repeating pattern that changes **colour and orientation**.

7 Complete the input/output table using the given pattern rule.

a Rule: Multiply by 10

Input	Output
1	
2	
3	
4	

b Rule: Add 20

Input	Output
1	
2	
3	
4	

I Can Checklist:

Equations & Inequalities

Describe how variables are used, and use them in various contexts as appropriate. For example,

- ***I can*** *talk about how a letter can stand for a number in math.*
- ***I can*** *use variables in different math situations.*

Determine whether given sets of addition, subtraction, multiplication, and division expressions are equivalent or not equivalent. For example,

- ***I can*** *check if different math sentences mean the same thing.*
- ***I can*** *do this with adding, subtracting, multiplying, and dividing.*

Identify and use equivalent relationships for whole numbers up to 1000 in various contexts. For example,

- ***I can*** *find and use equivalent relationships between numbers up to 1000.*

Matching Expressions

Number expressions are **equivalent** if both sides equal the same number.

20 + 20 and 15 + 25 both equal 40

1. Draw a line to match the equivalent addition expressions.

7 + 18	15 + 15
11 + 14 + 5	9 + 9 + 9
12 + 15	12 + 6 + 7

2. Draw a line to match the equivalent subtraction expressions.

100 − 64	80 − 14 − 13
78 − 25	94 − 72
39 − 17	55 − 19

3. Draw a line to match the equivalent multiplication expressions.

4 × 9	12 × 4
8 × 6	5 × 2 × 3
3 × 10	6 × 6

4. Draw a line to match the equivalent division expressions.

56 ÷ 7	30 ÷ 5
60 ÷ 12	16 ÷ 2
48 ÷ 8	5 ÷ 1

I can match equivalent expressions.

Exploring Variables

A **variable** is a letter or symbol that represents a number we don't know.

For example,

Joe has 10 stamps. He now has 15 stamps. How many stamps did he get?
The x represents the number we don't know.

$$10 + x = 15$$
$$10 + 5 = 15 \qquad x = 5$$

1 Circle the **variable** in the equation.

a $15 + n = 21$

b $y - 12 = 8$

c $6 + 4 = p$

2 Solve to find the **variable**.

a $p - 6 = 16$

$p =$

b $20 + 17 = m$

$m =$

c $y + 24 = 39$

$y =$

3 Circle the equation that matches the word problem.

a Caleb has 30 markers in his pencil case. Julie borrows n markers from Caleb. Caleb now has 18 markers in his pencil case.

$n - 18 = 30$ $\qquad$ $n + 18 = 30$ $\qquad$ $30 - n = 18$

b Lee has n gummy bears in a jar. Lee buys a package with 14 gummy bears and adds them to the jar. Now Lee has 56 gummy bears.

$n - 14 = 56$ $\qquad$ $n + 14 = 56$ $\qquad$ $56 - n = 14$

I can identify variables.

Exploring Balanced Equations

A **balanced equation** means both sides of the equal sign equal the same number.

Balanced: **$10 + 5 = 15$ ✓** Not Balanced: **$2 \times 4 \neq 10$**

1 Put a check mark in the box if the equation is *balanced*. (✓)
Put a line through the equal sign if the equation is *not balanced*. (≠)

a $20 + 15 = 35$	**b** $40 - 20 = 18$	**c** $3 \times 5 = 15$
d $28 \div 7 = 6$	**e** $16 + 21 = 30$	**f** $54 - 31 = 23$
g $6 \times 8 = 48$	**h** $36 - 18 = 18$	**i** $10 \times 4 = 45$

2 Fill in the blank with the missing number to balance the equation.

a 16 + ______ = 35	**b** 55 − 45 = ______	**c** ______ × 6 = 24
d 80 ÷ 10 = ______	**e** 3 × ______ = 33	**f** 60 + 18 = ______

Show What You Know!

1 Draw a line to match the equivalent expressions.

$13 + 19$	$54 - 20 - 22$
7×3	$54 \div 6$
$17 - 8$	8×4
$60 \div 5$	$7 + 14$

2 Solve to find the **variable**.

a $22 + m = 34$

$m =$

b $r + 12 = 25$

$r =$

c $15 - 11 = n$

$n =$

d $18 - k = 6$

$k =$

e $14 + 19 = p$

$p =$

f $h - 15 = 12$

$h =$

3 Write an equation that matches the word problem.

a There are n oranges in a basket. Shania adds 13 oranges to the basket Now there are 36 oranges in the basket.

b Charlie has 27 sweaters in his drawer. Charlie donates n sweaters to charity. Now Charlie has 11 sweaters.

Show What You Know! (continued)

4 Chris solves the math question below.

57 − 29 = 28

Which number sentence will help Chris check his answer?

- **a** 29 − 28 = 1
- **b** 57 + 29 = 86
- **c** 86 − 29 = 57
- **d** 28 + 29 = 57

5 Consider the number sentence below.

40 − 13 = 27

Pick the number sentence that belongs to the same fact family.

- **a** 35 − 8 = 27
- **b** 13 + 27 = 40
- **c** 40 − 10 = 30
- **d** 40 − 27 = 13

6 In which number sentence can 8 replace the question mark and make the number sentence true?

- **a** 35 − 10 = 1 + ?
- **b** 35 − 10 = 17 + ?
- **c** 35 − 10 = 19 + ?
- **d** 35 − 10 = 18 + ?

7 Pick the correct equation below.

- **a** 9 + 18 = 5 + 9 + 13
- **b** 9 + 18 = 10 + 2 + 9
- **c** 9 + 18 = 9 + 9 + 6
- **d** 9 + 18 = 8 + 12 + 4

8 Pick the number that completes the number sentence below.

18 − ? = 5 + 7

- **a** 4
- **b** 10
- **c** 6
- **d** 5

9 Pick the number that completes the number sentence below.

15 + 20 = 18 + ?

- **a** 15
- **b** 17
- **c** 12
- **d** 19

I Can Checklist:
Coding Skills

Solve problems and create computational representations of mathematical situations by writing and executing code, including code that involves sequential, concurrent, and repeating events. For example,

- ***I can*** *solve problems and show math situations by writing and running code.*
- ***I can*** *write code that does things in order (sequential), at the same time (concurrent), or over and over (repeating).*

Read and alter existing code, including code that involves sequential, concurrent, and repeating events, and describe how changes to the code affect the outcomes. For example,

- ***I can*** *read and change code that other people wrote.*
- ***I can*** *talk about how changing the code changes what it does.*

Introduction to Coding

Coding is when we tell computers what to do. We give them instructions called code. Coding is how we make websites, phone apps, and other things we use every day.

1. Colour the pictures of things that need coding to run.

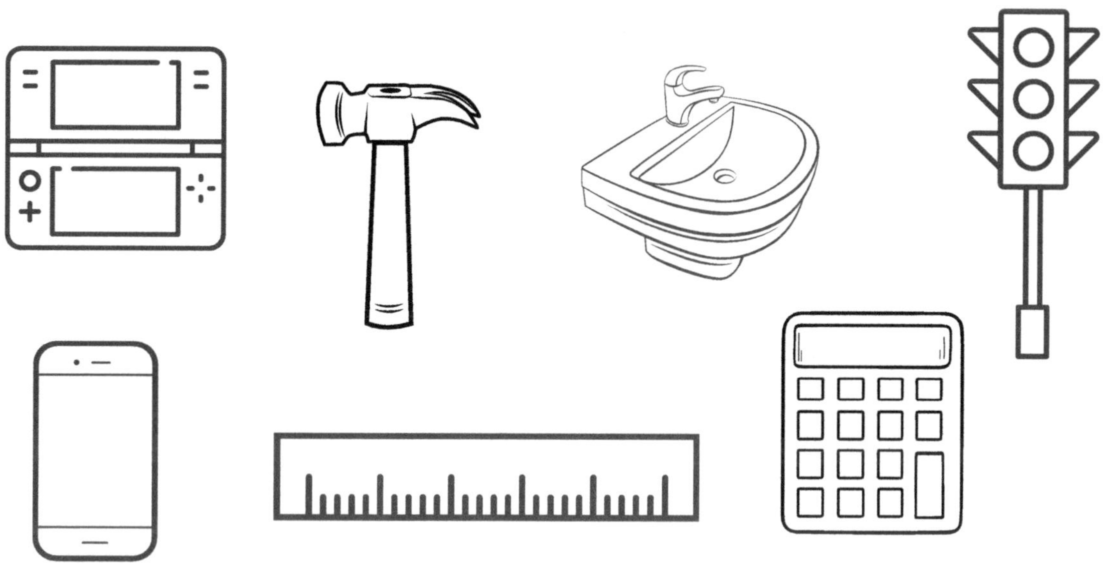

2. List some electronics that people use that need coding to run.

1 ______________________________

2 ______________________________

3 ______________________________

3. How does coding affect your daily life?

Complete the Code

A command is a specific instruction in a line of code that tells a device what to do.

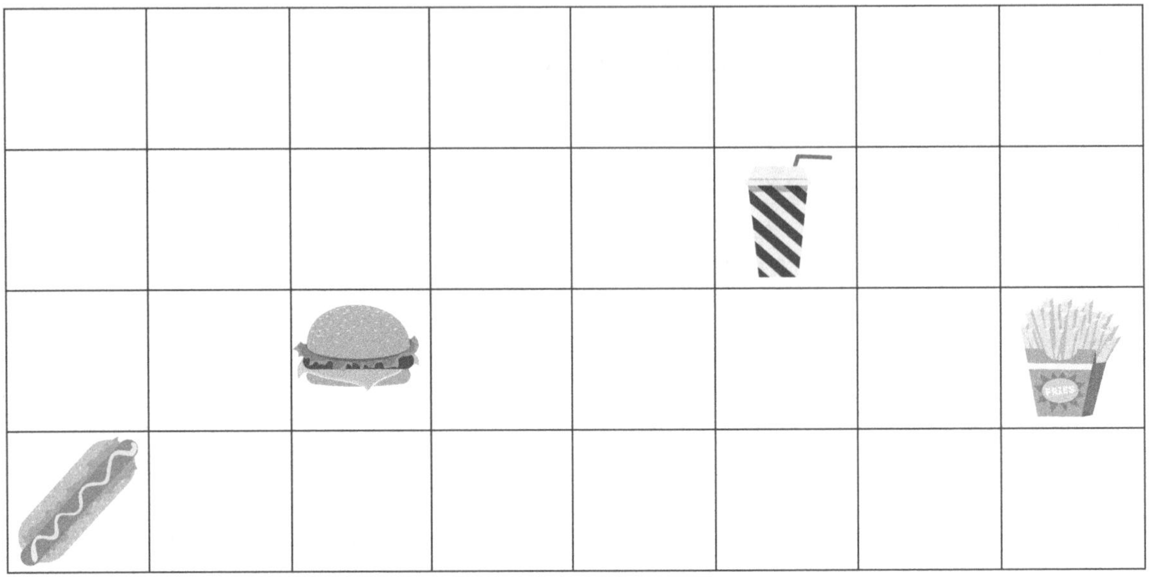

Complete the line of code by drawing the commands using arrows.

1

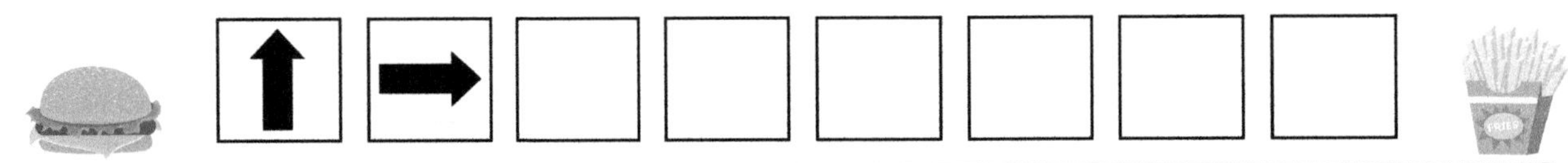

2

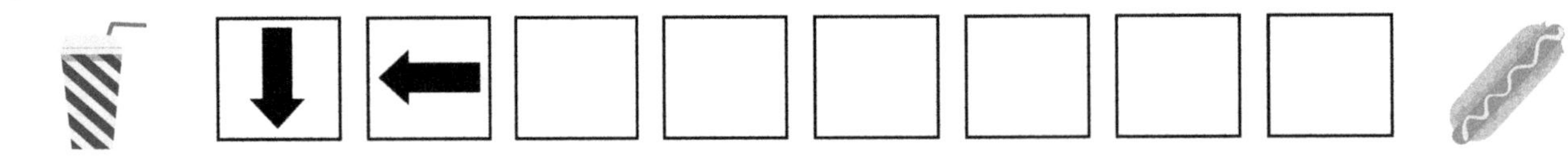

3

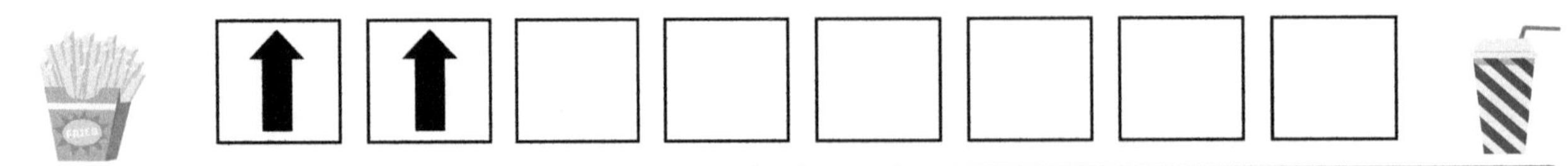

I can complete the code.

Exploring Writing Code

A command is a specific instruction in a line of code that tells a device what to do.

For example,

Line 1: go 4 spaces right

Line 2: go 1 space up

Line 3: collect chick

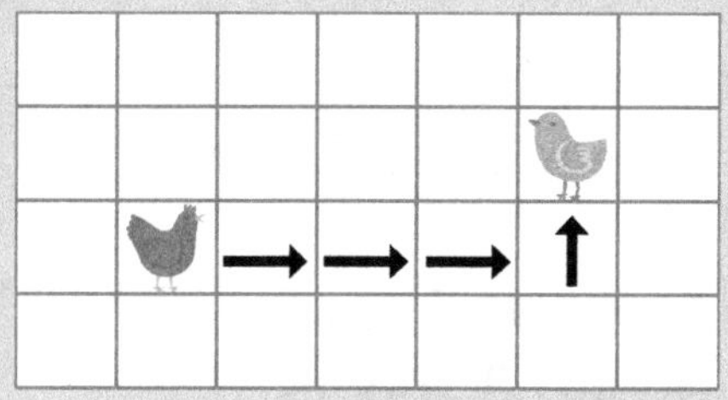

Write each line of code to move the hen to her chick and collect it.

1

Line 1: ______________________________

Line 2: ______________________________

Line 3: ______________________________

2

Line 1: ______________________________

Line 2: ______________________________

Line 3: ______________________________

3

Line 1: ______________________________

Line 2: ______________________________

Line 3: ______________________________

4

Line 1: ______________________________

Line 2: ______________________________

Line 3: ______________________________

Writing Concurrent Code

Concurrent codes are events that happen at the same time.

For example,
Who gets to school first?

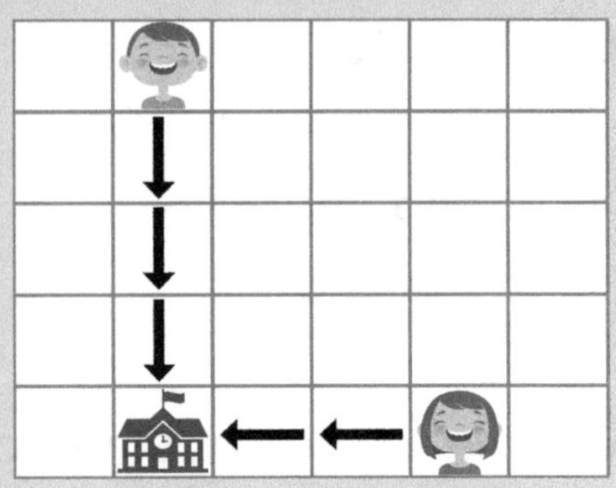

Boy: go down 4 spaces — 4 spaces total
Girl: go left 3 spaces — 3 spaces total

The girl gets to school first because she gets there in fewer spaces.

Write the code for each child to see who gets home in fewer spaces.

1

Girl Line 1: ______________________________

Girl Line 2: ______________________________

Total Spaces: __________

Boy Line 1: ______________________________

Boy Line 2: ______________________________

Total Spaces: __________

2

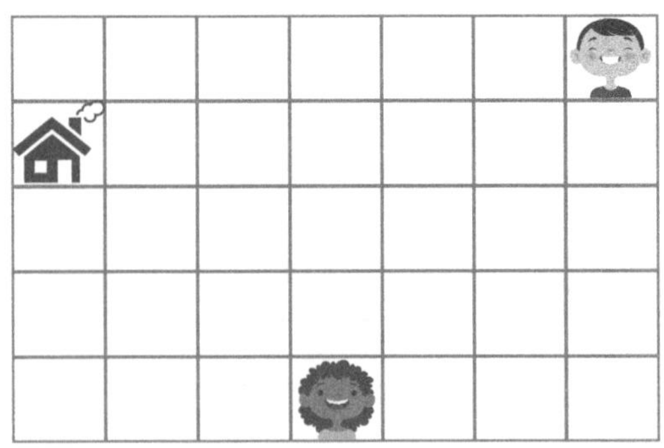

Girl Line 1: ______________________________

Girl Line 2: ______________________________

Total Spaces: __________

Boy Line 1: ______________________________

Boy Line 2: ______________________________

Total Spaces: __________

I can write concurrent code.

Exploring Loops

Loops are actions that repeat a specific number of times.

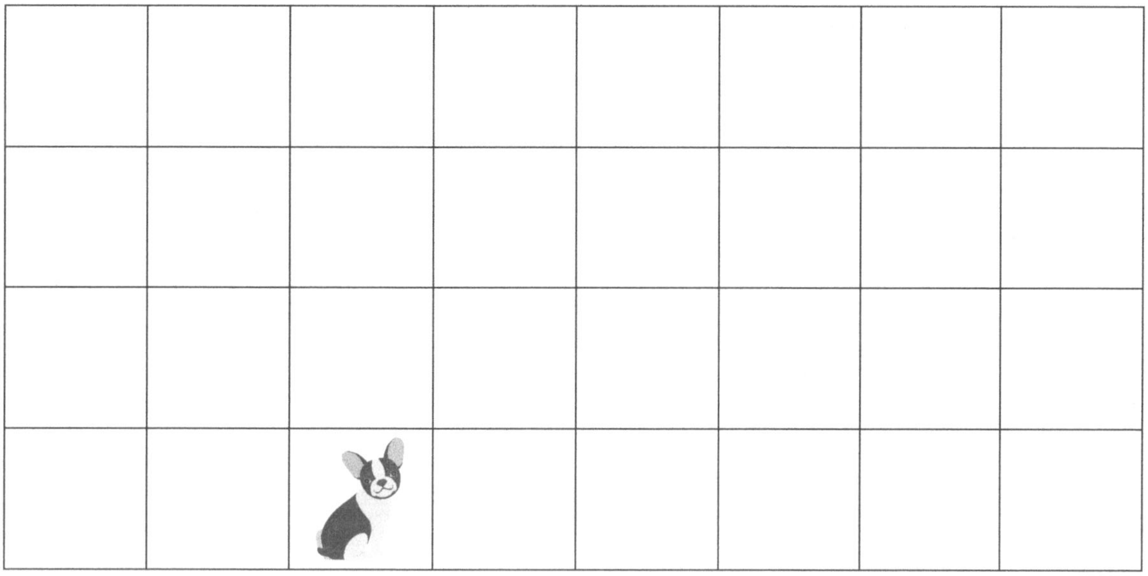

Oh no! Rufus buried his bone but doesn't remember where he put it! Follow the code to help Rufus retrace his steps. Mark an X on the map where Rufus finds his buried bone!

Line 1: go up 1 space

Line 2: repeat 4 times
go right 1 space

Line 3: repeat 2 times
go up 1 space

Line 4: repeat 5 times
go left 1 space

Line 5: go down 1 space

Line 6: go right 1 space

The Same or Different Outcomes

Changing the **order** that code is written can sometimes produce the same outcome, and can sometimes produce a different outcome.

The cat is going to the fish. Follow the sets of code.
Colour if they produce the same or different outcome.

1 **Set 1**

Line 1: go up 1 space
Line 2: go right 1 space
Line 3: go down 2 spaces
Line 4: go right 2 spaces

Set 2

Line 1: go down 2 spaces
Line 2: go right 1 space
Line 3: go up 1 space
Line 4: go right 2 spaces

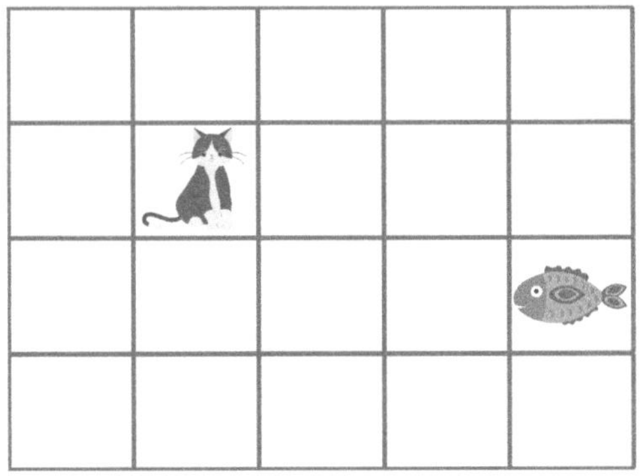

same outcome

different outcome

2 **Set 1**

Line 1: go left 3 spaces
Line 2: go up 2 spaces
Line 3: go right 1 space
Line 4: go up 1 space

Set 2

Line 1: go up 2 spaces
Line 2: go up 1 space
Line 3: go left 3 spaces
Line 4: go right 1 space

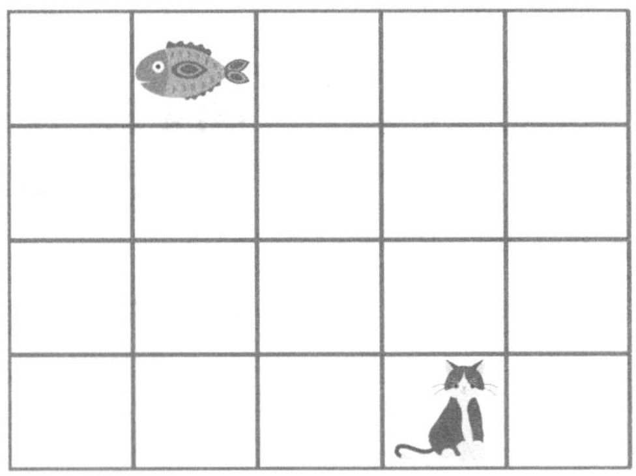

same outcome

different outcome

I can read code with different orders.

Altering Code

The word **alter** means to change.
To alter the code means to write the same code in a different way or order.

The dog is trying to get to its bowl. Alter one line of code so that the code has a **different** outcome, and the dog goes to the bone instead.

1

Line 1: go up 1 space
Line 2: go right 1 space
Line 3: go up 2 spaces
Line 4: go right 1 space

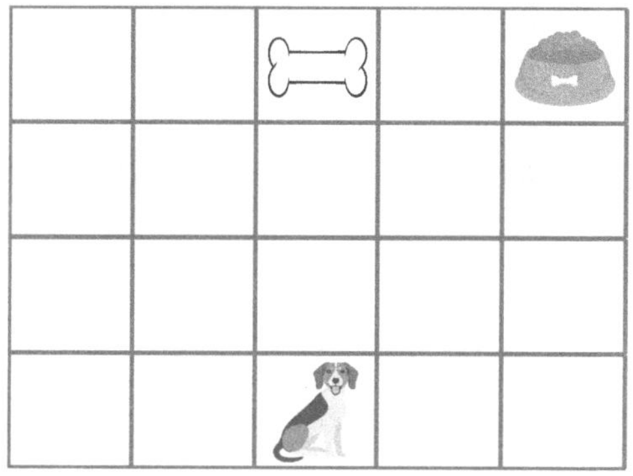

Altered Code:

Line 1: ______________________________

Line 2: ______________________________

Line 3: ______________________________

Line 4: ______________________________

2

Line 1: go left 1 space
Line 2: go down 2 spaces
Line 3: go left 2 spaces
Line 4: go down 1 space

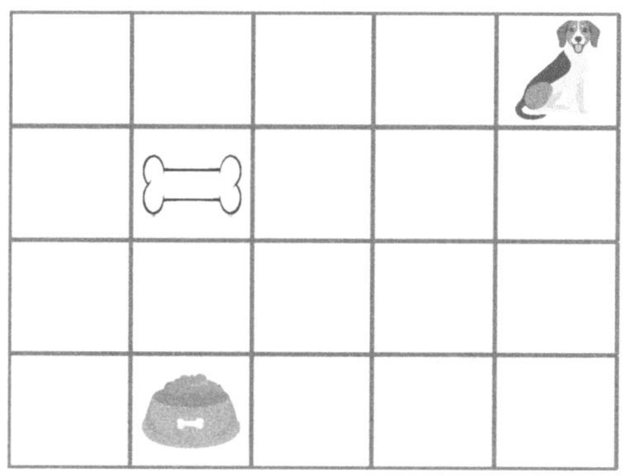

Altered Code:

Line 1: ______________________________

Line 2: ______________________________

Line 3: ______________________________

Line 4: ______________________________

I can write altered code.

Debugging Code

Debug code by fixing a problem or "bug" in your code.

For example,

Jay writes code to get the boy to school but it is not working.

Line 1: move left 3 spaces
Line 2: move down 2 spaces

Jay debugs the code by changing "move down" to "move up."

1 Read and test the code. Debug the code to get the bird to its nest.

a Line 1: move left 4 spaces
Line 2: move up 1 space

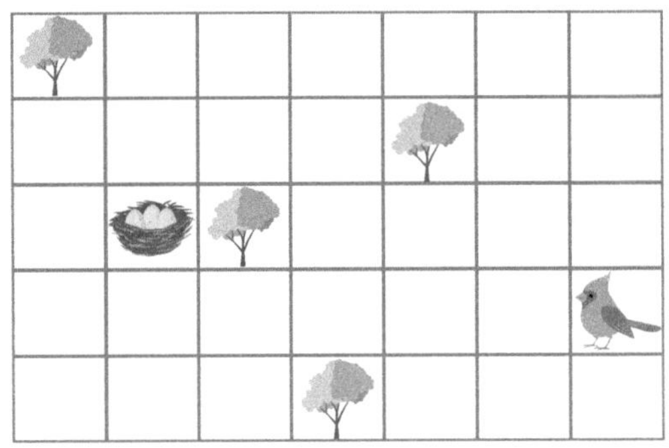

This is how I debug the code:

____

____

b Line 1: move right 3 spaces
Line 2: move up 2 spaces
Line 3: move left 3 spaces

This is how I debug the code:

____

____

I can debug code.

Debugging Code (continued)

2 Oh no! Anita's code is scrambled and no longer works.
Help Anita debug the code by ordering the lines of code from 1 to 5 so the bird collects its egg and drops the egg off at its nest.

a

Line _______: collect egg

Line _______: drop egg in nest

Line _______: move up 2 spaces

Line _______: move right 2 spaces

Line _______: move right 4 spaces

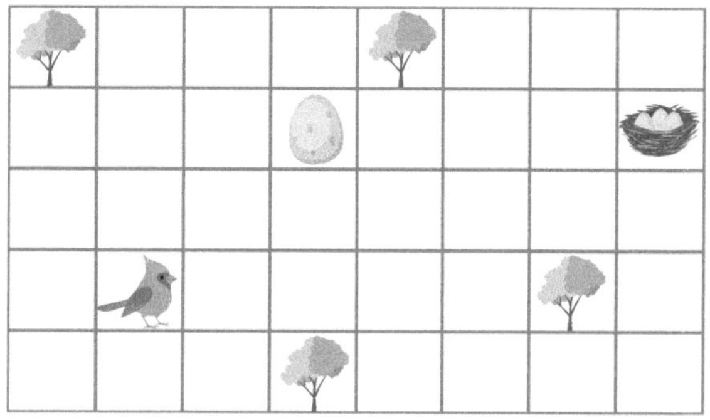

b

Line _______: move down 1 space

Line _______: move down 3 spaces

Line _______: drop egg in nest

Line _______: move left 4 spaces

Line _______: collect egg

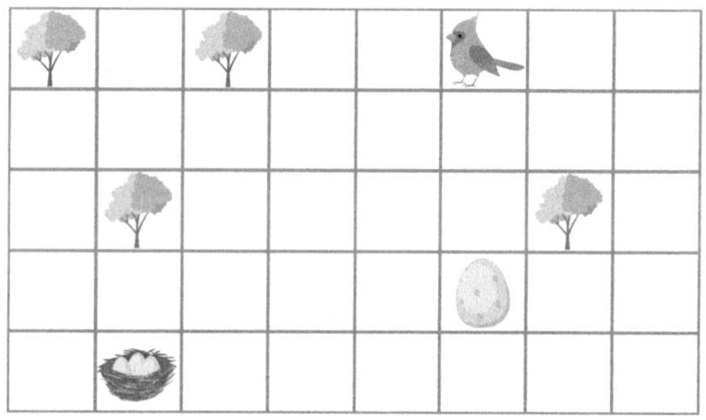

c

Line _______: collect egg

Line _______: move right 4 spaces

Line _______: move right 3 spaces

Line _______: drop egg in nest

Line _______: move up 2 spaces

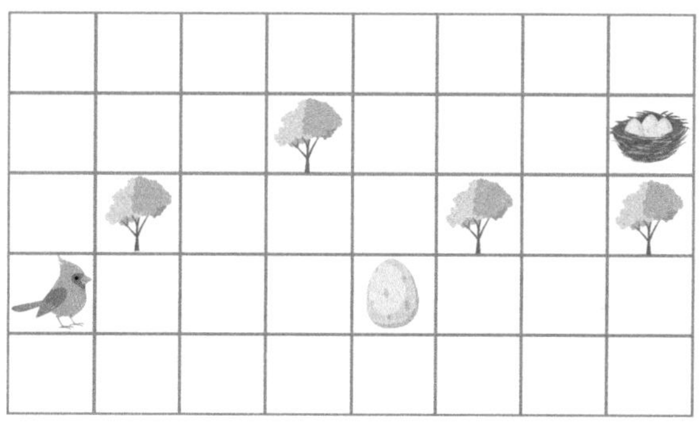

Show What You Know!

1. Write each line of code to move the duck to her duckling and collect it.

a

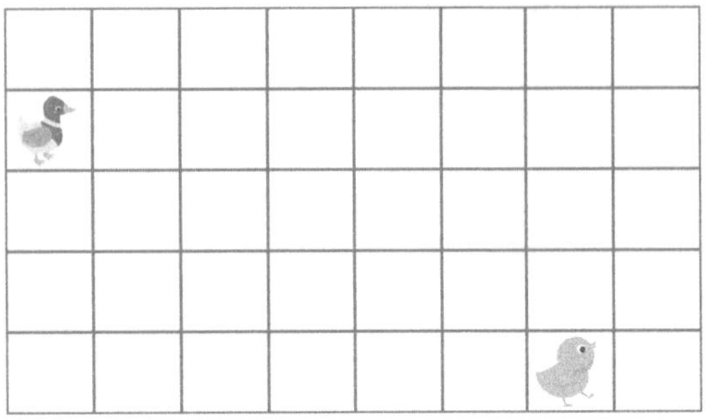

Line 1: ____________________

Line 2: ____________________

Line 3: ____________________

b

Line 1: ____________________

Line 2: ____________________

Line 3: ____________________

2. The dog is trying to get to its bowl. Alter one line of code so that the code has a **different** outcome, and the dog goes to the bone instead.

Line 1: go down 1 space
Line 2: go left 1 space
Line 3: go up 1 space
Line 4: go left 2 spaces

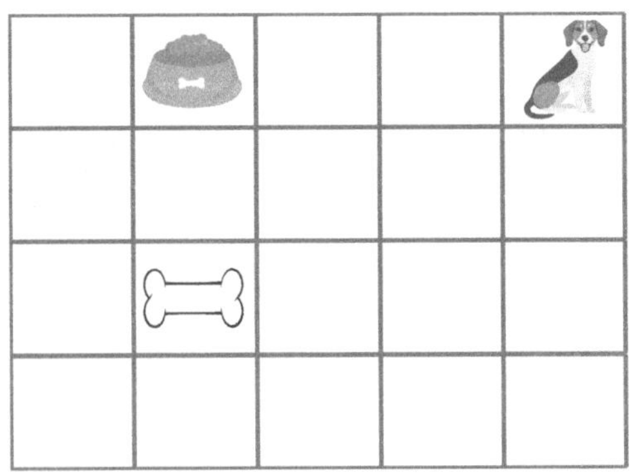

Altered Code:

Line 1: ____________________

Line 2: ____________________

Line 3: ____________________

Line 4: ____________________

Show What You Know! (continued)

3 Julie lost her backpack on the way home! Follow the code to help Julie retrace her steps. Mark an X on the map where Julie finds her lost backpack!

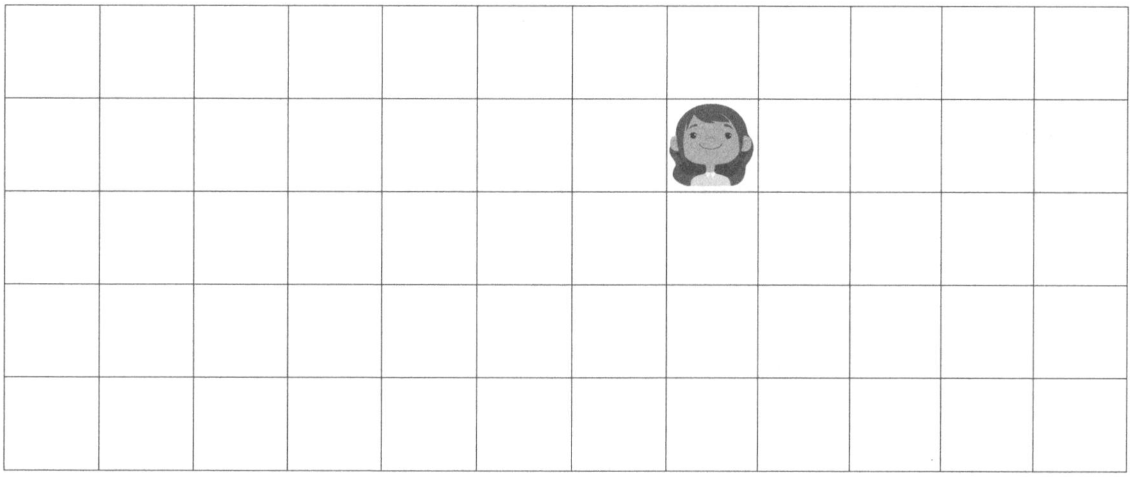

Line 1: repeat 4 times
go left 1 space

Line 2: repeat 2 times
go down 1 space

Line 3: repeat 3 times
go right 1 space

Line 4: go down 1 space

4 Read and test the code. Debug the code to get the bird to its nest.

Line 1: move right 3 spaces
Line 2: move down 1 space

This is how I debug the code:

____

____

I Can Checklist:
Data Literacy

Sort sets of data about people or things according to two and three attributes, using tables and logic diagrams, including Venn, Carroll, and tree diagrams, as appropriate. For example,

- ***I can*** *sort data about things or people by two or three things at once.*
- ***I can*** *use tables and diagrams like Venn, Carroll, and tree diagrams to sort data.*

Collect data through observations, experiments, and interviews to answer questions of interest that focus on qualitative and quantitative data, and organize the data using frequency tables. For example,

- ***I can*** *gather information by watching, doing experiments, and asking questions.*
- ***I can*** *organize this information in a frequency table.*

Display sets of data, using many-to-one correspondence, in pictographs and bar graphs with proper sources, titles, and labels, and appropriate scales. For example,

- ***I can*** *show data in pictures and bar graphs.*
- ***I can*** *make sure my pictures and graphs have sources, titles, labels, and scales.*

Determine the mean and identify the mode(s), if any, for various data sets involving whole numbers, and explain what each of these measures indicates about the data. For example,

- ***I can*** *find the mean (average) and mode (most common) of data sets.*
- ***I can*** *talk about what the mean and mode tell me about the data.*

Analyze different sets of data presented in various ways, including in frequency tables and in graphs with different scales, by asking and answering questions about the data and drawing conclusions, then make convincing arguments and informed decisions. For example,

- ***I can*** *ask and answer questions about data and draw conclusions.*
- ***I can*** *use the information to make good decisions and strong arguments.*

Exploring Venn Diagrams

A **Venn diagram** is a way to sort data into two or three circles that overlap in the middle. The right and left sides show things that are different about the two. The overlapping part in the middle shows things that are the same.

Use the Venn Diagram to answer the questions about the clubs Paul and Sia have joined.

What School Clubs Have You Joined?

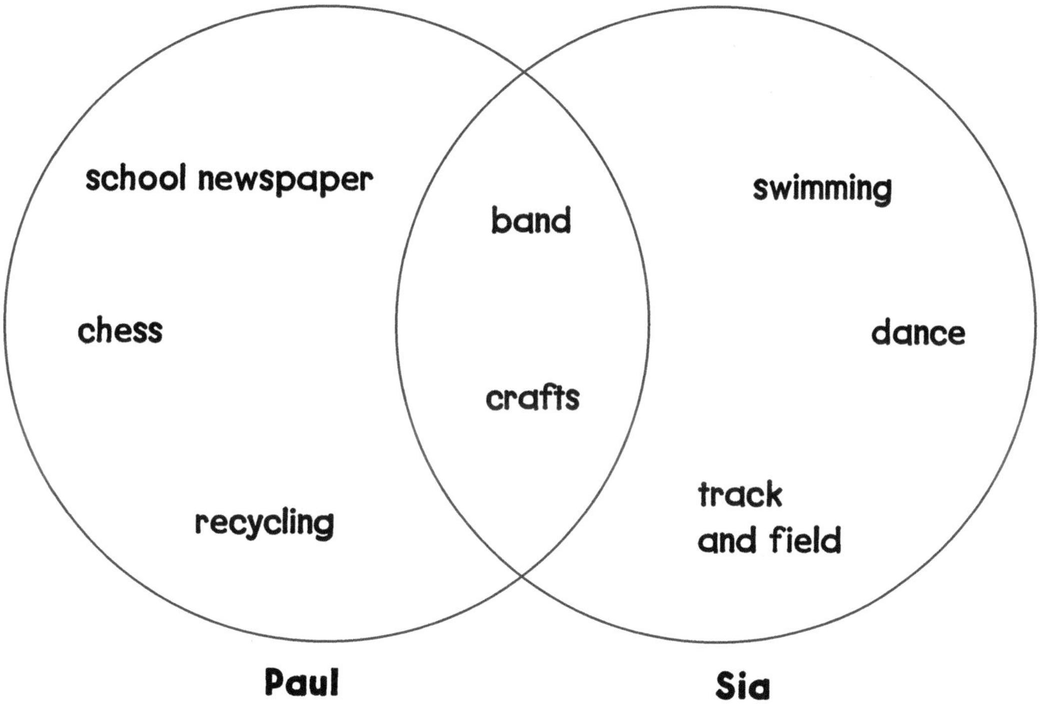

1. Which clubs has Paul joined? ______________________________

2. Which clubs has Sia joined? ______________________________

3. Which clubs have they both joined? ______________________________

I can read Venn diagrams.

Sorting Using a Carroll Diagram

Carroll diagram is a way of sorting objects, numbers, and shapes by their attributes.

1 Sort the creatures based on the attributes in the Carroll diagram.

	Can Fly	Cannot Fly
Has more than 2 legs		
Has 2 legs or less		

Duck 	Owl 	Fish 	Cat 
Bee 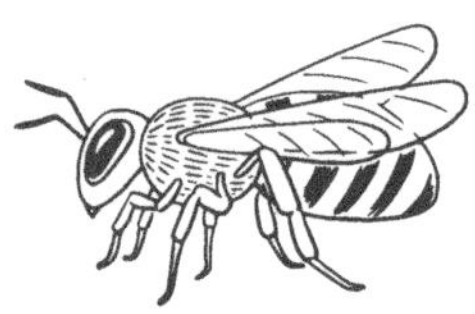	Lion 	Penguin 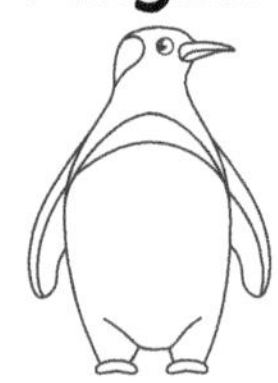	Ladybug 
Bear 	Cockatoo 	Snake 	Fly 

a How many creatures are in the "Can Fly" category? ______________

b How many creatures can fly and have 2 legs or less? ______________

I can sort using a Carroll diagram.

Sorting Using a Carroll Diagram (continued)

2 Sort the shapes based on the attributes in the Carroll diagram.

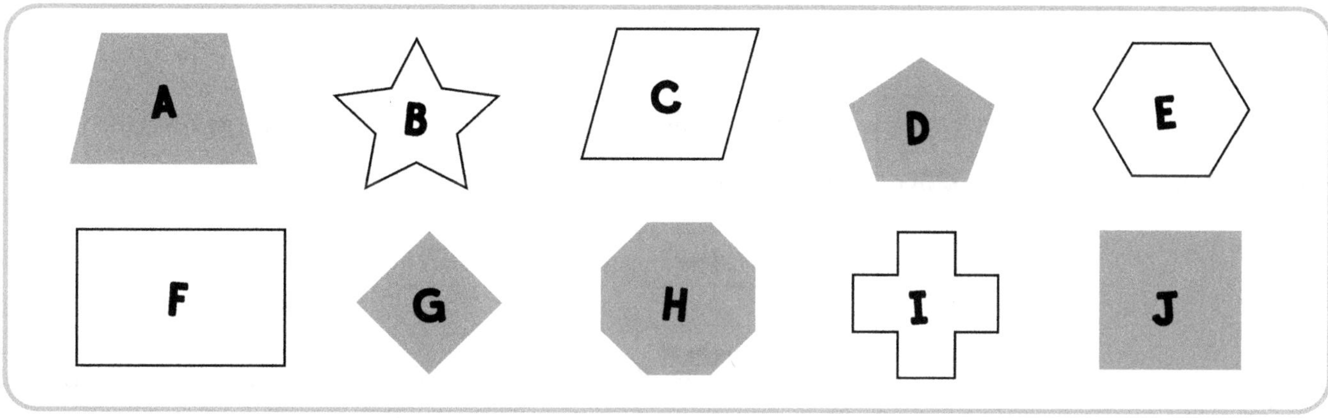

	Is Grey	Is Not Grey
Has 4 sides		
Has more than 4 sides		

a What kinds of shapes have 4 sides? ______________________

b Name three of the shapes that have more than 4 sides. ______________________

____

c How many shapes fit into the "Is Grey" category? ______________________

d How many shapes are there altogether? ______________________

I can sort using a Carroll diagram.

Exploring Tree Diagrams

A **tree diagram** is a diagram with branches that is used to sort data to show all possible combinations for multiple attributes.

The tree diagram below shows all possible outcomes for getting an ice cream with two different flavours, and two different toppings.

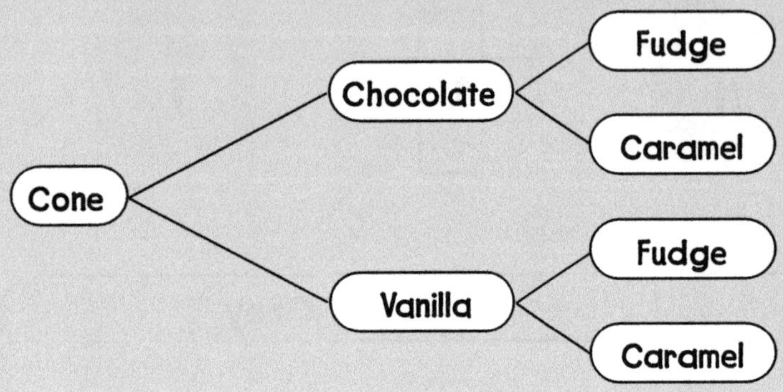

There are 4 different possible outcomes for getting an ice cream treat.

1 Look at the tree diagram. Answer the questions.

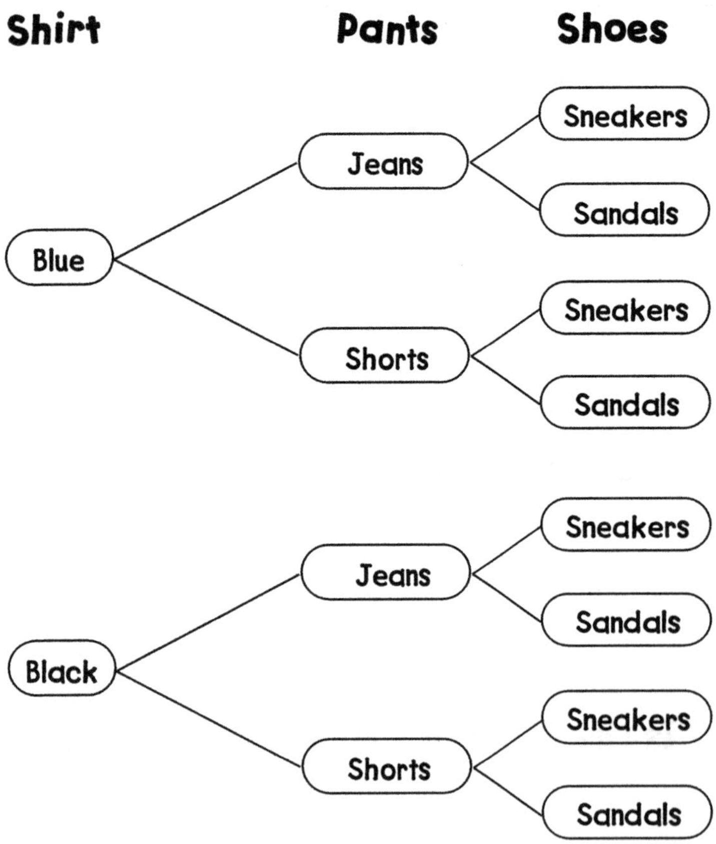

a) How many total possible outcomes are there?

____

b) How many total possible outcomes are there for the blue shirt?

____

c) What are the two options for bottoms?

____

d) What are the two shoe options for shorts?

____

I can read tree diagrams.

Exploring Tree Diagrams (continued)

2 Create a tree diagram to show all the possible outcomes.

a **Harry's Hamburgers**

Meat: Beef or Chicken **Toppings:** Cheese, Lettuce, or Tomato

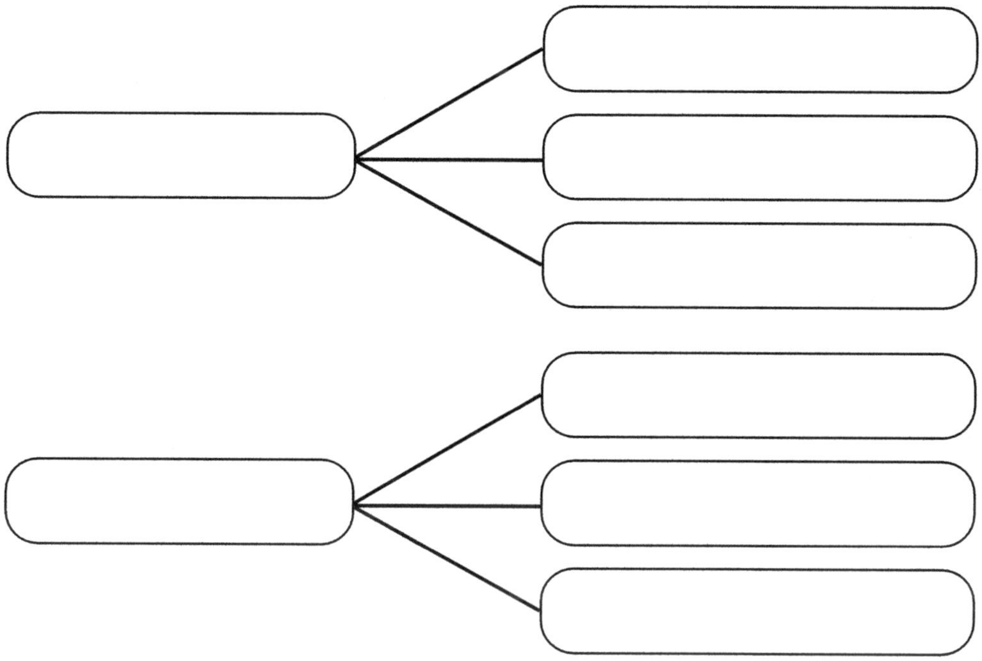

b **Lisa's Pizzas**

Crust: Thin or Stuffed **Toppings:** Pepperoni, Olives, or Beef

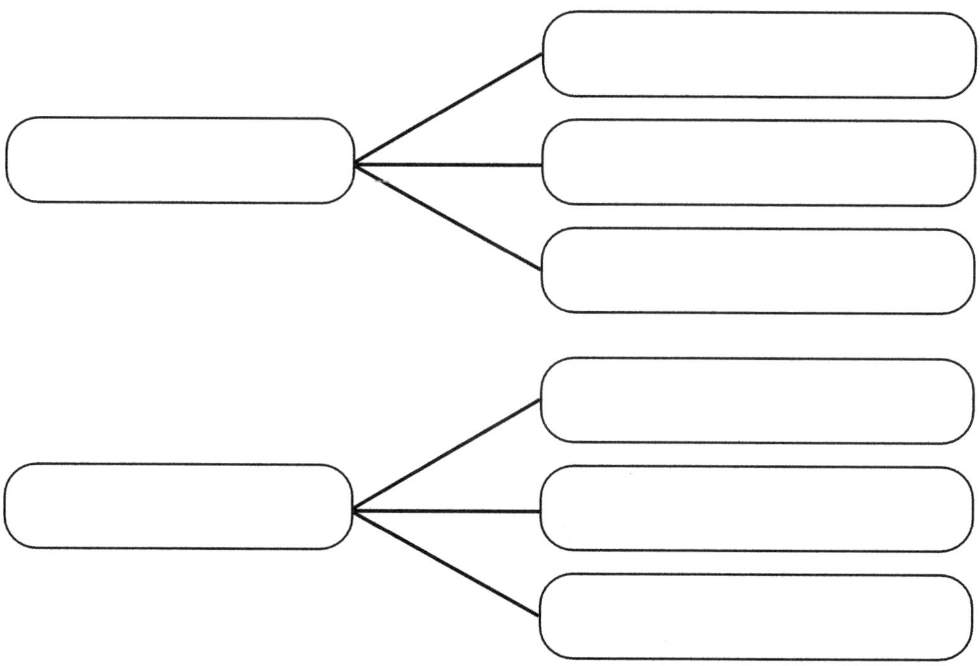

I can write tree diagrams.

Organizing Data: Frequency Tables

A **frequency table** lists items and shows the number of times the items occur.

1. Students were surveyed about their favourite colours.
Use the survey results to fill in the frequency table and answer the questions.

Survey Results

Colour	
green	green
red	purple
red	blue
green	green
purple	green
blue	purple
green	green
purple	red
red	blue

Frequency Table

Colour	Tally	Frequency
Red		
Blue		
Green		
Purple		

a. What is the most popular colour? ____________________

b. What is the least popular colour? ____________________

c. Which two colours have the same number of votes? ____________

d. How many votes are for red compared to blue? ____________

e. How many votes are there altogether? ____________________

 I can organize data in a frequency table.

Organizing Data: Frequency Tables (continued)

2. Students were surveyed on their favourite fruits.
Use the survey results to fill in the frequency table and answer the questions.

Survey Results

Fruit										
	cherries	apples	kiwis	kiwis	apples	cherries	grapes	kiwis	cherries	apples
	apples	grapes	pears	kiwis	apples	grapes	cherries	apples	kiwis	cherries

Frequency Table

Fruit	Tally	Frequency
apples		
grapes		
pears		
kiwis		
cherries		

a. What is the most popular fruit? ______________________

b. Which fruit has only one vote? ______________________

c. Which fruits have the same number of votes? ______________________

d. How many votes are for grapes compared to cherries? ______________________

e. How many votes are there for apples and grapes? ______________________

Reading a Pictograph

A **pictograph** uses pictures or icons to show data and to compare information. Each picture or icon can represent more than one object. A key is used to tell what each picture represents.

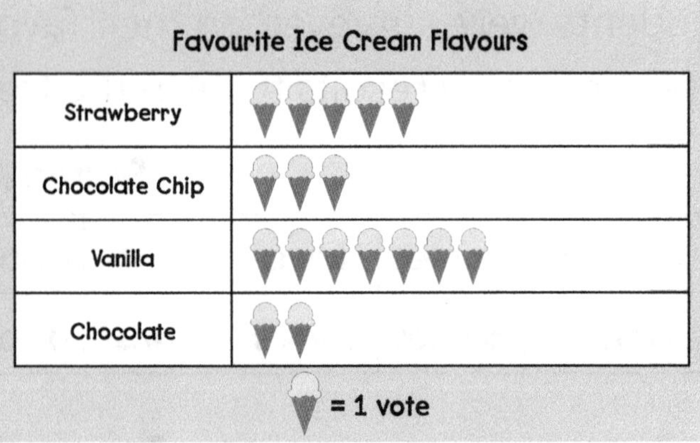

The grade 3 classes were surveyed on how many books they've read. Use the pictograph to answer the questions.

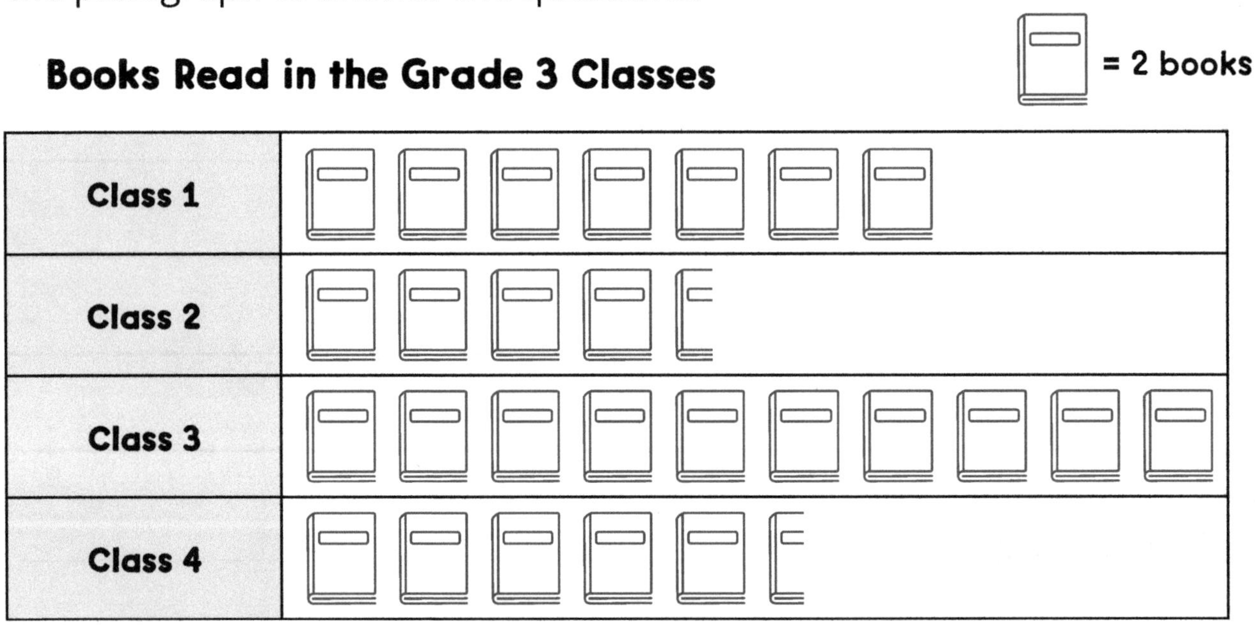

1. What is one book worth in the pictograph? ________________

2. Which class read the most books? ________________

3. How many fewer books did class 2 read compared to class 4? ________

4. How many books did class 2 read? ________________

I can read pictographs.

Exploring Pictographs

Meghan took a survey on students' favourite ice cream flavours.

Here are the results of the survey.

Favourite Ice Cream Flavours

 **= 4 people**

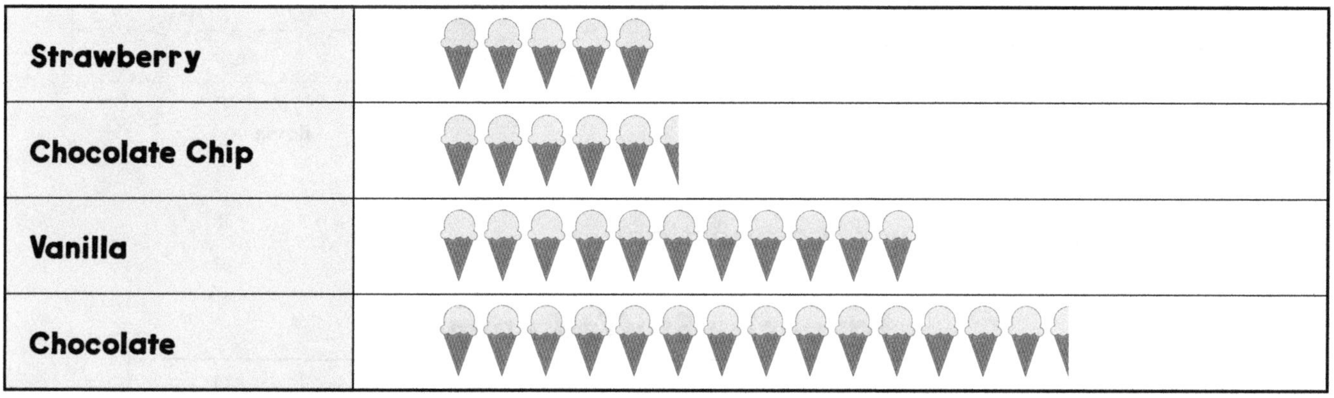

1. Which flavour is the most popular? ______________________

2. Which flavour is the least popular? ______________________

3. How many students chose chocolate chip? ______________________

4. How many students chose either strawberry or vanilla? ______________________

5. How many students chose chocolate? ______________________

6. How many students voted altogether? ______________________

Exploring Bar Graphs

A **bar graph** uses horizontal or vertical bars that display data.

Bar graphs are a good choice to display data that you want to compare.

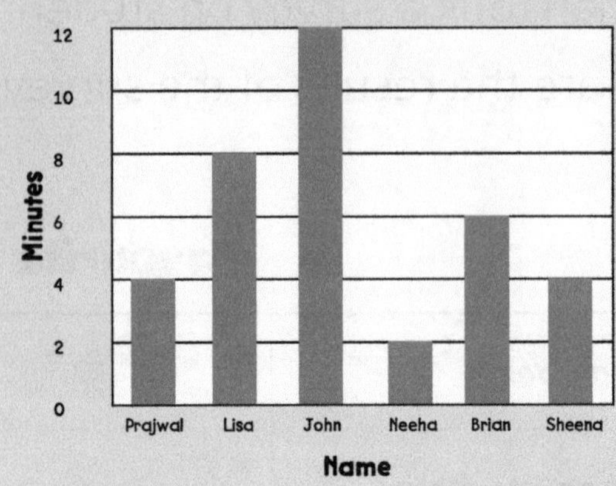

Read the bar graph to answer the questions.

Favourite Stuffed Animals

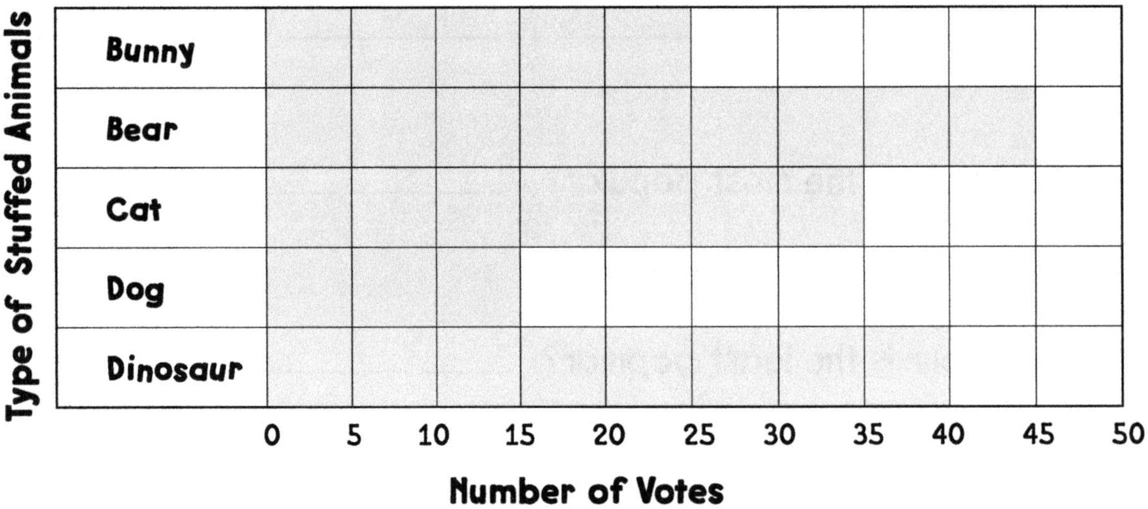

1. Which type of stuffed animal is the most popular? ______________________

2. Which type of stuffed animal is the least popular? ______________________

3. How many voted for dinosaurs? ______________________

4. How many fewer students like bunnies than bears? ______________________

5. Which type of stuffed animal had 40 votes? ______________________

I can read bar graphs.

Reading a Bar Graph

Use the bar graph to answer the questions.

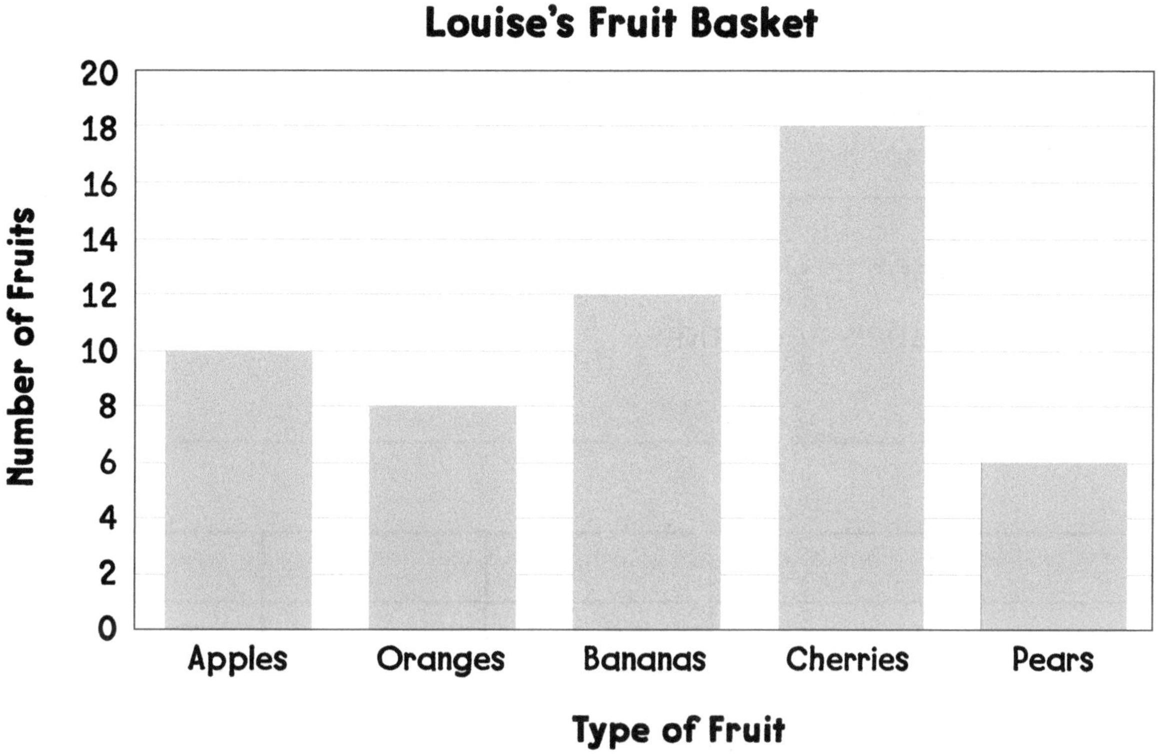

1. What fruit does Louise have the most of? ______________________

2. What fruit does Louise have the least of? ______________________

3. How many pears are in Louise's basket? ______________________

4. How many more bananas does Louise have than oranges? __________

5. How many fruits in total are in Louise's basket? ________________

6. Which fruit does Louise have 8 of? __________________________

Making Bar Graphs

All of the students in two Grade 3 classes were surveyed about their favourite pizza toppings. The classes combined their data to make this chart.

Pepperoni	Cheese	Tomatoes	Peppers	Mushrooms
25	40	10	25	5

1. Complete the bar graph to show the information on the chart. Make sure you add labels and a title.

____

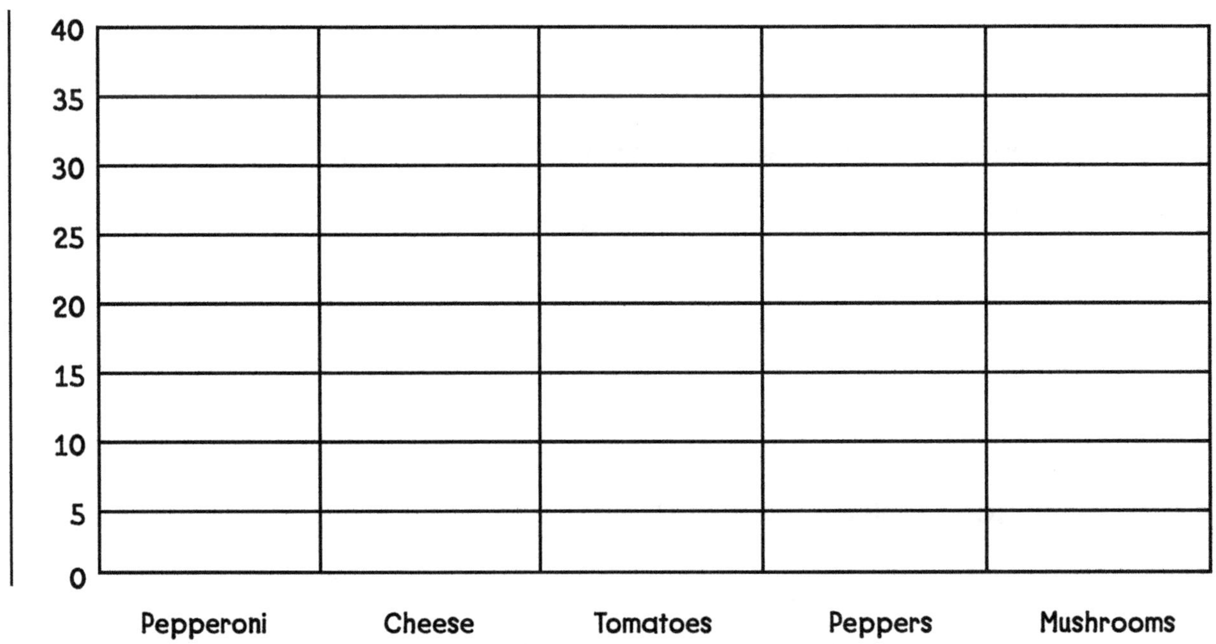

____

2. Write three statements about the bar graph.

____

____

____

I can make bar graphs.

Making Bar Graphs (continued)

3 Students went apple picking and wrote their data in this chart.

Create a pictograph and a bar graph to represent the data.

Anita	Tariq	Rana	Lea	Paul
30	25	10	40	50

Apples Picked

Apples Picked

Reading a Tally Chart

A tally chart shows data by counting by groups of five. Each line, or tally, represents 1. Once you reach a group of 5, you start another group.

𝍸 = 5

Colour	Tally	Number
Red	𝍸 ||	
Blue	𝍸 𝍸 |||	
Green	||||	
Purple	𝍸 |||	

Students were surveyed on their favourite kinds of animals. Complete the tally chart. Use the tally chart to answer the questions.

Favourite Animals

Animal	Tally	Number
Dogs	𝍸 ||||	
Cats	𝍸 |	
Birds	||||	
Lizards	𝍸	

1. What is the most popular animal? ______________________

2. What is the least popular animal? ______________________

3. Which animal has 6 votes? ______________________

4. How many votes are there altogether? ______________________

I can read tally charts.

Exploring Bar Graphs and Tally Charts

Complete the tally chart and bar graph. Answer the questions.

Coins in the Piggy Bank

Kind of Coin	Tally	Number
Nickels	𝍸 𝍸	
Dimes		12
Quarters	𝍸 ||||	
Loonies		4

Coins in the Piggy Bank

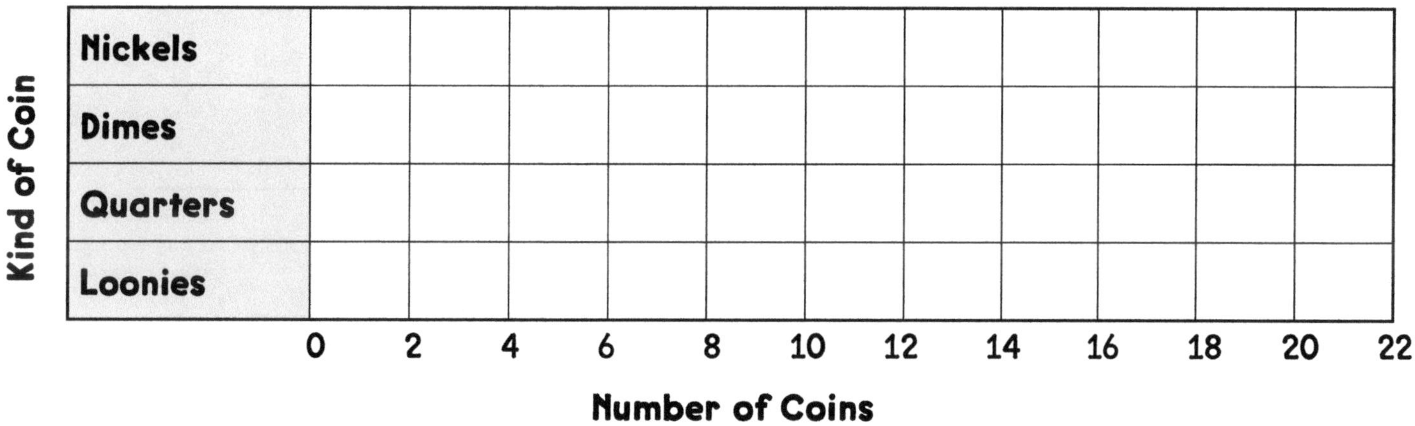

1. Which kind of coin is there most of? ____________________

2. Which kind of coin is there least of? ____________________

3. How many fewer quarters are there than nickels? ____________________

4. How many coins are there altogether? ____________________

Exploring Mean

The **mean** is the average number in a set of numbers.

For example,

2, 4, 1, 5, 3

Step 1: Add the values together: $2 + 4 + 1 + 5 + 3 = 15$

Step 2: Divide by the number of values in the set: $15 \div 5 = 3$

The mean is 3.

Find the mean of the data set.

1. 1, 3, 6, 2

   Mean: ____________________

2. 4, 2, 3, 7

   Mean: ____________________

3. 10, 6, 8, 4

   Mean: ____________________

4. 15, 11, 9, 5

   Mean: ____________________

5. 5, 3, 7, 4, 1

   Mean: ____________________

6. 12, 6, 5, 3, 4

   Mean: ____________________

I can find the mean.

Exploring Mode

The **mode** is the value that appears the most often in a data set.

For example,

1, 6, 4, 8, 6, 7, 6

Step 1: Rewrite the numbers in order: 1, 4, 6, 6, 6, 7, 8

Step 2: Find the number that appears the most often: 6

The mode is 6.

1. Find the mode of the data set.

a) 1, 5, 5, 2, 6

Mode: ______________________

b) 7, 1, 7, 10, 5, 7

Mode: ______________________

c) 8, 9, 12, 5, 8

Mode: ______________________

d) 3, 15, 20, 15, 6, 15

Mode: ______________________

2. Look at the graph. Find the mode.

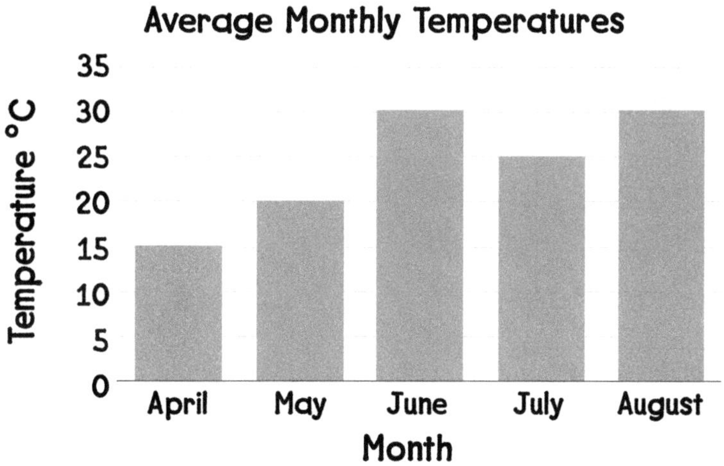

Mode: ______________________

I can find the mode.

Show What You Know!

1 Consider the following graph.

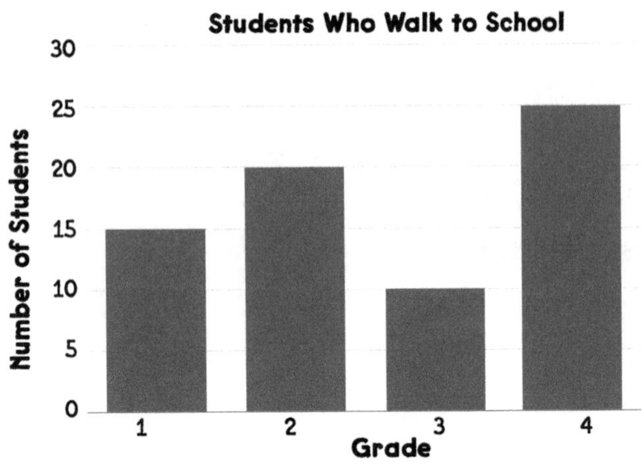

Choose the table that matches the data in the graph.

a

Grade	Number of Students
1	10
2	20
3	15
4	25

b

Grade	Number of Students
1	15
2	20
3	10
4	25

c

Grade	Number of Students
1	20
2	15
3	25
4	10

d

Grade	Number of Students
1	5
2	15
3	25
4	10

2 The children in Mr. Rypan's Grade 3 class recorded the number of books they read each month for 6 months.

Month	Number of Books
January	40
February	35
March	28
April	23
May	35
June	21

Choose the mode of this data set.

a 35 **b** 23

c 28 **d** 21

3 Find the mean of the data set.

a 5, 9, 10, 8, 3

Mean: ____________________

b 8, 12, 9, 14, 7

Mean: ____________________

Show What You Know! (continued)

4 The pictograph below shows the number of students who participated in some Earth Day activities.

Activity	Number of Students
Plant a tree	★ ★ ★ ★
Hand out flyers	★ ★ ½★
Plant seeds	★ ★ ★ ½★

Key
Each ★ represents 10 students.

Use the data from the pictograph to make a bar graph.
Be sure to include labels and titles.

Complete the scale provided.

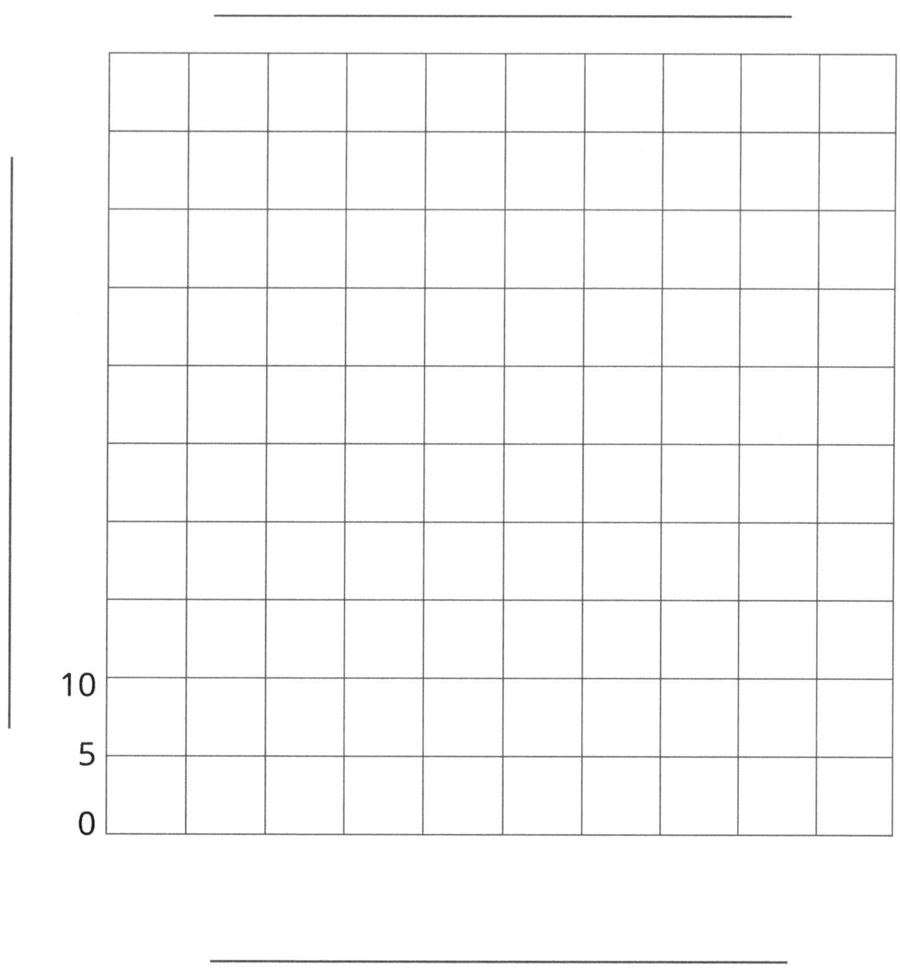

I Can Checklist:

Probability

Use mathematical language, including the terms “impossible,” “unlikely,” “equally likely,” “likely,” and “certain,” to describe the likelihood of events happening, and use that likelihood to make predictions and informed decisions. For example,

- ***I can*** *use words like “impossible,” “unlikely,” “equally likely,” “likely,” and “certain,” to talk about how possible it is that something will happen.*
- ***I can*** *use these chances to guess what will happen and make good choices.*

Make and test predictions about the likelihood that the mean and the mode(s) of a data set will be the same for data collected from different populations.
For example,

- ***I can*** *guess and check if the mean (average) and mode (most common) will be the same for different groups.*

What Is Probability?

Probability is the likelihood of an event happening. Use the words *impossible*, *unlikely*, *likely*, and *certain* to describe the probability of an event happening.

1 Circle the best answer for each question.

a 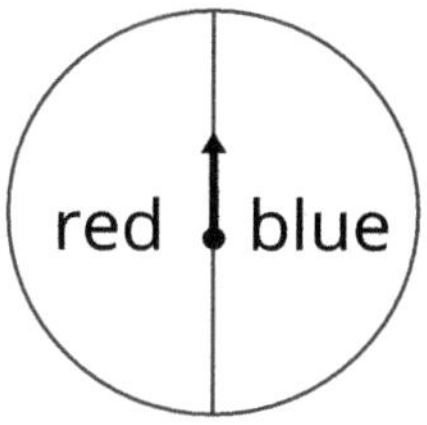

What is the probability of spinning red?

likely **unlikely** **certain** **impossible**

b 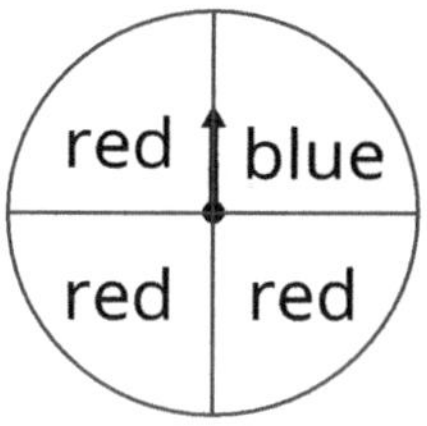

What is the probability of spinning blue?

likely **unlikely** **certain** **impossible**

c 

What is the probability of spinning yellow?

likely **unlikely** **certain** **impossible**

d 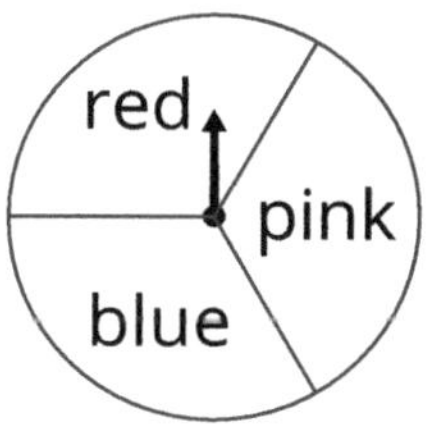

What is the probability of spinning green?

likely **unlikely** **certain** **impossible**

2 Draw spinners that show different probabilities of spinning **red**.

likely

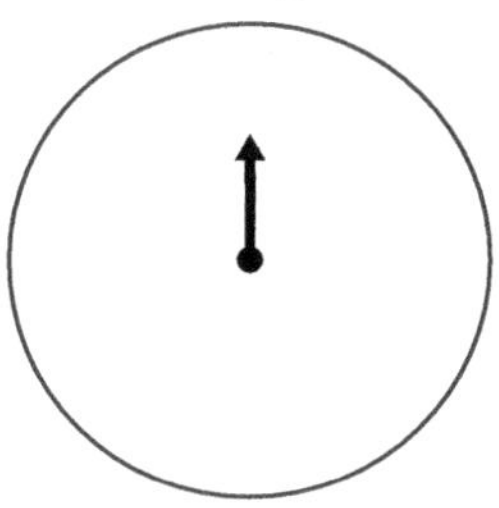

unlikely

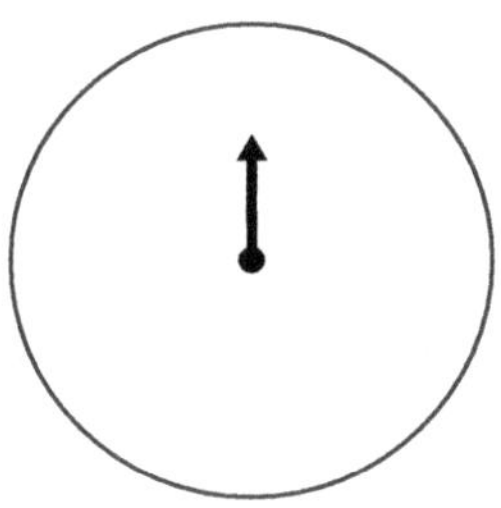

impossible

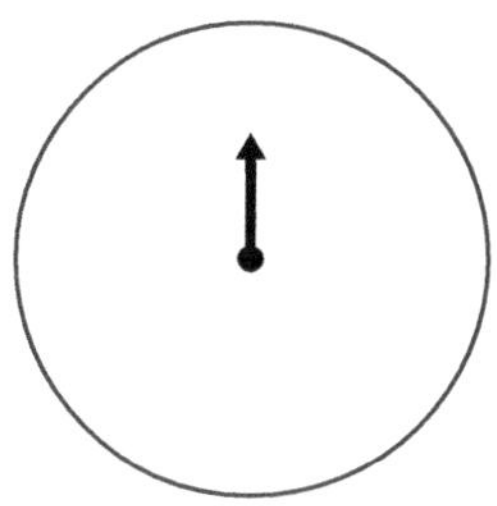

What Is the Probability?

1 Circle the best answer.

a

What is the probability of drawing a  ?

likely **unlikely** **certain** **impossible**

b

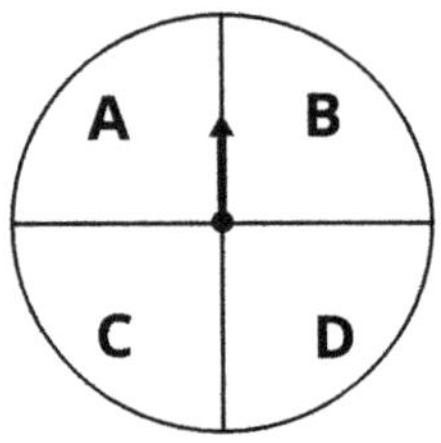

John spins the arrow on the spinner 40 times. What is the probability of the arrow landing on D?

likely **unlikely** **certain** **impossible**

c

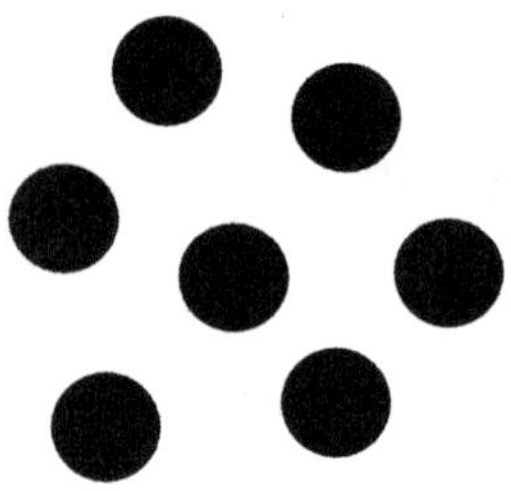

Look at the circles. What is the probability of choosing a solid white circle?

likely **unlikely** **certain** **impossible**

2 Circle the best answer.

a What is the probability of seeing a rainbow today?

likely **unlikely** **certain** **impossible**

b What is the probability of snow falling during the summer?

likely **unlikely** **certain** **impossible**

I can identify probability.

Making Predictions About Likelihood

Circle if the given statement is likely or unlikely to happen.

1. Most students in Mrs. Roger's Grade 3 class dislike Brussels sprouts. Is it likely or unlikely that most of the Grade 3 students in Mr. Smith's class will also dislike Brussels sprouts?

   likely **unlikely**

2. All of the beansprouts in the Grade 3 class grew under 10 cm in a week. Is it likely or unlikely that the beansprouts in the Grade 4 class will grow above 20 cm in a week?

   likely **unlikely**

3. This week, the mean amount of time the Grade 3 class watched television after school was one hour. Is it likely or unlikely that the time spent watching television will be the same next week?

   likely **unlikely**

4. The students in the Grade 3 class spend a mean of 20 minutes on homework each night. Is it likely or unlikely the Grade 8 class spends the same amount of time on homework each night?

   likely **unlikely**

5. Most of the Grade 3 students like pepperoni on their pizza. Is it likely or unlikely that most of the Grade 4 students will like pepperoni on their pizza?

   likely **unlikely**

I can predict likelihood.

Show What You Know!

1. Amy, Sally, Quinn, and Liz are playing a game using a spinner. Each gets a point when the arrow lands on their first initial.

   Choose the spinner that is fair to all the players.

   a. 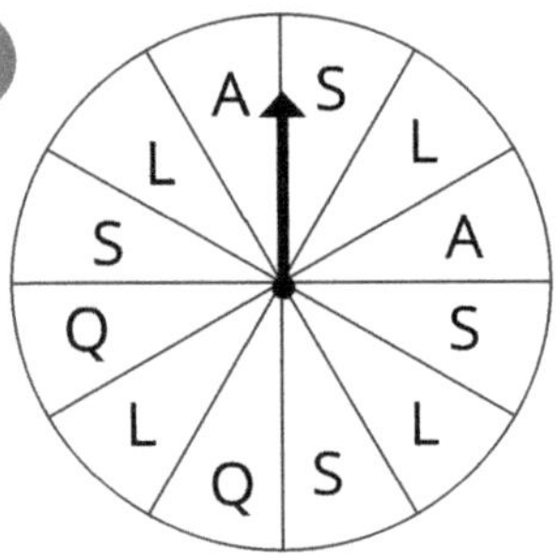

   b. 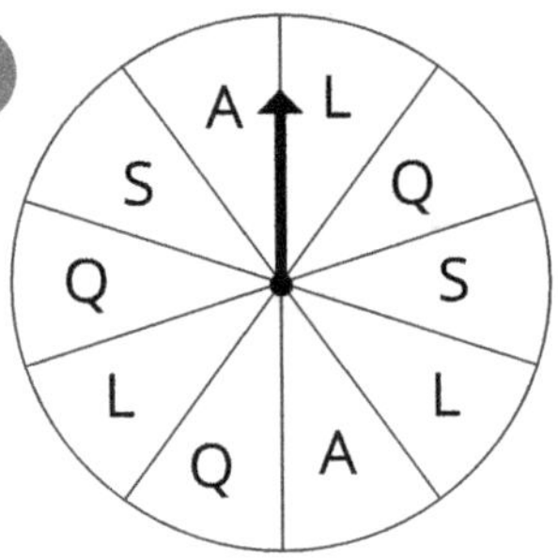

   c. 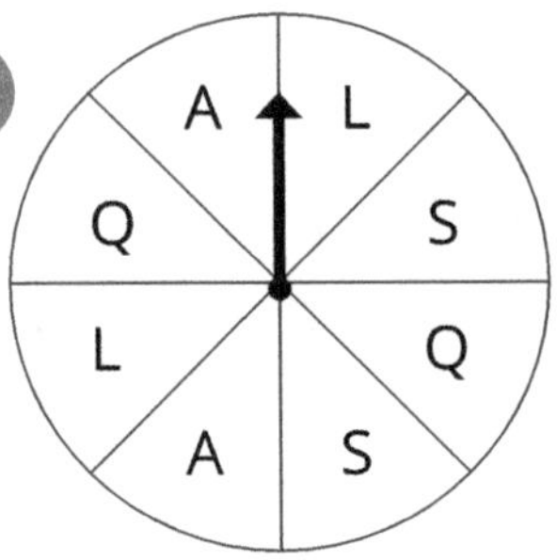

   d. 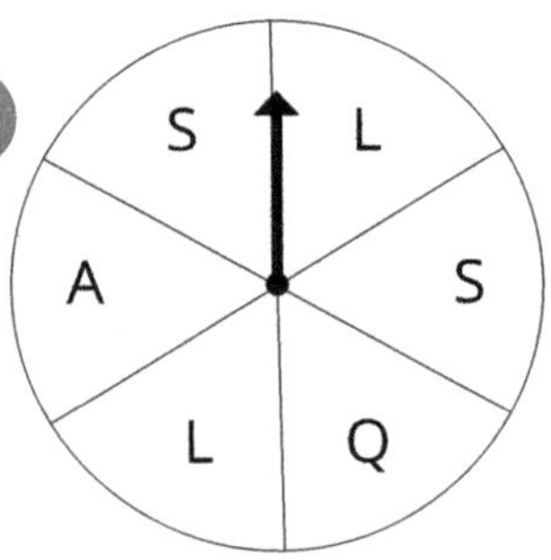

2. Mr. Gomez places the names below in a bag.

   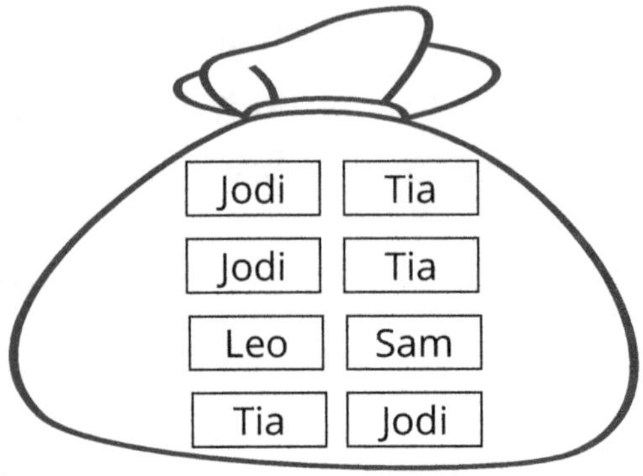

   He chooses 1 name from the bag without looking. Which names are most likely to be chosen?

   a. Jodi and Tia
   b. Leo and Sam
   c. Tia and Sam
   d. Jodi and Leo

3. Lucy has 15 tiles in a bag. The tiles are red, blue, and green.

   Choose the number of tiles of each colour to make all colours equally likely to be drawn.

   a. 4
   b. 5
   c. 3
   d. 2

Show What You Know! (continued)

4 Matthew and Ryley choose a spinner to play a game. If the arrow lands on M, Matthew wins. If the arrow lands on R, Ryley wins. Which spinner gives Matthew and Ryley equal chances of winning?

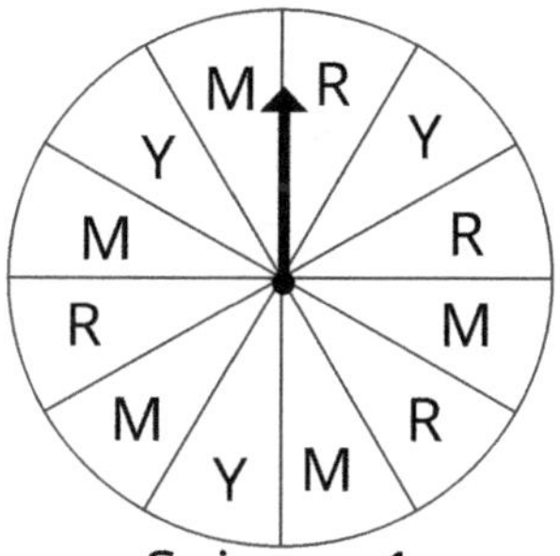

Spinner 1

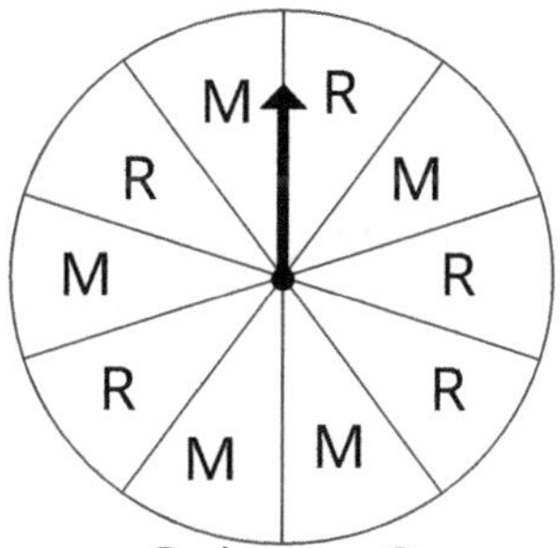

Spinner 2

Circle one: **Spinner 1** **Spinner 2**

Justify your answer.

I Can Checklist:

Geometric & Spatial Reasoning

Sort, construct, and identify cubes, prisms, pyramids, cylinders, and cones by comparing their faces, edges, vertices, and angles. For example,

- ***I can*** *sort, make, and name different shapes like cubes, prisms, pyramids, cylinders, and cones by looking at their faces, edges, vertices, and angles.*
- ***I can*** *build and break down different structures, and name the flat (2D) shapes and solid (3D) objects in these structures.*

Compose and decompose various structures, and identify the two-dimensional shapes and three-dimensional objects that these structures contain. For example:

- ***I can*** *make a robot using different 3D objects like cubes (for the body), cylinders (for the arms and legs), and a sphere (for the head), then I can take it apart and tell you about all the shapes I used.*
- ***I can*** *look at a picture of a house and tell you about the different 2D shapes (like squares for the windows, triangles for the roof) and 3D objects (like rectangular prisms for the body of the house) that it contains.*
- ***I can*** *build a tower using my blocks, then deconstruct it and show you all the different shapes I used, like cubes, rectangular prisms, and cylinders.*

Identify congruent lengths, angles, and faces of three-dimensional objects by mentally and physically matching them, and determine if the objects are congruent. For example,

- ***I can*** *match the same lengths, angles, and faces of solid shapes in my mind and with my hands.*
- ***I can*** *tell if solid shapes are the same (congruent).*

Location & Movement

Give and follow multistep instructions involving movement from one location to another, including distances and half and quarter turns. For example,

- ***I can*** *tell someone how to move from one place to another with many steps, including distances and turns.*

Three-Dimensional Objects

The **vertex** is the corner of a 3D object.
The plural of vertex is **vertices**.

An **edge** is the line where two faces meet.

A **face** is the flat surface of a 3D object.

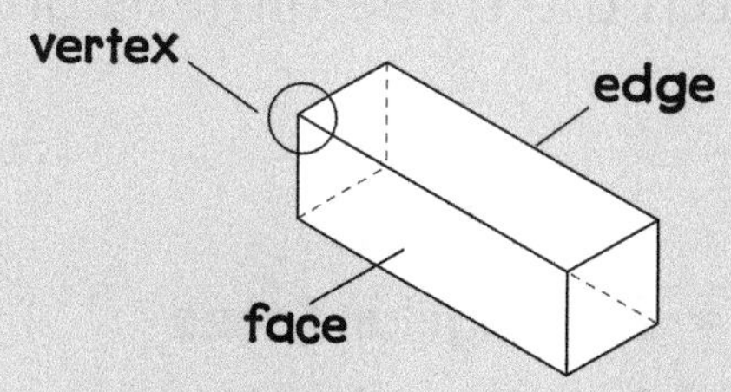

Name of Object	Object	Faces	Edges	Vertices
Rectangular Prism	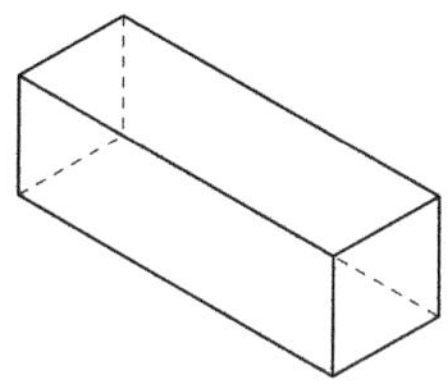	**6 faces** • 2 square faces • 4 rectangular faces	**12**	**8**
Triangular Prism	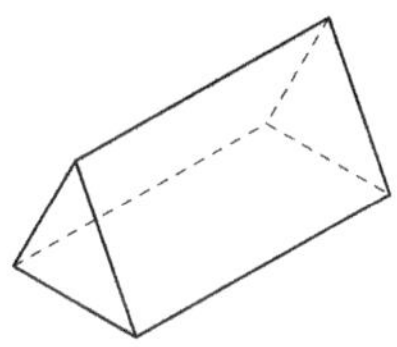	**5 faces** • 2 triangular faces • 3 rectangular faces	**9**	**6**
Cube	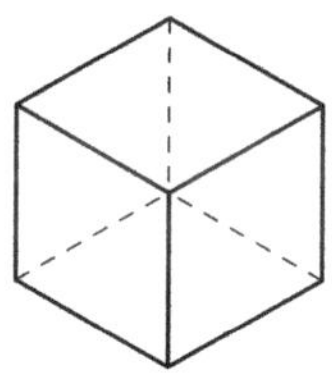	**6 faces** • 6 congruent square faces	**12**	**8**
Cylinder	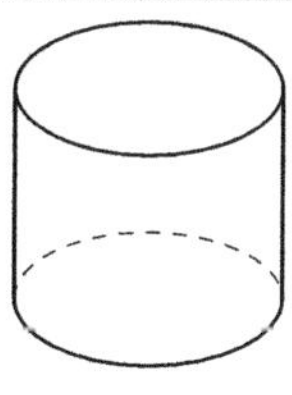	**3 faces** • 2 circular faces • 1 rectangular face	**0**	**0**
Square-Based Pyramid	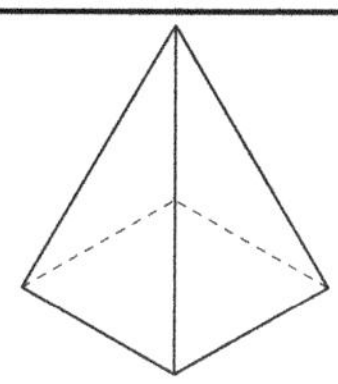	**5 faces** • 1 square face • 4 triangular faces	**8**	**5**
Cone	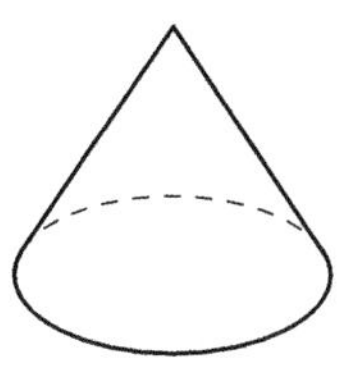	**2 faces** • 1 circular face • 1 curved face	**1**	**1**

Matching Three-Dimensional Objects

Match the three-dimensional object to its name and correct faces.

5 faces • 2 triangular faces • 3 rectangular faces	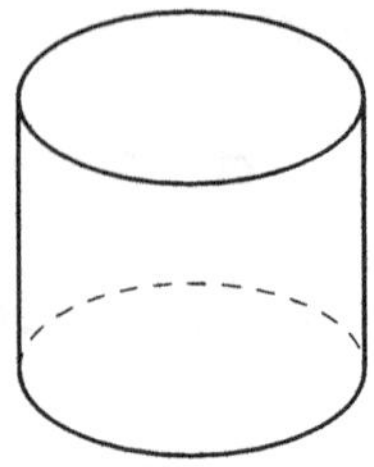	rectangular prism
3 faces • 2 circular faces • 1 rectangular face	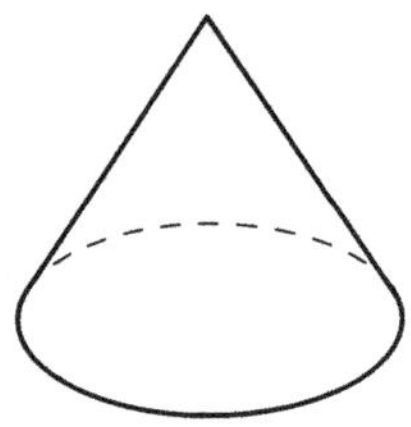	cube
6 faces • all congruent squares	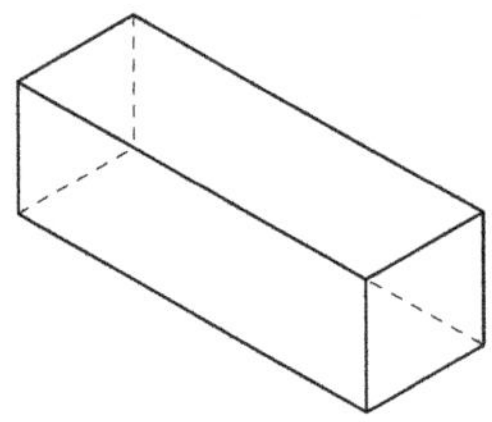	cylinder
2 faces • 1 circular face • 1 curved face	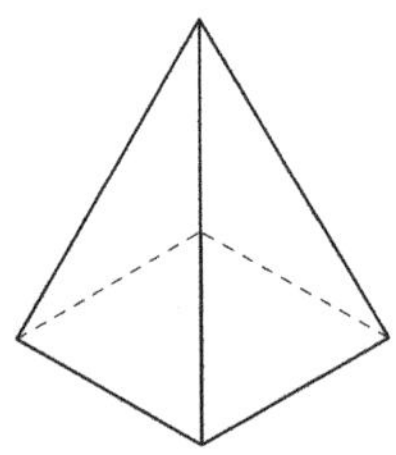	triangular prism
6 faces • 2 square faces • 4 rectangular faces	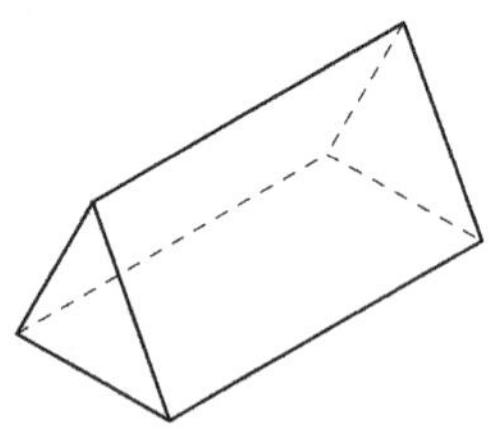	cone
5 faces • 1 square face • 4 triangular faces	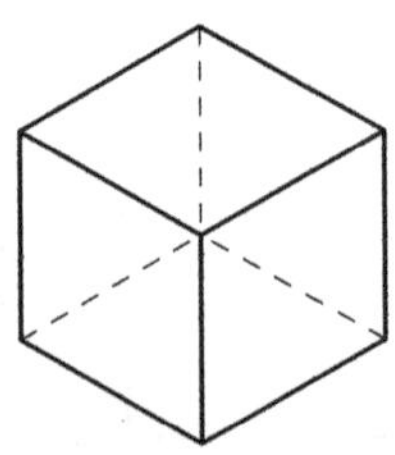	square-based pyramid

I can match three-dimensional objects.

3D Objects: Edges and Vertices

Circle the correct name for the 3D object. Then, identify the number of edges and vertices.

1 Rectangular Prism   Cube

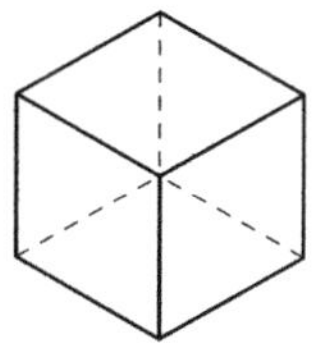

Number of edges: ______________

Number of vertices: ______________

2 Triangular Prism   Cone

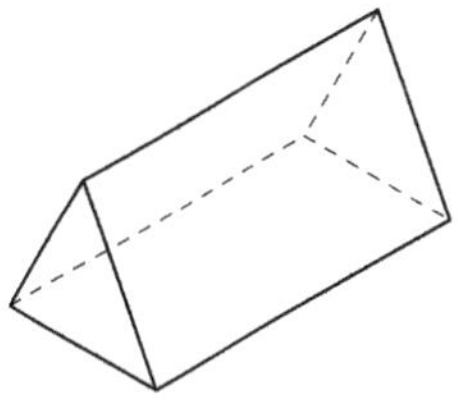

Number of edges: ______________

Number of vertices: ______________

3 Cube   Rectangular Prism

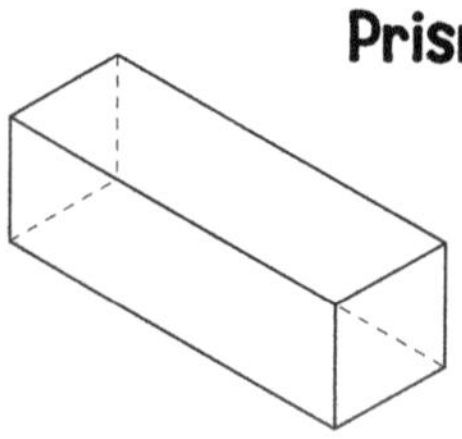

Number of edges: ______________

Number of vertices: ______________

4 Cylinder   Square-Based Pyramid

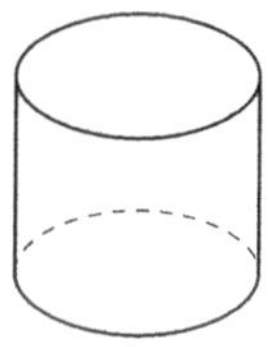

Number of edges: ______________

Number of vertices: ______________

5 Cone   Triangular Prism

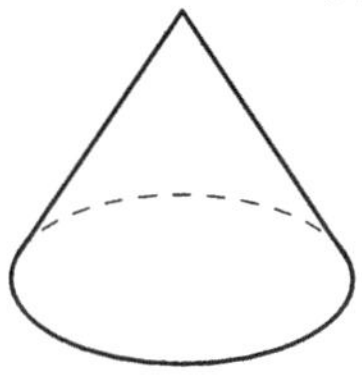

Number of edges: ______________

Number of vertices: ______________

6 Square-Based Pyramid   Cube

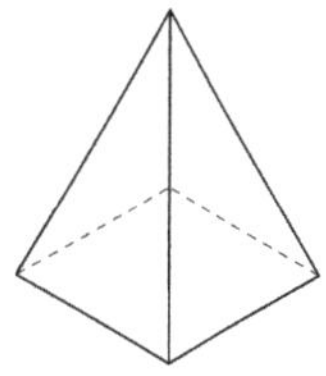

Number of edges: ______________

Number of vertices: ______________

I can identify the number of vertices and edges.

Matching Nets

Match the 3D object name to its net and picture.

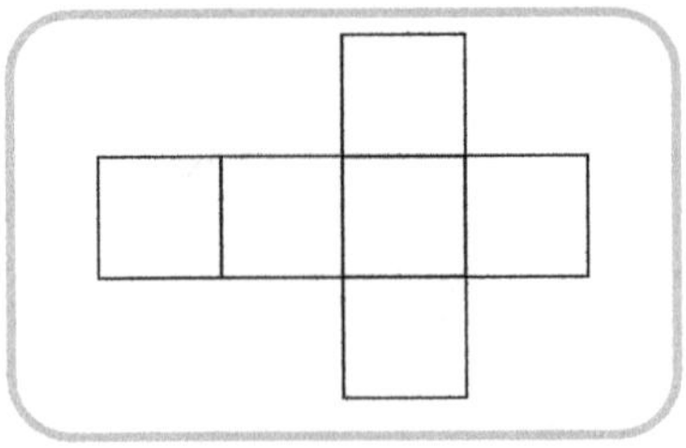

Rectangular Prism

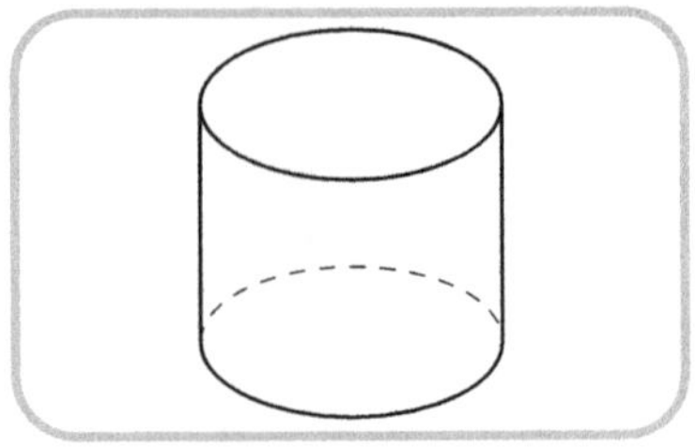

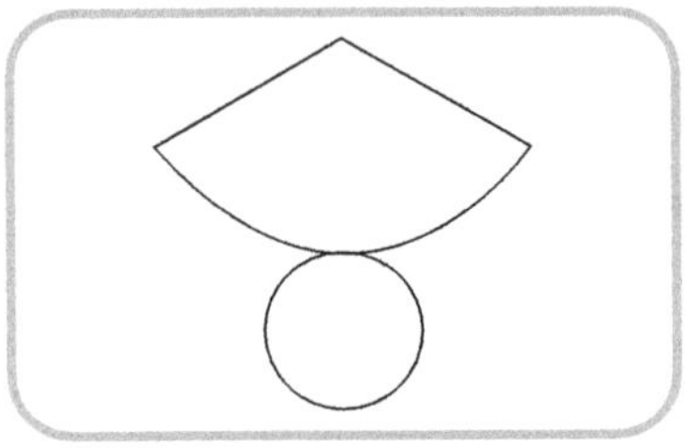

Cube

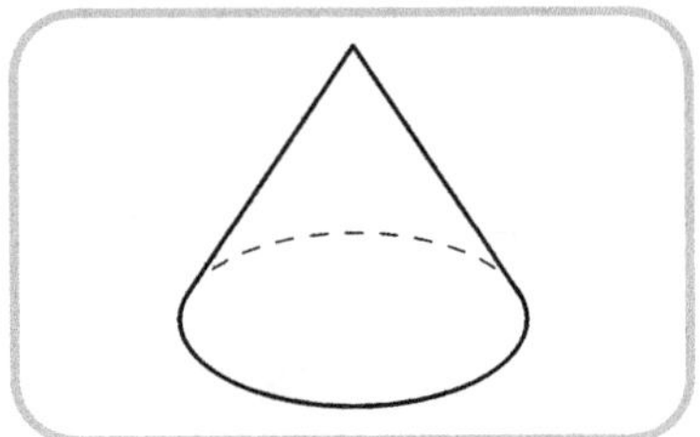

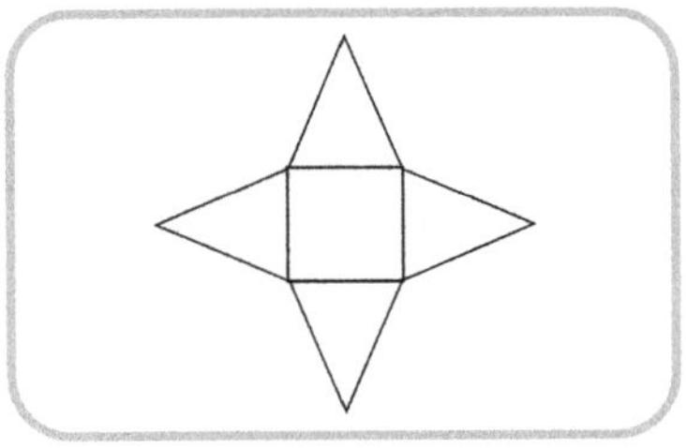

Triangular Prism

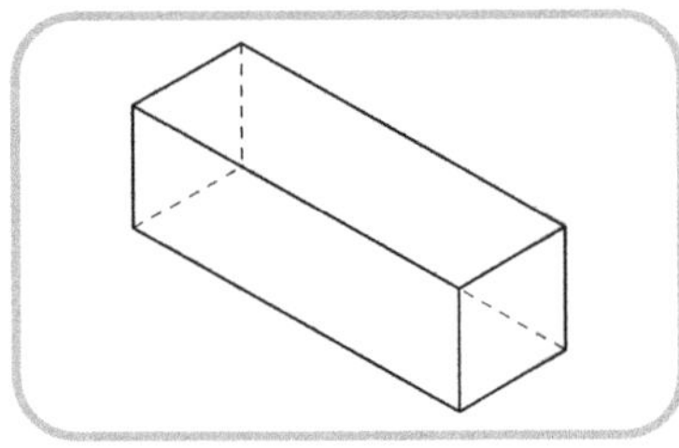

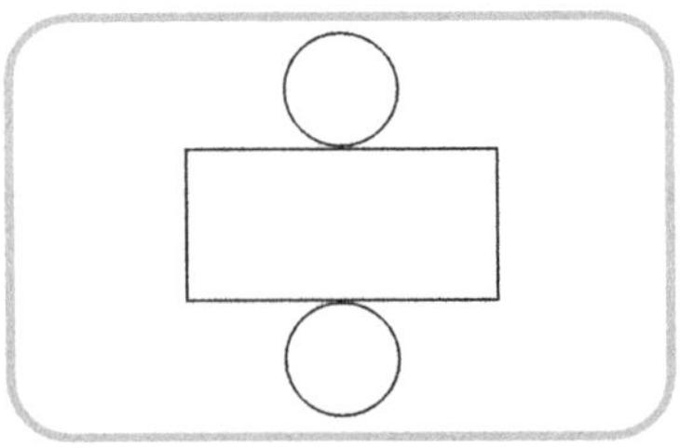

Cylinder

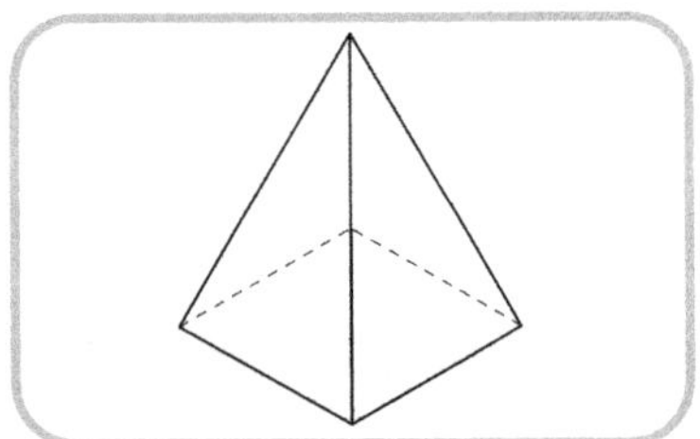

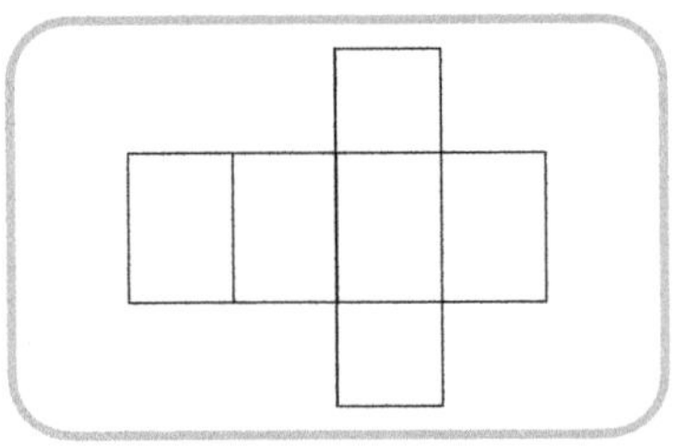

Cone

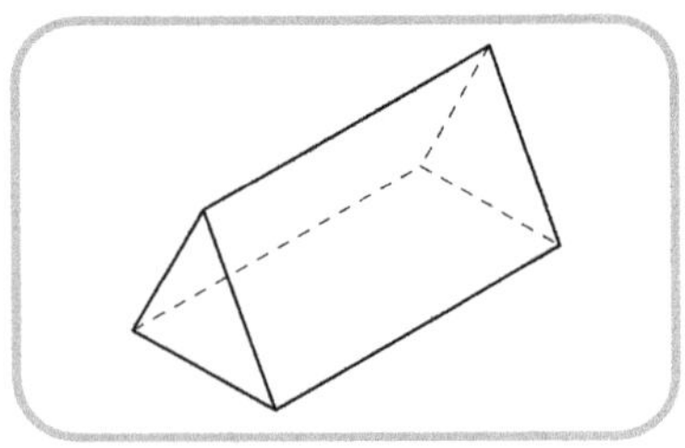

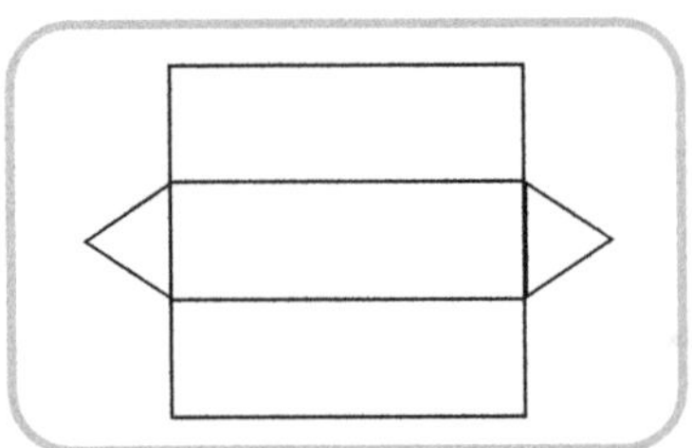

Square-Based Pyramid

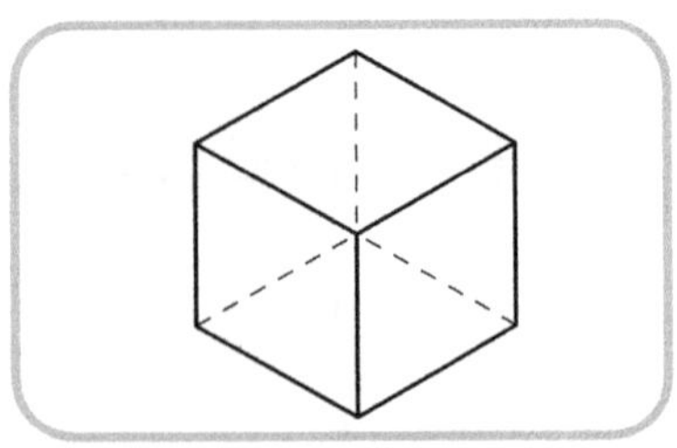

I can match 3D objects to their nets.

Sorting 2D Shapes and 3D Objects

Identify the 2D shapes and 3D objects. Write the names of the shapes and objects in the correct column in the chart.

2D Shapes	3D Objects

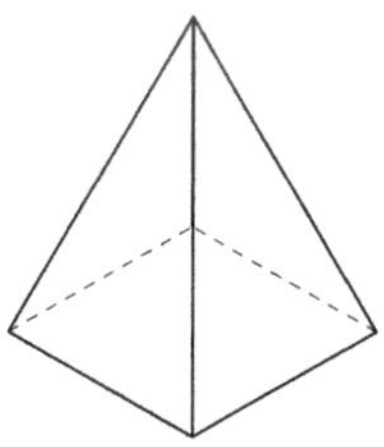

Square-Based Pyramid

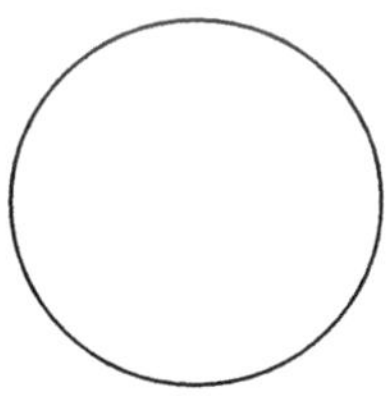

Circle

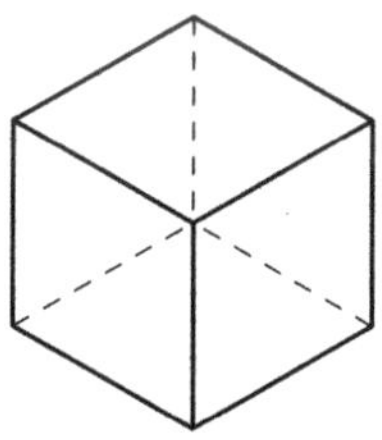

Cube

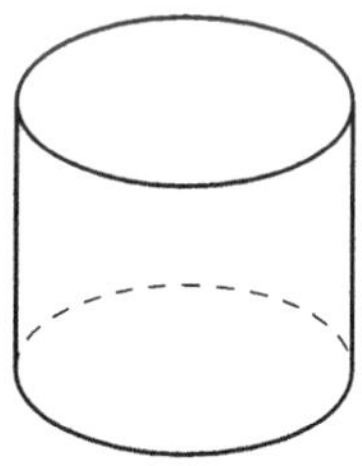

Cylinder

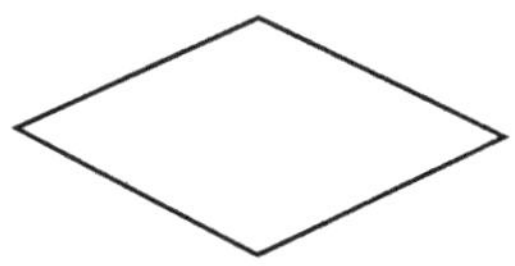

Rhombus

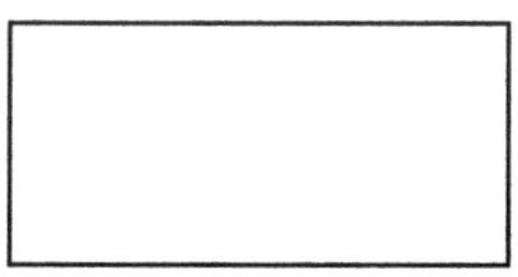

Rectangle

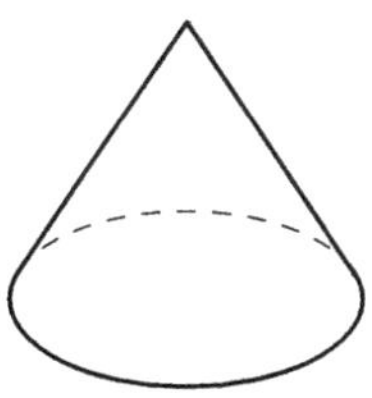

Cone

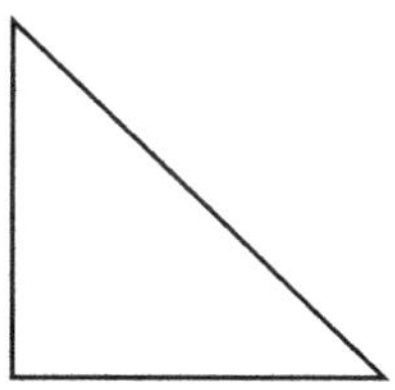

Triangle

Square

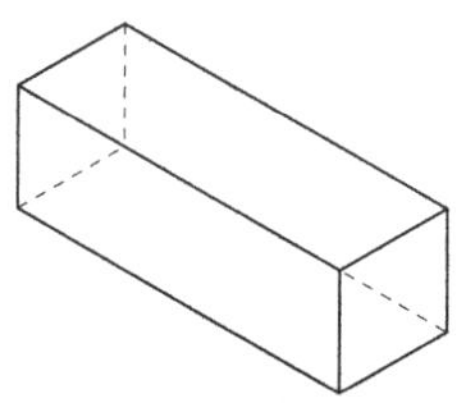

Rectangular Prism

I can sort 2D shapes and 3D objects.

Identifying 3D Objects

Think about how 3D objects are found in real life. Draw a line to match the 3D object on the left to the correct picture on the right.

Sphere 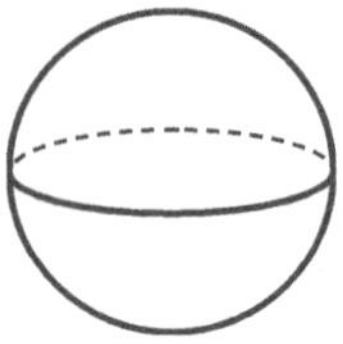

 Pyramid

Cube 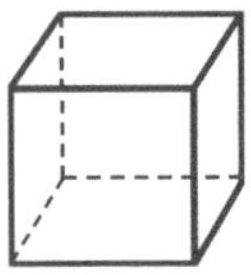

 Tissue Box

Square-based Pyramid 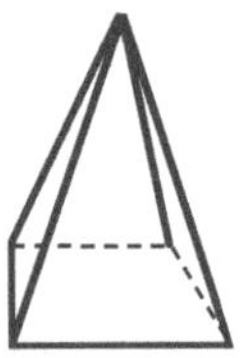

 Die

Cone 

 Globe

Cylinder 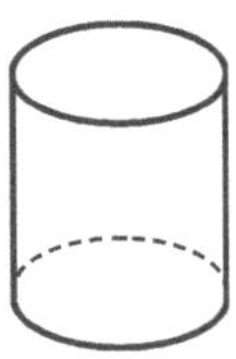

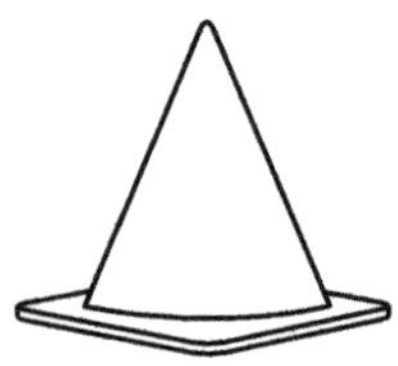 Pylon

Rectangular Prism 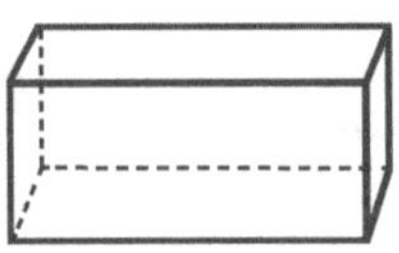

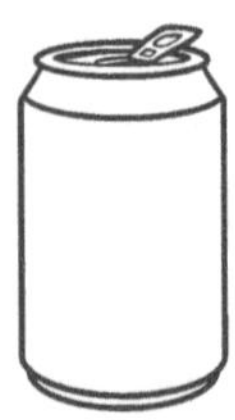 Can

I can identify 3D objects.

Take a 3D Shape Walk

No matter where you live, you can see 3D objects that are human-made or found in nature. Make a list of 3D objects you find in real life or in magazines.

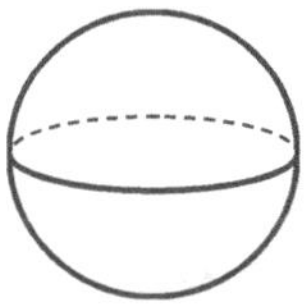

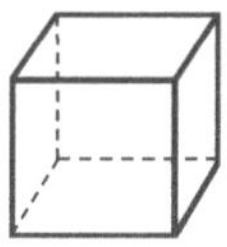

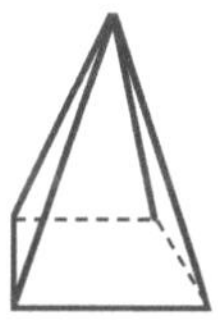

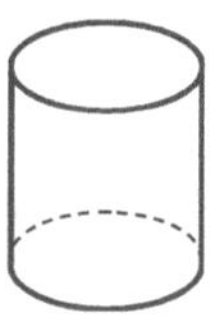

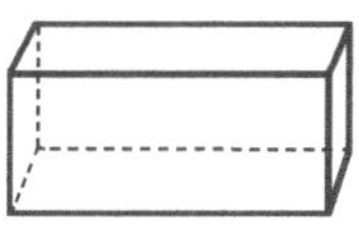

I can find 3D objects.

Exploring Polygons

A **polygon** is a 2D shape with three or more sides.

A corner of a **polygon** is called a **vertex**.
The plural of vertex is **vertices**.

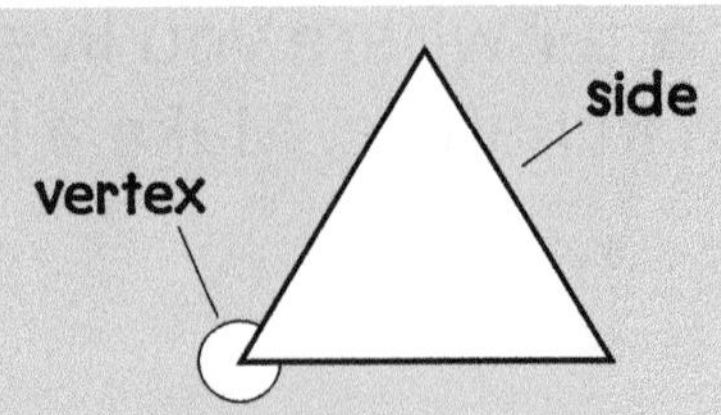

Shape	Trace the Shape	Name of Shape	Number of Sides	Number of Vertices
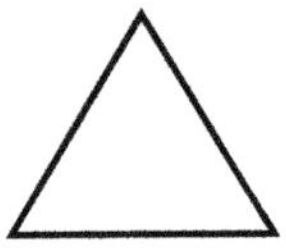				

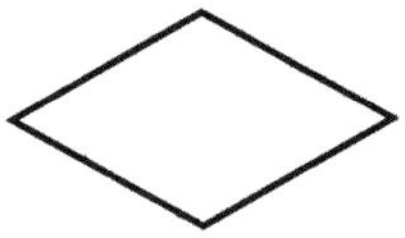	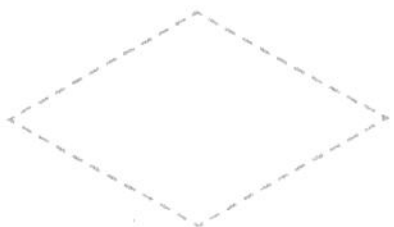			

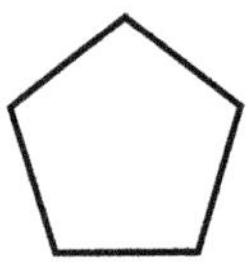				
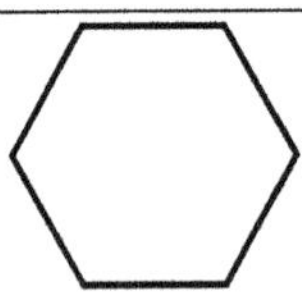	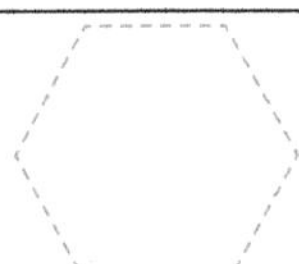			
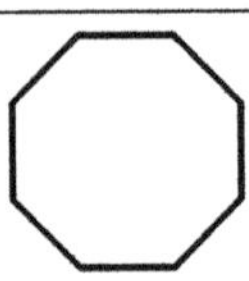	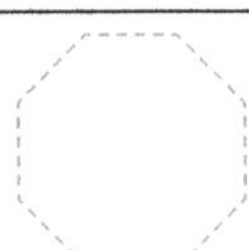			

I can identify polygons.

Exploring Polygons (continued)

A **regular polygon** is a shape with three or more sides that has all sides equal and all angles equal.

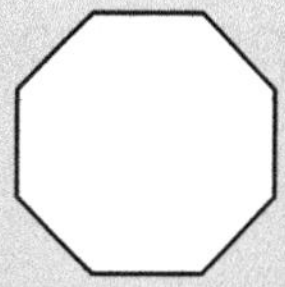

An **irregular polygon** is a shape with three or more sides that does not have all sides equal or all angles equal.

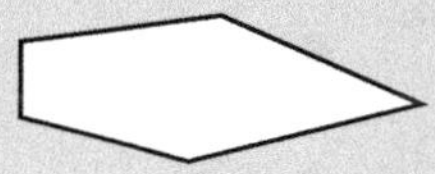

1 Put an **X** if the shape is not a polygon.
Colour the regular polygons blue. Colour the irregular polygons red.

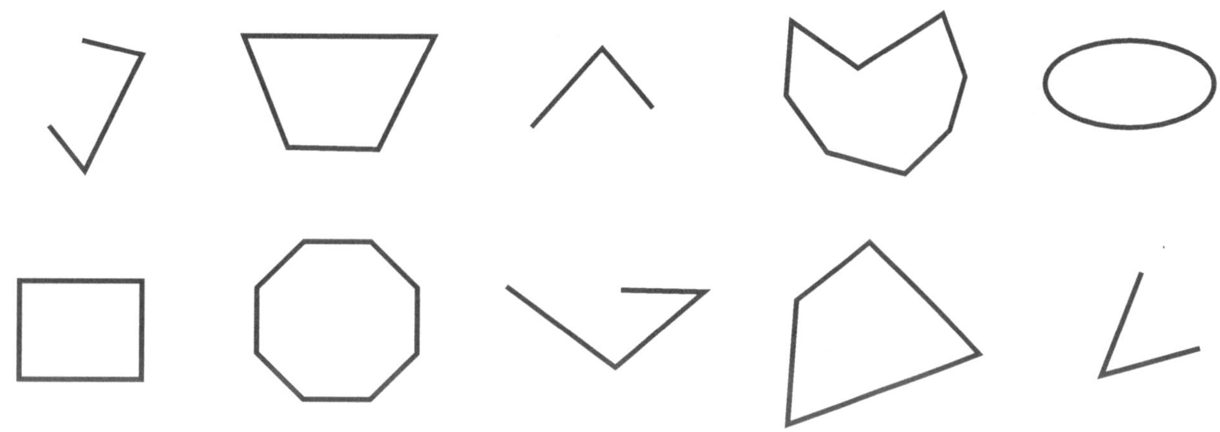

Quadrilaterals are polygons with 4 sides.

2 Colour the quadrilaterals yellow. Put an **X** if the polygon is not a quadrilateral.

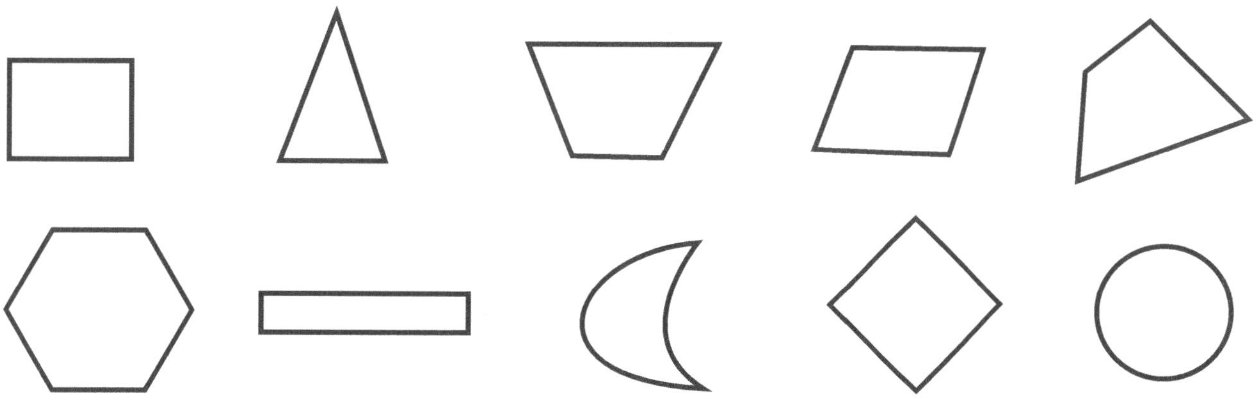

I can identify polygons.

Sorting Polygons

Sort the 2D shapes into groups.

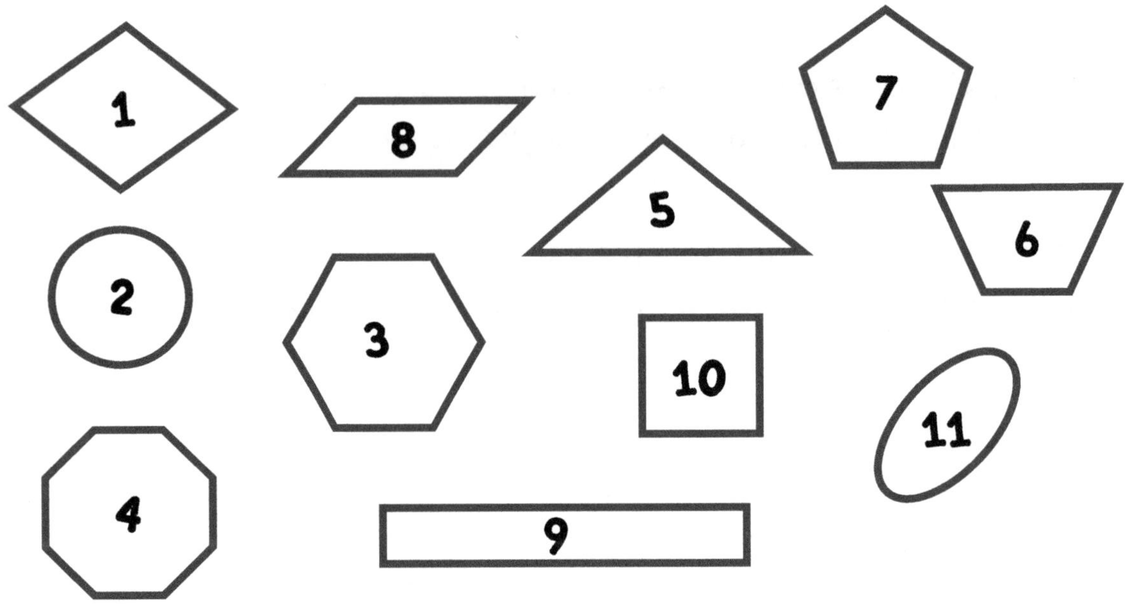

2D Shape Number	Polygon Sorting Rule
	more than 5 sides
	4 vertices
	only 3 sides
	more than 1 set of parallel lines
	square corners

I can sort polygons.

Exploring 3D Figures

Complete the attribute chart.

3D Figure	Number of Faces	Shape of Faces	Number of Edges	Number of Vertices
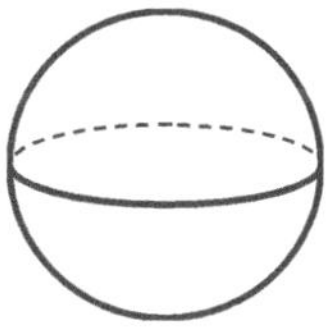 Sphere				
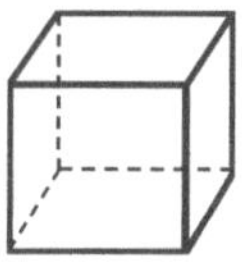 Cube				
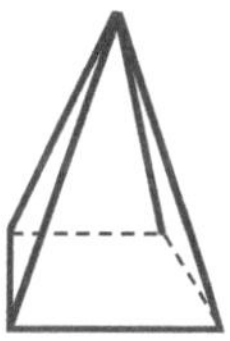 Square-based Pyramid				
 Cone				
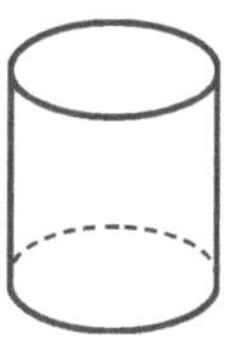 Cylinder				
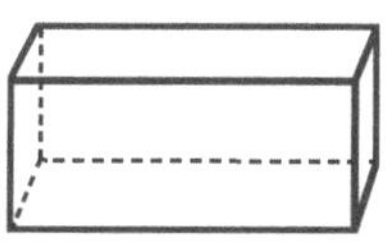 Rectangular Prism				

I can identify attributes of 3D figures.

Exploring Symmetry

A **line of symmetry** divides a shape into 2 parts that are the exact same size and shape.

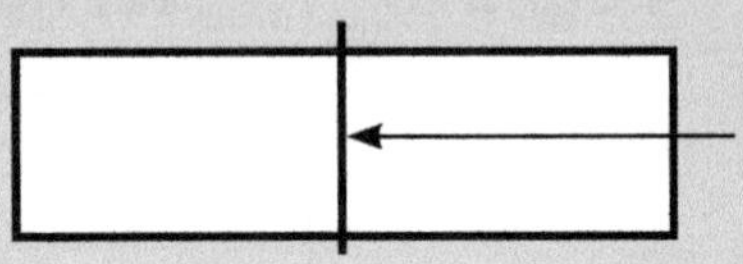

This shape does not have a line of symmetry.

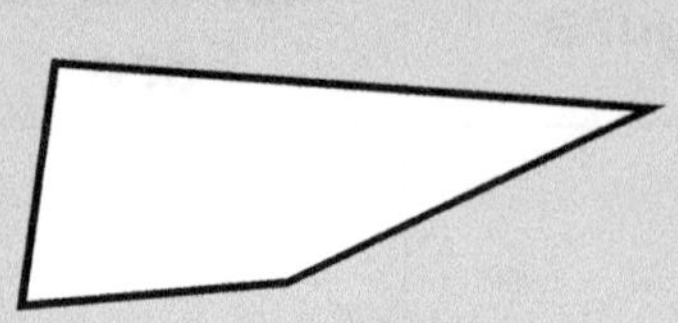

Draw the line of symmetry for the shapes that are symmetrical.
Put an **X** on the shapes that do not have a line of symmetry.

I can identify symmetry.

Exploring Congruent Figures

Congruent figures have the exact same shape and size.

Is the pair of shapes congruent? Circle the correct answer.

1. 

   yes **no**

2. 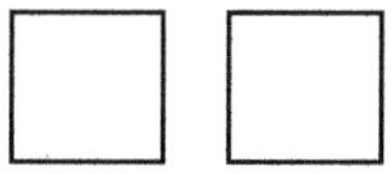

   yes **no**

3. 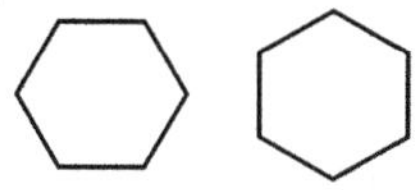

   yes **no**

4. 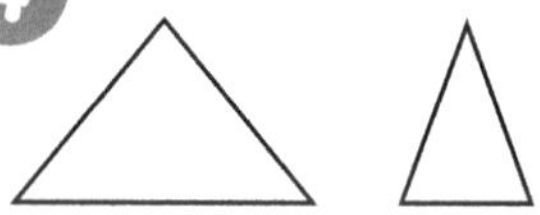

   yes **no**

5. 

   yes **no**

6. 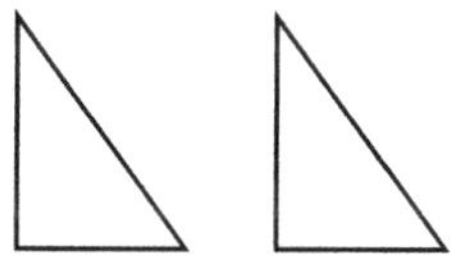

   yes **no**

7. 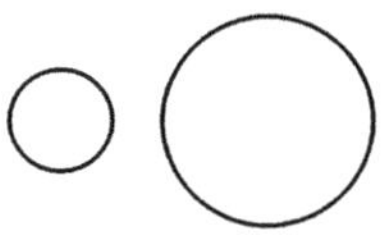

   yes **no**

8. 

   yes **no**

9. 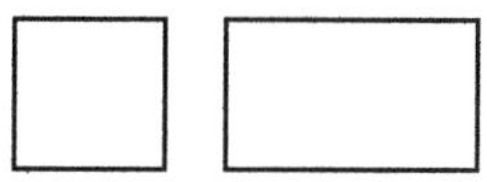

   yes **no**

10. 

    yes **no**

11. 

    yes **no**

12. 

    yes **no**

I can identify congruent shapes.

Reflections, Translations, and Rotations

These are types of transformations.

This is a **reflection**.

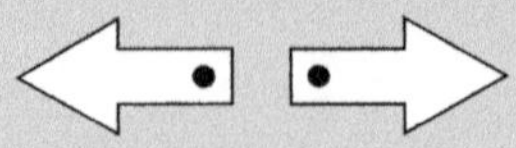

The shape flips so they are mirror images.

This is a **translation**.

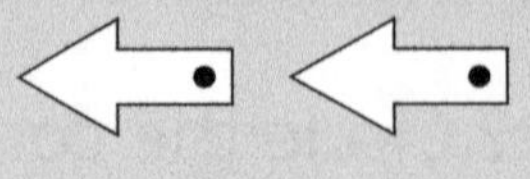

The shape slides in the same direction.

This is a **rotation**.

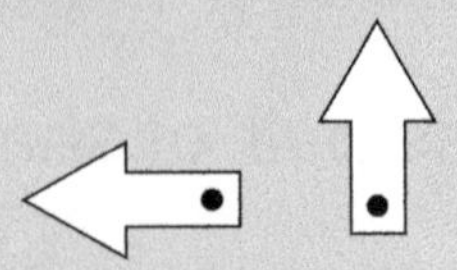

The shape turns.

1 Write whether the transformation is a reflection, a translation, or a rotation.

a

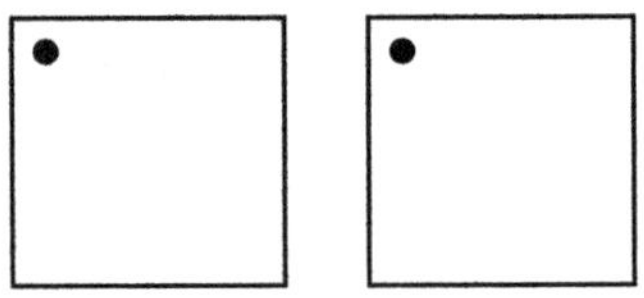

____

b

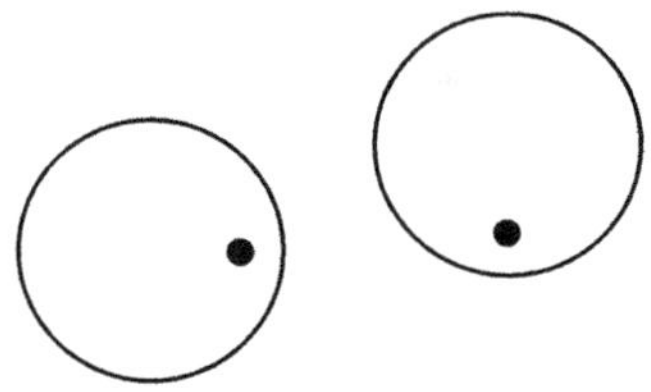

____

c

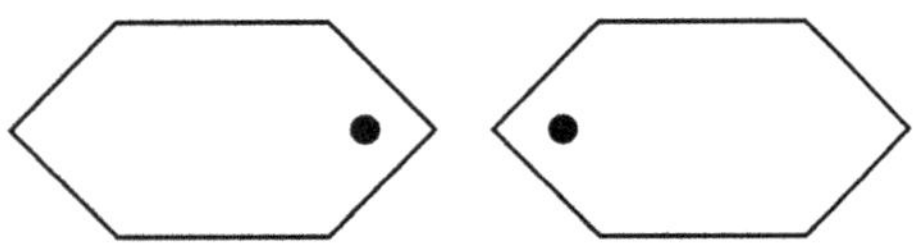

____

d

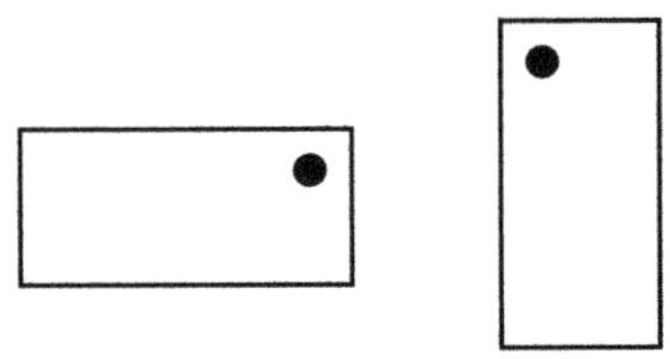

____

2 Draw and name your own transformation.

a

____

b

____

I can identify reflections, translations, and rotations.

Reflections, Translations, and Rotations (continued)

3 Write whether the transformation is a reflection, a translation, or a rotation.

a

____

b

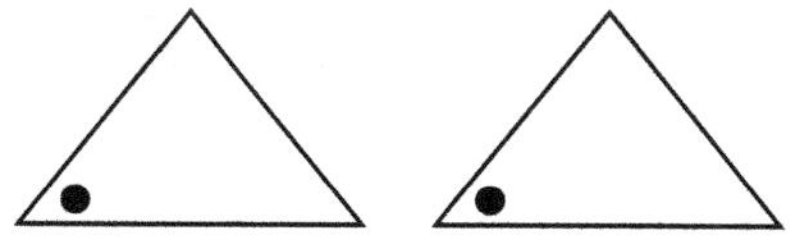

____

c

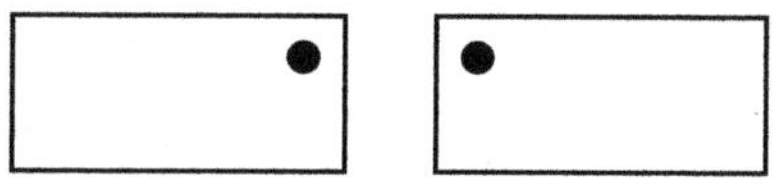

____

d

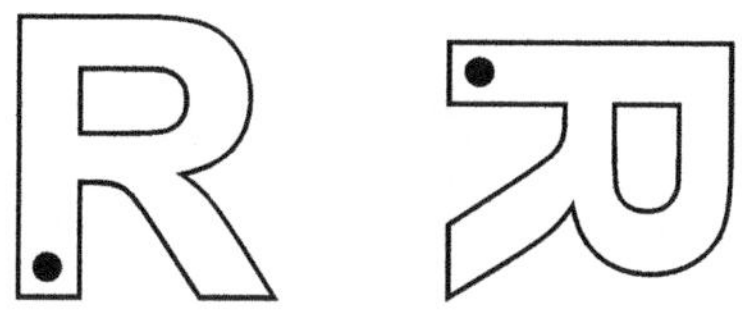

____

e

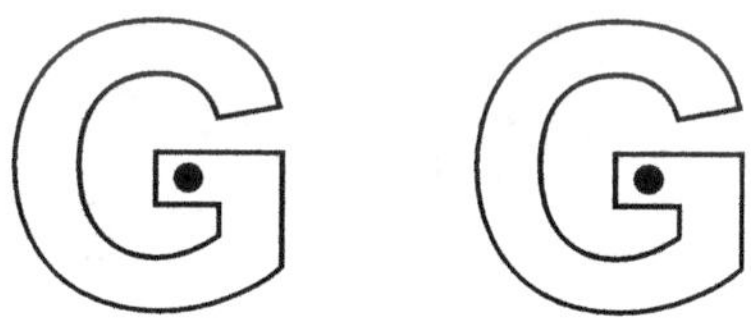

____

f

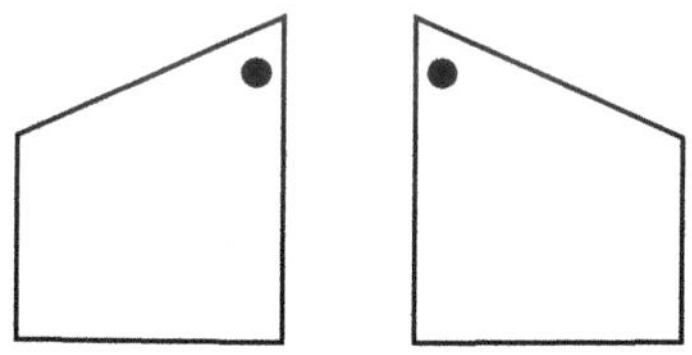

____

g

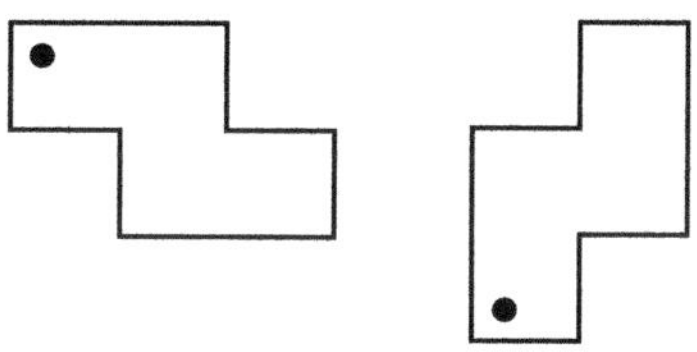

____

h

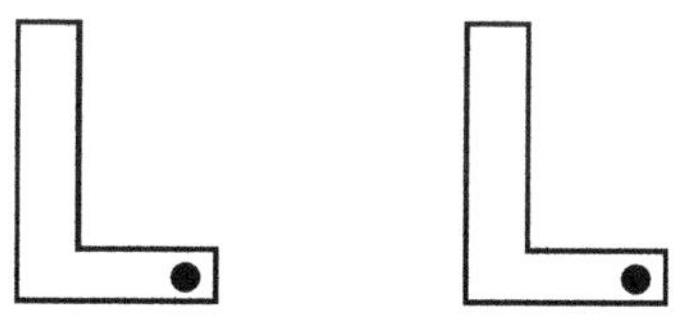

____

Transformations in Everyday Objects

Write whether the transformation is a reflection, a translation, or a rotation.

1

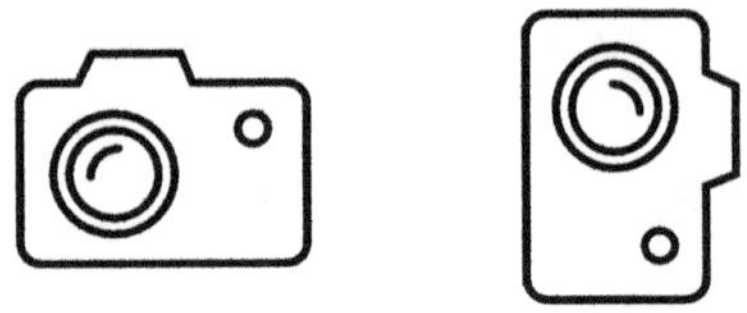

____

2

____

3

____

4

____

5

____

6

____

7

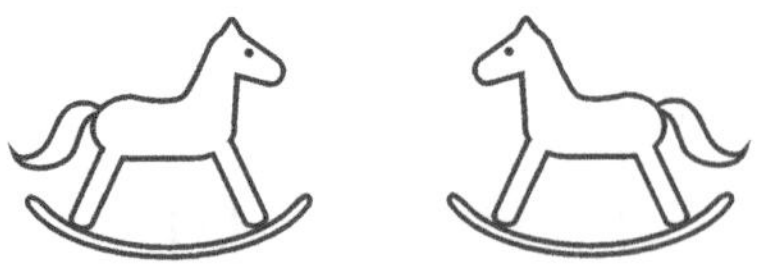

____

8

____

I can identify transformations in everyday objects.

Describing Turns

A **turn** is when a figure rotates around one of its vertices.

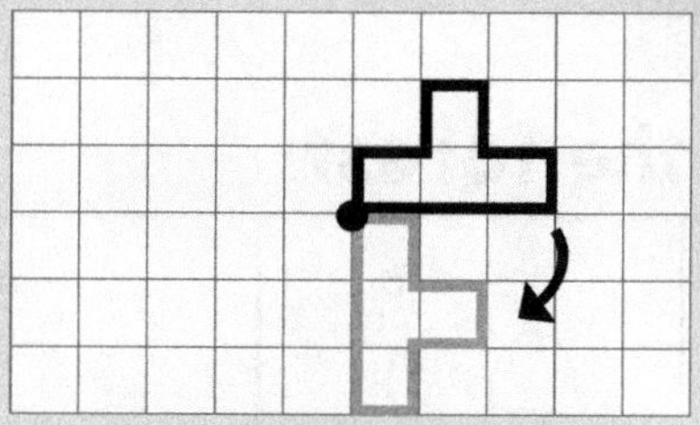

quarter turn

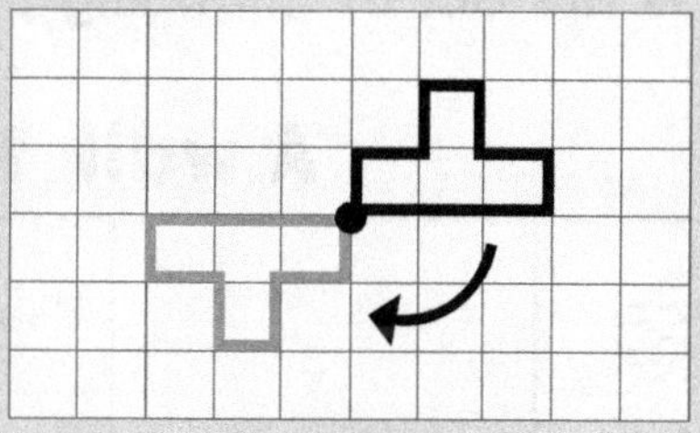

half turn

Circle whether the shape rotated a *quarter turn* or a *half turn*.

1. quarter turn   half turn

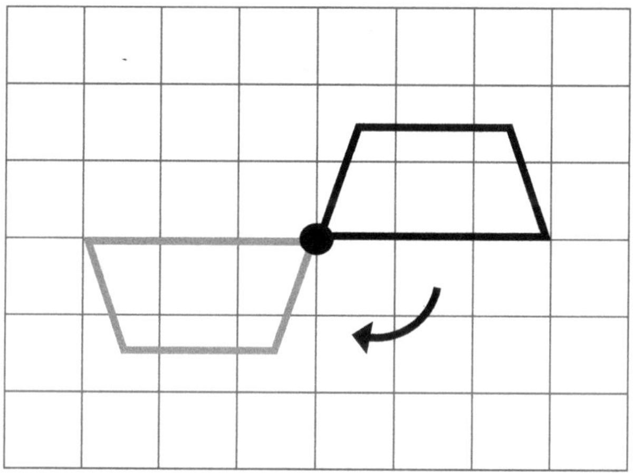

2. quarter turn   half turn

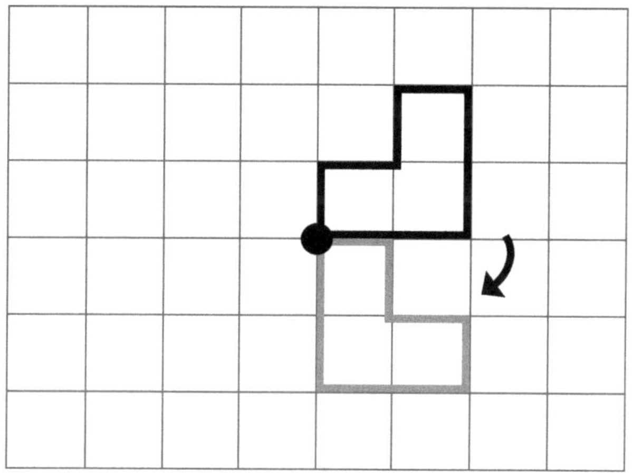

3. quarter turn   half turn

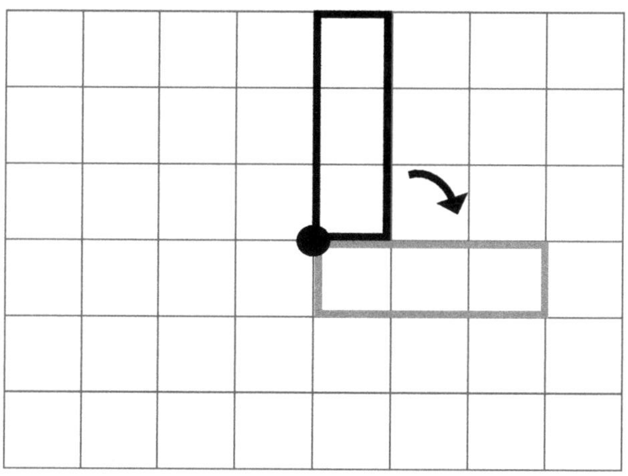

4. quarter turn   half turn

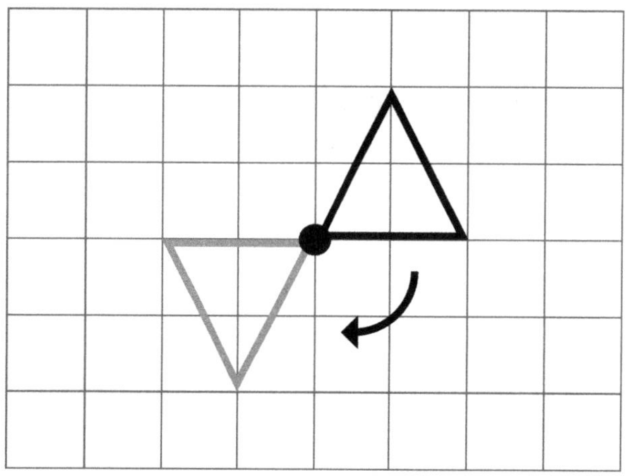

I can describe turns.

Exploring Location and Movement

A **location** is a place or position.
Movement is the act of changing place or position.

A walk through the forest

1. If I start on the ✕ and go **1** space up and **1** space to the left, what will I find?

   ____

2. If I start on the ✕ and go **3** spaces to the right, what will I find?

   ____

3. Describe how to get from the raccoon to the berry bush.

   ____

I can follow movement on a map.

Describing Movement on a Grid

Describe **movement** on a grid.

⇧ ⇩ ⇦ ⇨

Up, down, left, and right are directions to describe movement.

Go 4 squares to the right and 2 squares down.

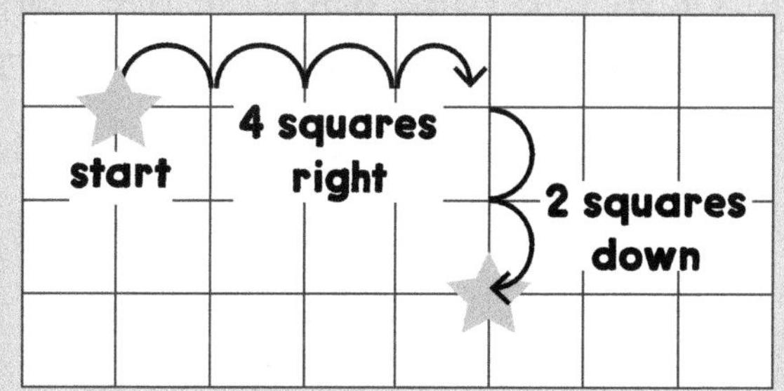

Describe the movement from Point A to Point B. Circle the correct direction.

1

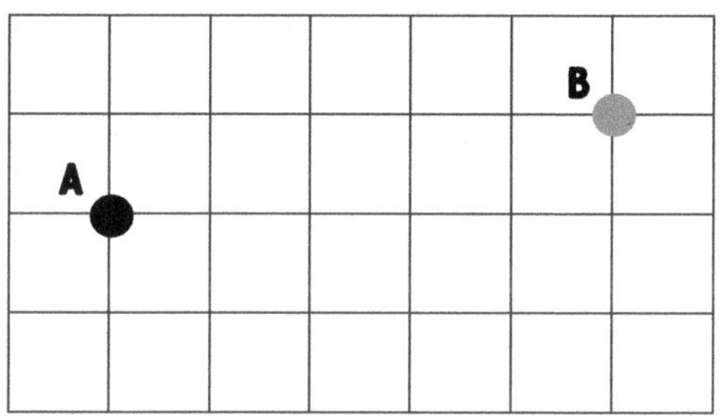

Go ______ squares left right

and go ______ squares up down.

2

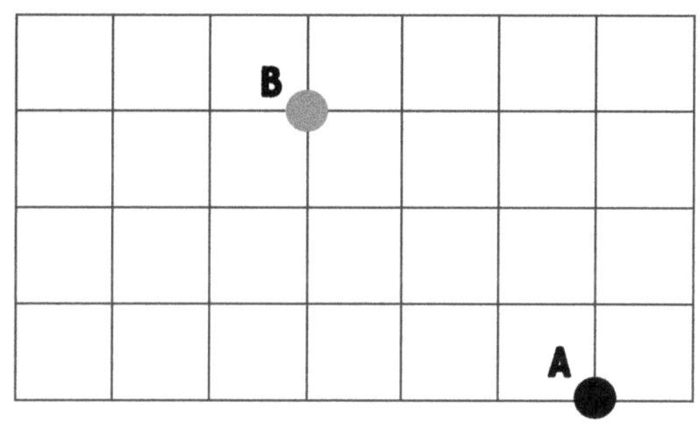

Go ______ squares left right

and go ______ squares up down.

3

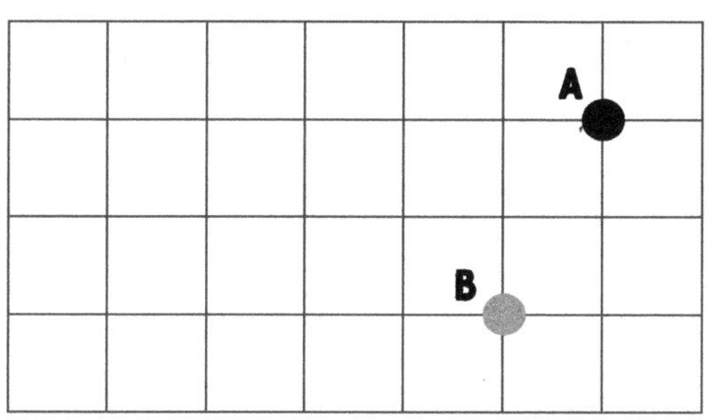

Go ______ squares left right

and go ______ squares up down.

4

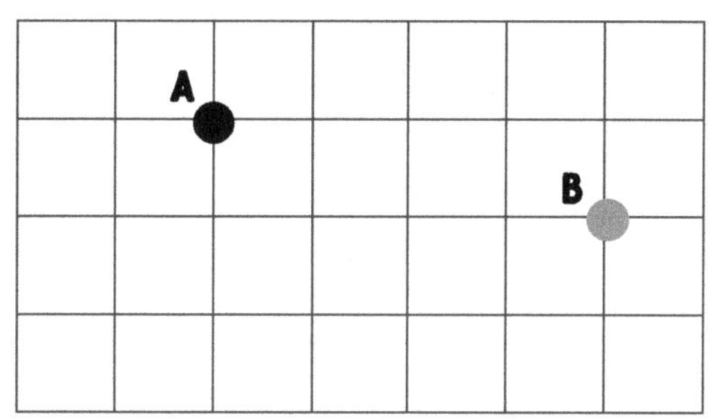

Go ______ squares left right

and go ______ squares up down.

I can describe movement on a grid.

Describing Movement on a Map

Look at the map and use the compass to write what direction you would need to travel to move from one location to the other. Use the word bank to help you.

North	East	South	West

1. Vancouver to Victoria: ___________
2. Kelowna to Vancouver: ___________
3. Fort Nelson to Prince George: ___________
4. Kitimat to Prince George: ___________
5. Vancouver to Prince George: ___________
6. Dease Lake to Fort Nelson: ___________

I can describe movement on a map.

Performing Movement

1 Help the animal find its way home by following the directions. Mark the animal's home with a circle.

a 4 squares left and 3 squares up

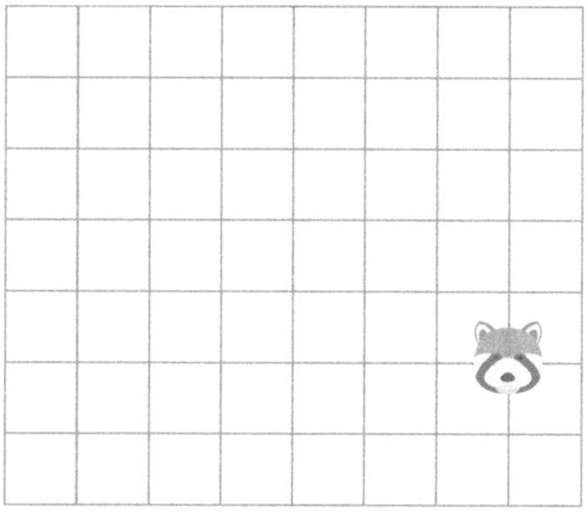

b 2 squares right and 6 squares down

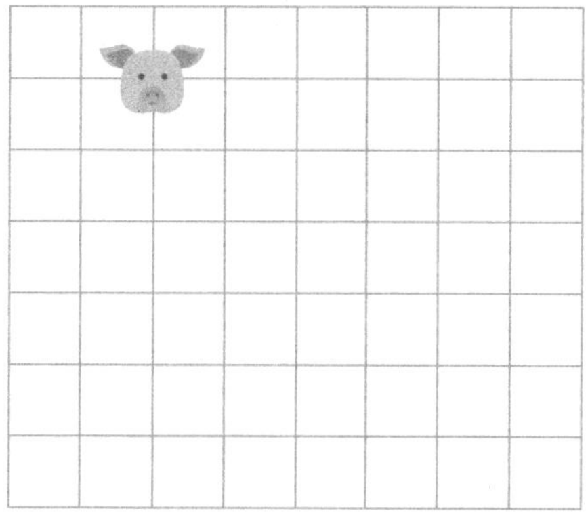

c 5 squares right and 2 squares up

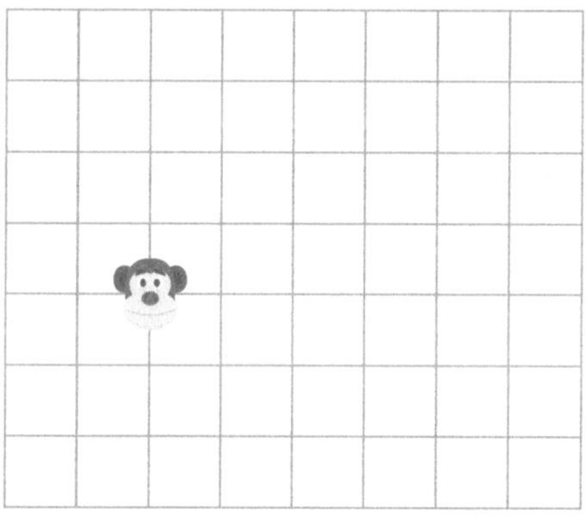

d 3 squares left and 5 squares down

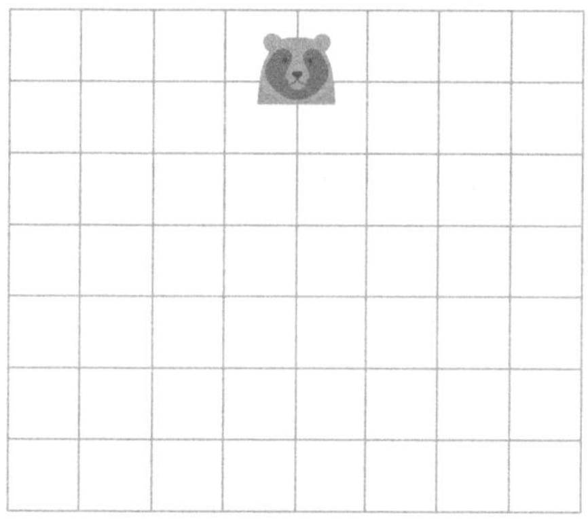

2 Mark the animal's home on the grid. Write the directions to get the animal home.

a ______________________________

____

b ______________________________

____

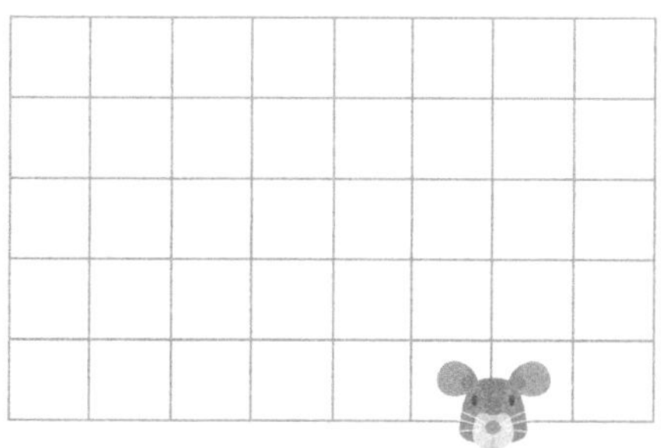

I can perform movement on a grid.

Show What You Know!

1. Choose the transformations in order that move the shape in Box 1 to Box 2, then to Box 3.

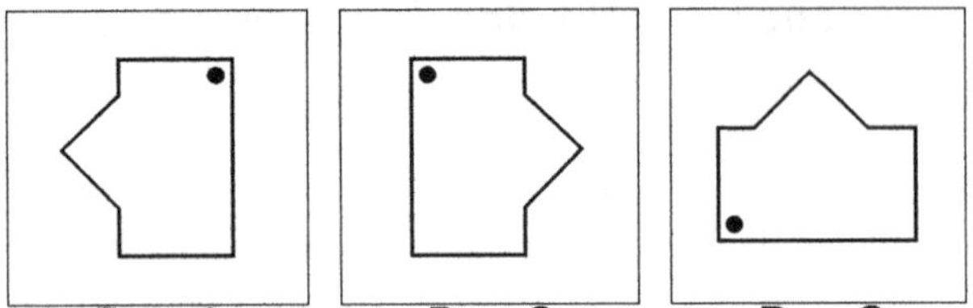

Box 1 Box 2 Box 3

   a. translation and reflection
   b. rotation and reflection
   c. reflection and rotation
   d. reflection and translation

2. Consider the shapes below.

Choose the 3-D figure you can make using all of the shapes.

   a. triangular prism
   b. rectanulgar prism
   c. square-based pyramid
   d. triangular-based pyramid

3. Identify the number of edges and vertices for the object.

a

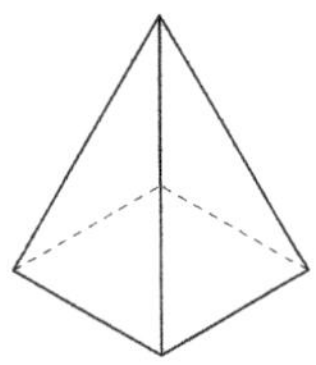

Number of edges: ______________

Number of vertices: ______________

b

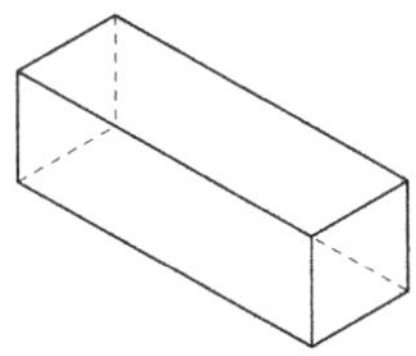

Number of edges: ______________

Number of vertices: ______________

4. Help the animal find its way home by following the directions. Mark the animal's home with a circle.

a **5 squares left and 2 squares up.**

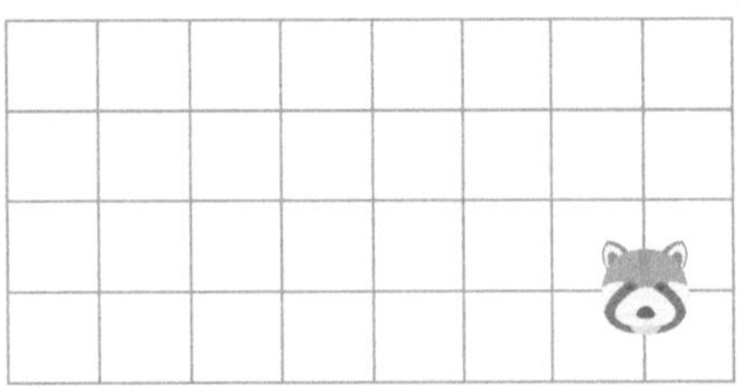

b **4 squares right and 3 squares down.**

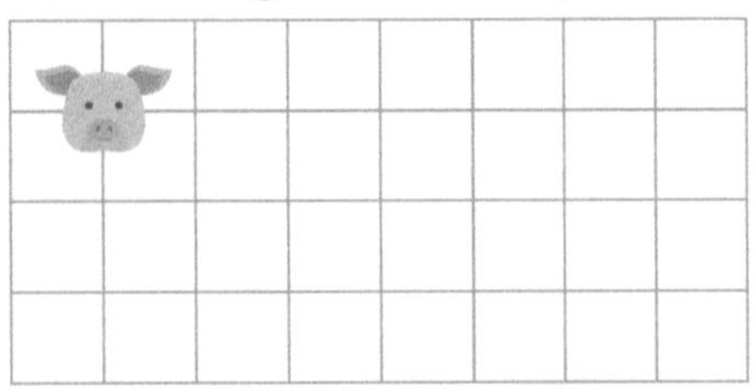

Show What You Know! (continued)

5. Look at the letters below.

M T H X

Which of the letters have more than one line of symmetry?

Justify your answer. Write about each letter.

M	**T**
H	**X**

I Can Checklist:
Measurement

Use appropriate units of length to estimate, measure, and compare the perimeters of polygons and curved shapes, and construct polygons with a given perimeter. For example,

- ***I can*** *draw a rectangle that has a perimeter of 12 cm..*

Explain the relationships between millimetres, centimetres, metres, and kilometres as metric units of length, and use benchmarks for these units to estimate lengths. For example,

- ***I can*** *explain that there are 10 mm in 1 cm, 100 cm in 1 m, and 1000 m in 1 km.*

Use non-standard units appropriately to estimate, measure, and compare capacity, and explain the effect that overfilling or underfilling, and gaps between units, have on accuracy. For example,

- ***I can*** *use a cup to measure the capacity of a larger container and explain that if I overfill or underfill the cup each time, my measurement will not be accurate.*

Compare, estimate, and measure the mass of various objects, using a pan balance and non-standard units. For example,

- ***I can*** *estimate the mass of my pencil, then check my estimate.*

Use various units of different sizes to measure the same attribute of a given item, and demonstrate that even though using different-sized units produces a different count, the size of the attribute remains the same. For example,

- ***I can*** *measure the length of my notebook using paper clips and erasers.*

Compare the areas of two-dimensional shapes by matching, covering, or decomposing and recomposing the shapes, and demonstrate that different shapes can have the same area. For example,

- ***I can*** *show that a square and two triangles that are the same size cover the same area.*

Use appropriate non-standard units to measure area, and use square centimetres (cm^2) and square metres (m^2) to estimate, measure, and compare the areas of various two-dimensional shapes, including those with curved sides. For example,

- ***I can*** *use square tiles to measure the area of my book's cover in non-standard units.*

Exploring Perimeter

The **perimeter** is the total distance around a figure.

We can use a unit grid to find the perimeter of any figure.

Each square is 1 unit by 1 unit.

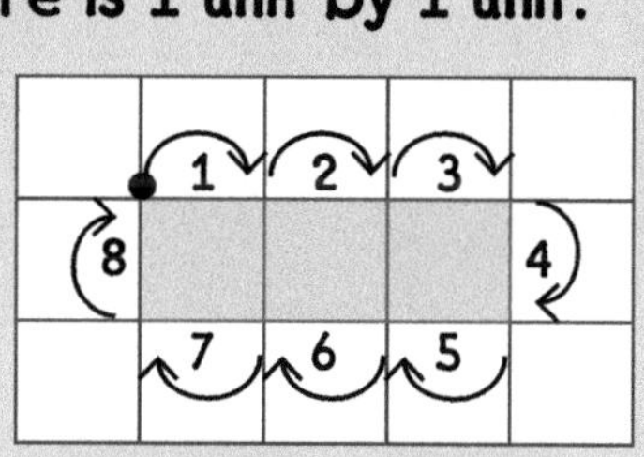

Perimeter = 8 units

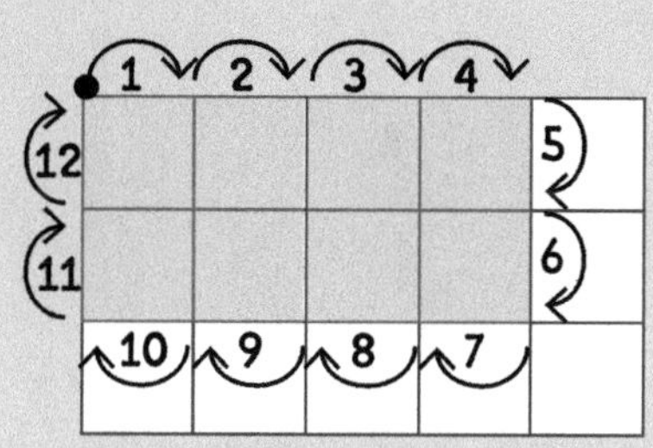

Perimeter = 12 units

Find the perimeter of the figure.

1

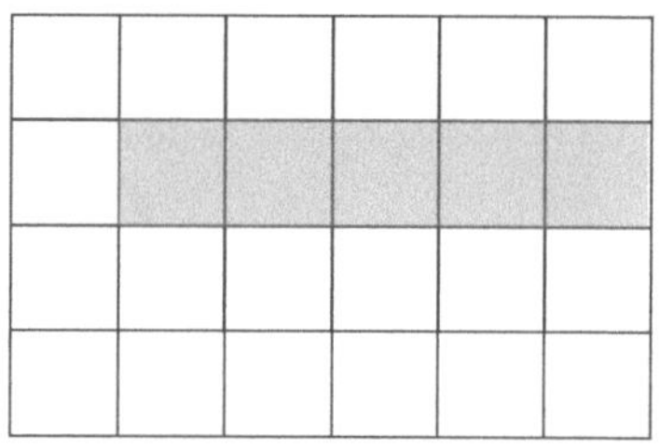

P = ________________ units

2

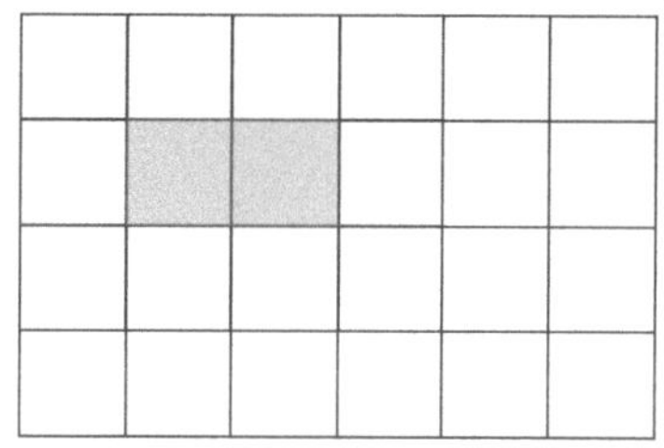

P = ________________ units

3

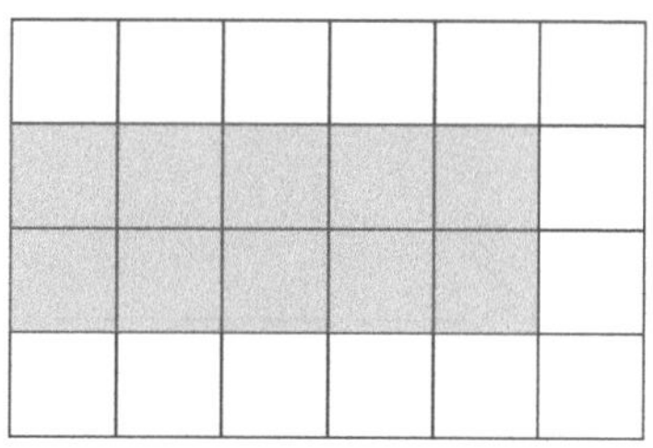

P = ________________ units

4

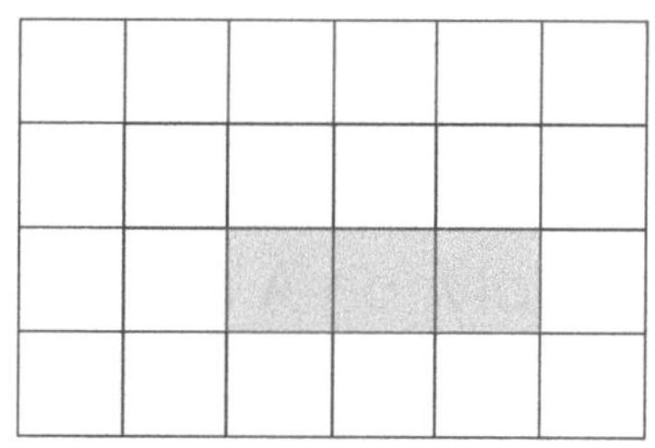

P = ________________ units

5

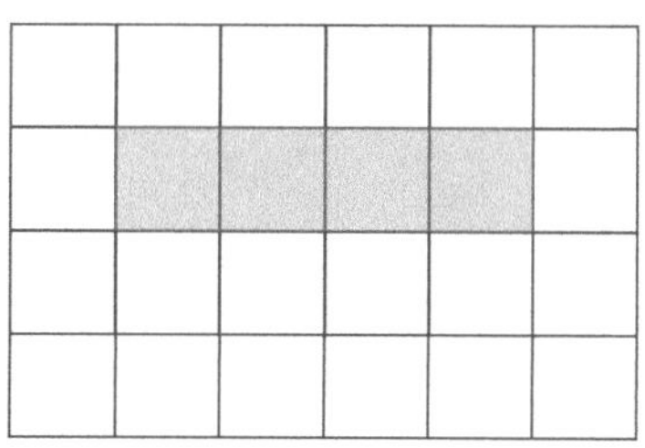

P = ________________ units

6

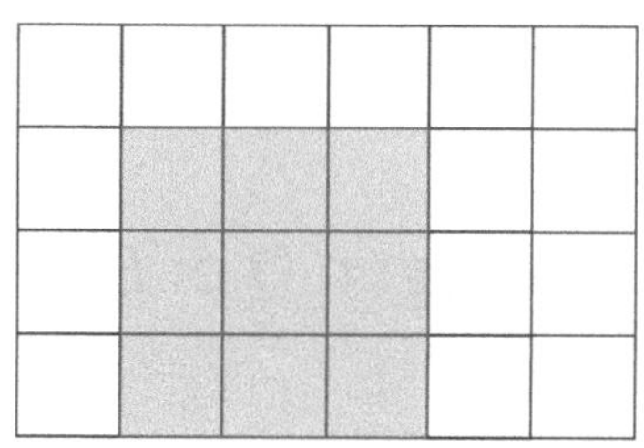

P = ________________ units

Comparing Perimeter: Polygons

Find and compare the perimeter of each polygon to answer the questions.

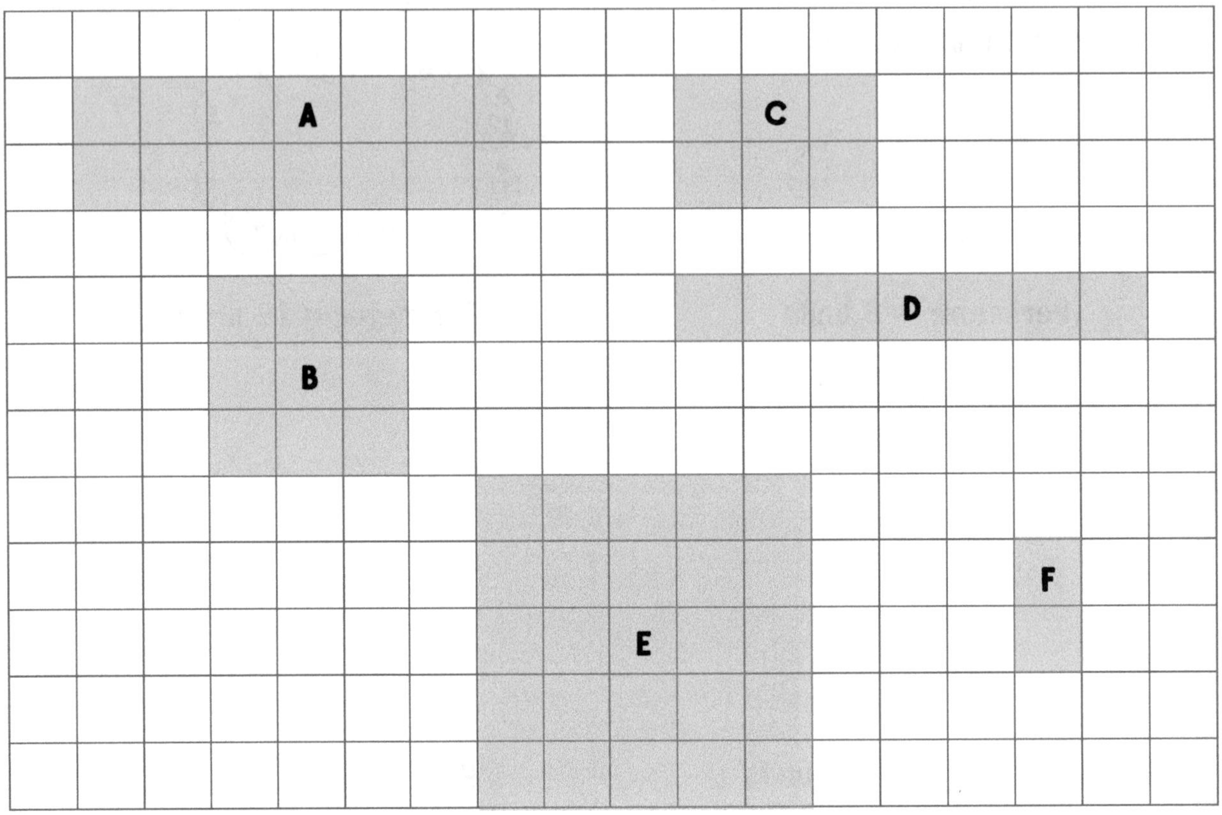

1. Which polygon has the largest perimeter? ____________________
2. Does polygon A or B have a smaller perimeter? ____________________
3. Which polygon has a perimeter of 18 units? ____________________
4. Which polygon has the smallest perimeter? ____________________
5. Does polygon D or E have a larger perimeter? ____________________
6. Which polygon has a perimeter of 16 units? ____________________

I can compare perimeters.

Drawing Perimeter

Construct a polygon with the specified perimeter given below.

1. **Construct a square with a perimeter of 8 units.**
2. **Construct a rectangle with a perimeter of 16 units.**
3. **Construct a rectangle and a square both with a perimeter of 12 units.**
4. **Construct a four-sided polygon with a perimeter of 14 units.**
5. **Construct a rectangle and a square both with a perimeter of 20 units.**

I can draw polygons using their perimeter.

Exploring Perimeter

To find the **perimeter**, or the distance around, add the lengths of each side of the shape.

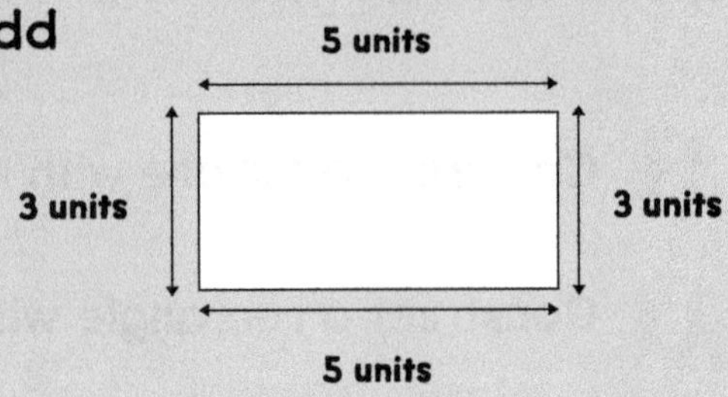

P = 5 + 3 + 5 + 3 = 16 units

The perimeter is 16 units.

Find the perimeter.

1

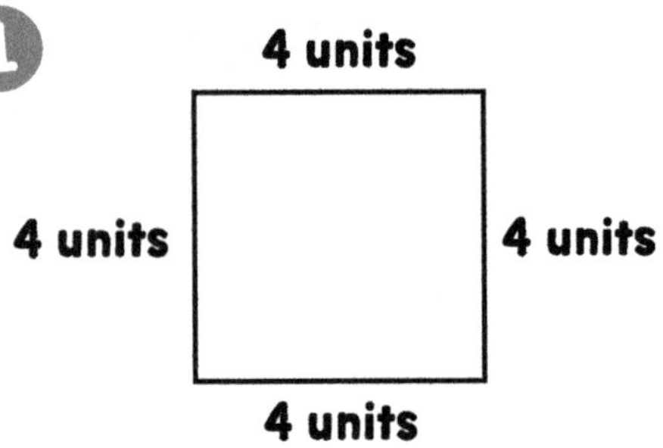

_____ + _____ + _____ + _____ = ______ units

2

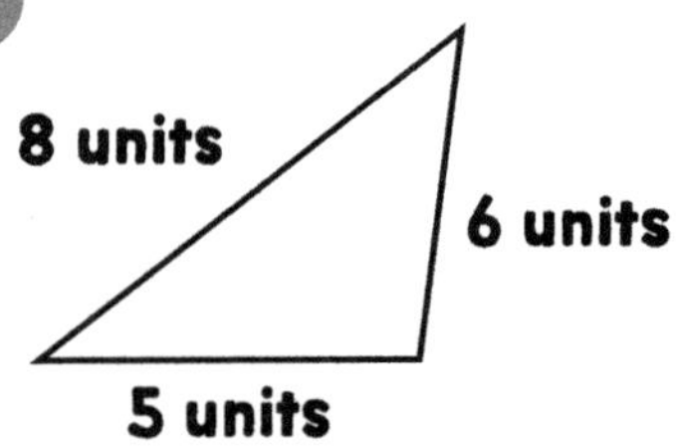

_____ + _____ + _____ = ______ units

3

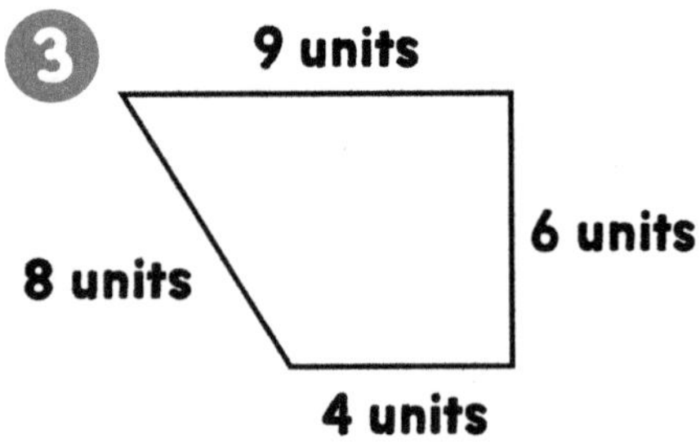

_____ + _____ + _____ + _____ = ______ units

I can calculate perimeter.

Finding the Perimeter: Polygons

To find the perimeter of a polygon, add the lengths of all of its sides.

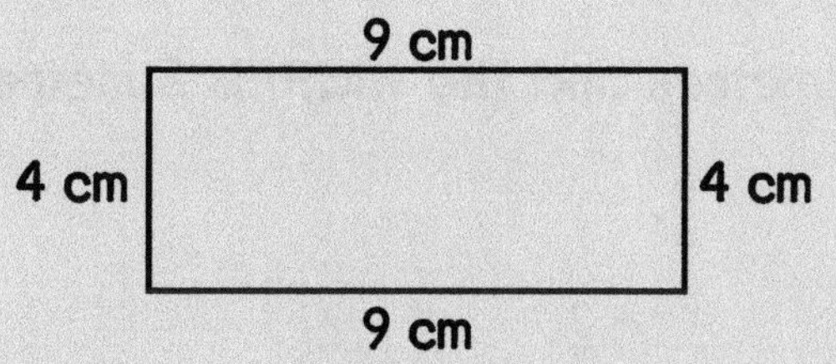

P = 4 cm + 9 cm + 4 cm + 9 cm
= 26 cm

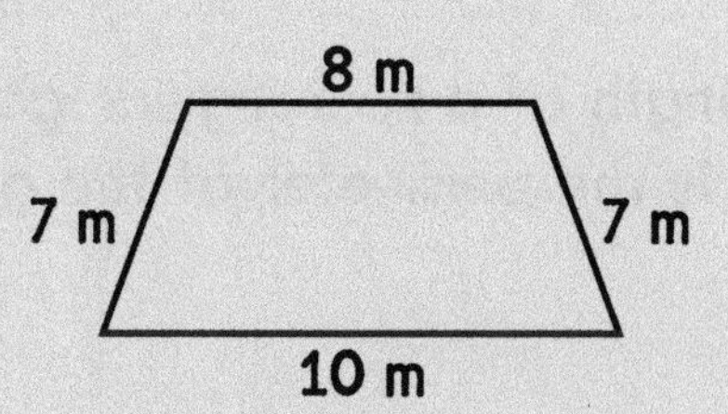

P = 7 m + 8 m + 7 m + 10 m
= 32 m

Find the perimeter.

1

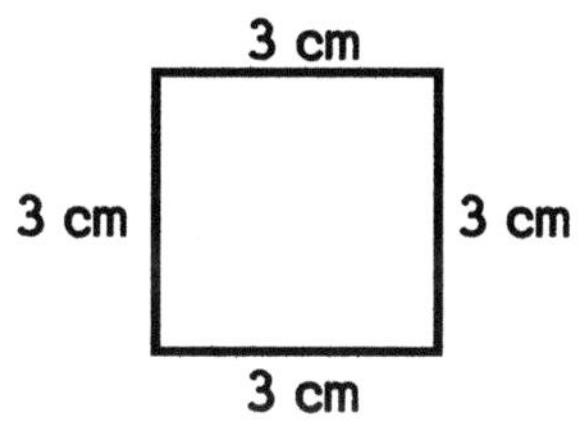

P = ______________________________

= __________ cm

2

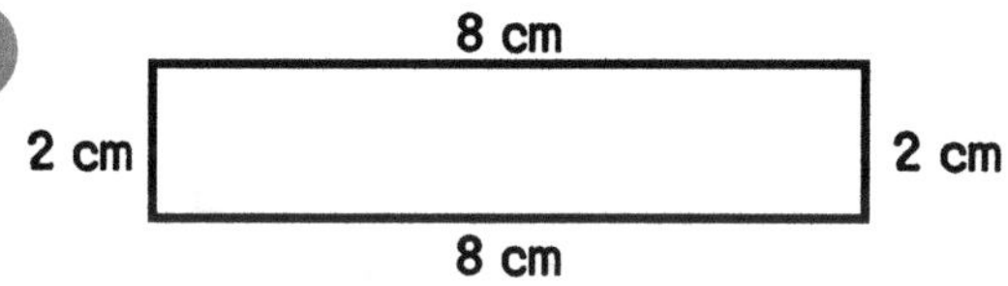

P = ______________________________

= __________ cm

3

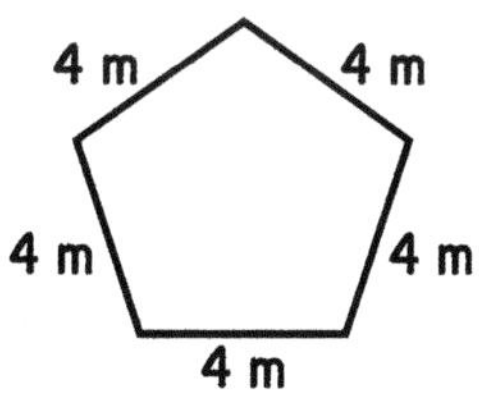

P = ______________________________

= __________ m

4

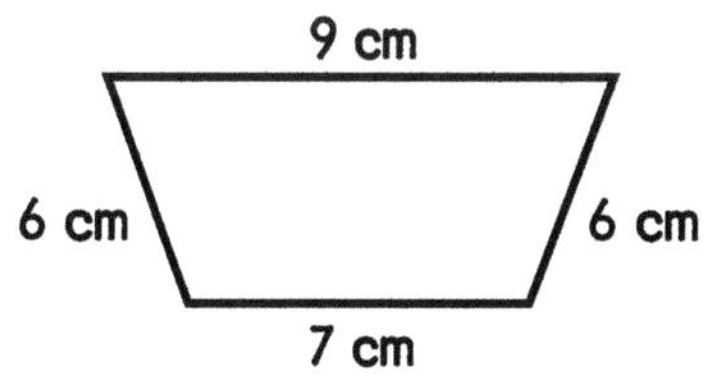

P = ______________________________

= __________ cm

5

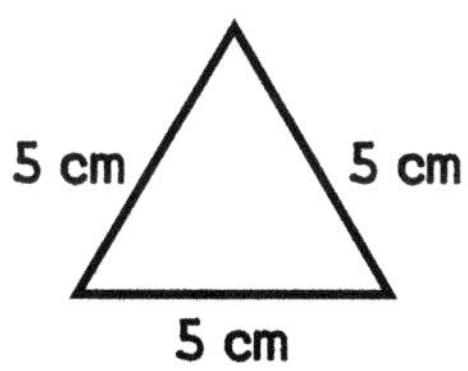

P = ______________________________

= __________ cm

6

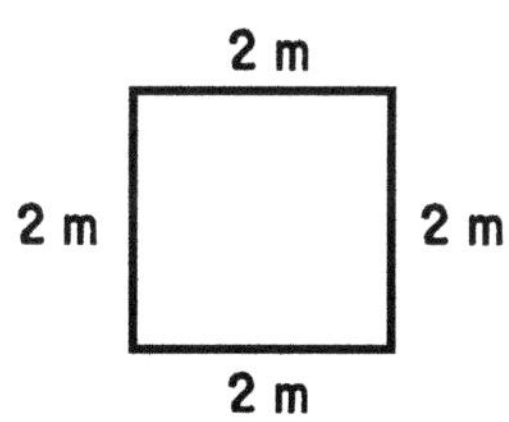

P = ______________________________

= __________ m

I can calculate perimeter.

Perimeter Word Problems

1 Solve.

a The length of a rectangular garden is 8 metres and the width is 5 metres
What is the perimeter of the garden?

b A square playground has sides that are each 12 metres long. What is the perimeter of the playground?

c An irregularly shaped swimming pool has sides measuring 9 metres, 6 metres, 12 metres, and 8 metres. What is the perimeter of the pool?

I can solve perimeter problems.

Perimeter Word Problems (continued)

2 Western School wants to build a new kindergarten playground. The principal has two models to choose from and wants the playground with the largest perimeter.

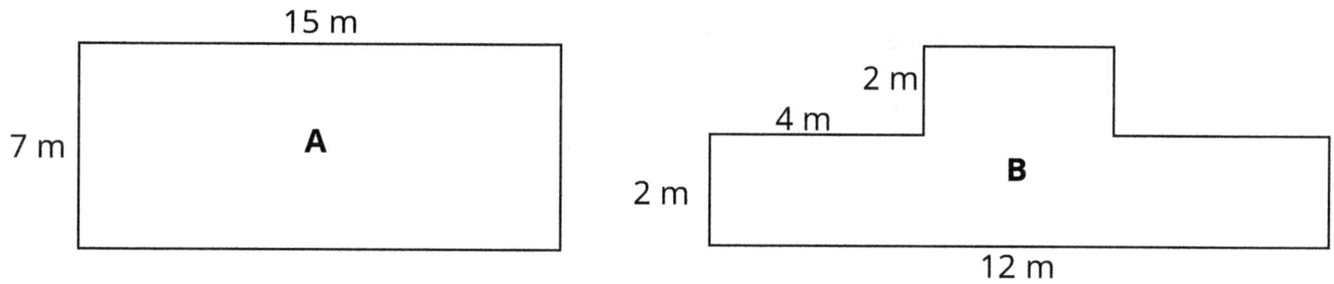

Which playground has the largest perimeter?

Show your work.

Playground _______ has the largest perimeter.

I can compare perimeters.

Exploring Area

Area is the number of units that cover a figure.

1 square = 1 unit

Count the number of shaded square units.

The area of the shaded figure is 9 square units.

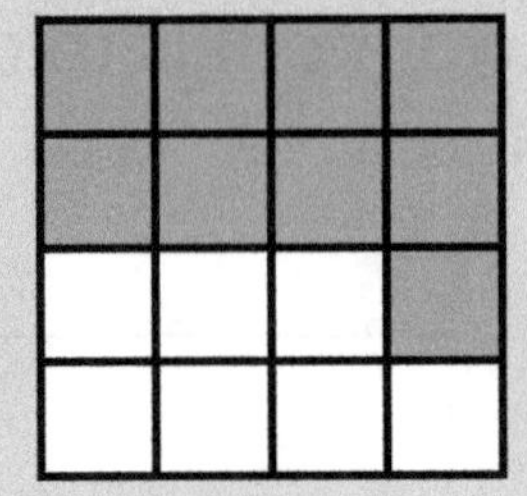

1. Count the number of shaded squares to find the area.

a

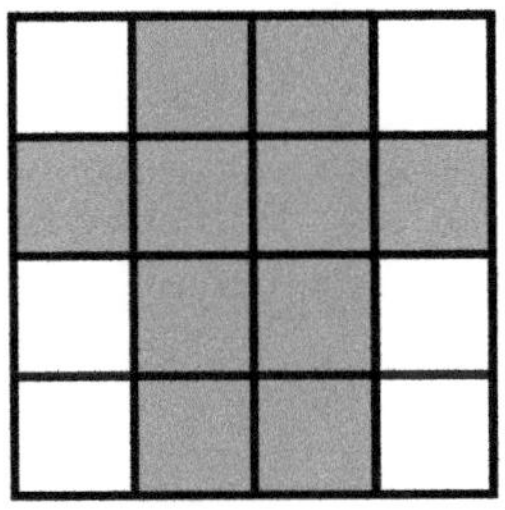

________ square units

b

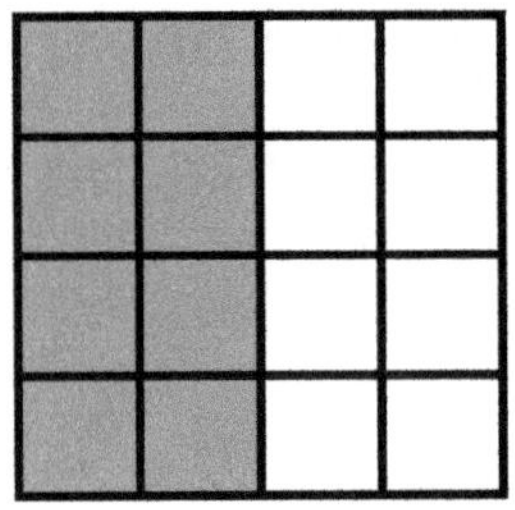

________ square units

c

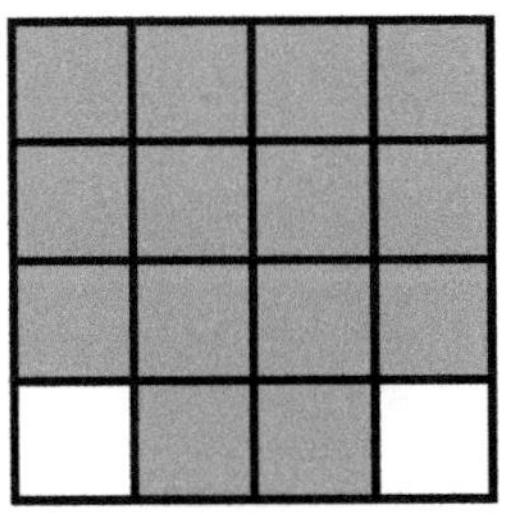

________ square units

d

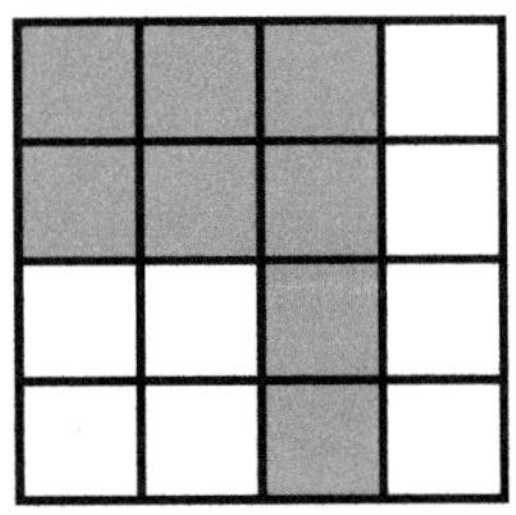

________ square units

e

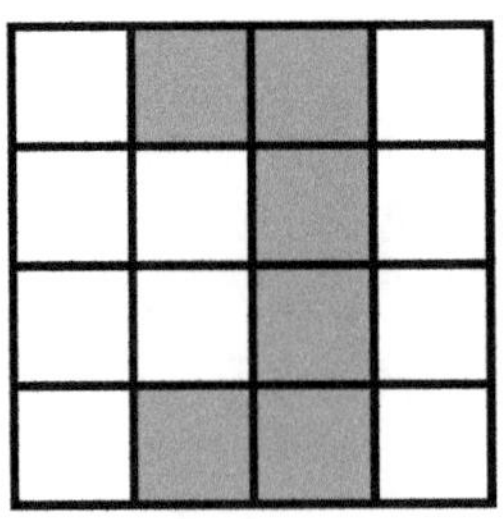

________ square units

f

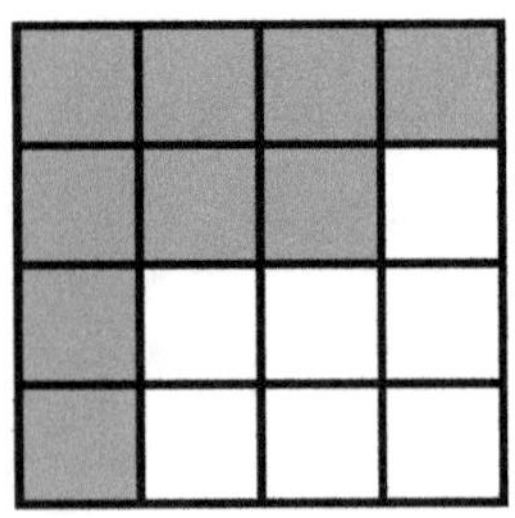

________ square units

I can calculate area.

Exploring Area (continued)

2 Peter and Leah both want to design their own farm. Help them design their own farm using the grids below.

Ideas: a barn, a garden, a house, a chicken coop, and a pasture

Peter's Farm

Leah's Farm

Comparing Area

Area is the amount of space a figure covers.

Figures that look different can have the same area.

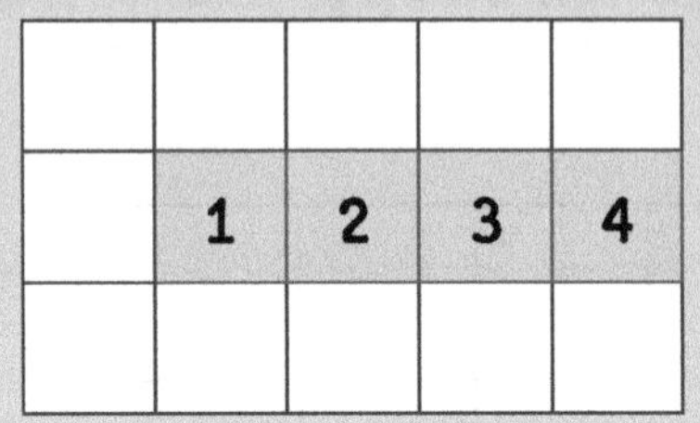

Area = 4 units

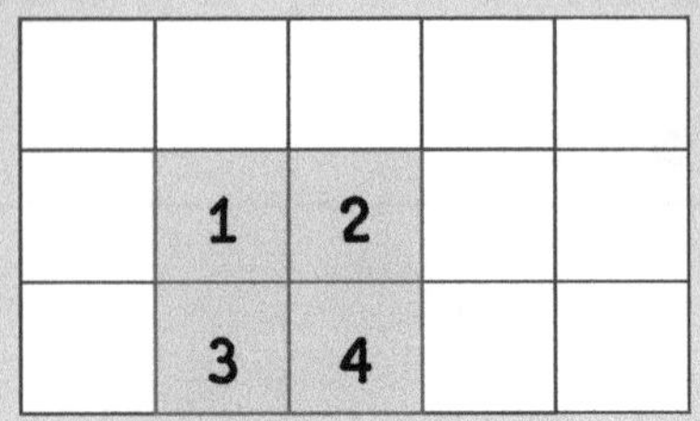

Area = 4 units

1. Circle the two figures that have the same area.

a

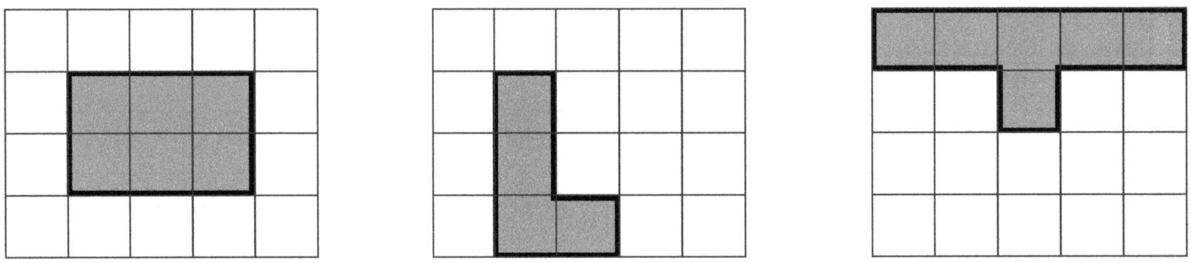

b

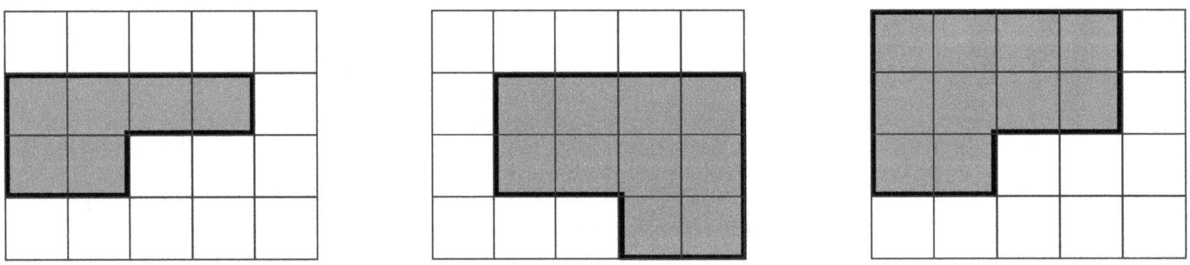

c

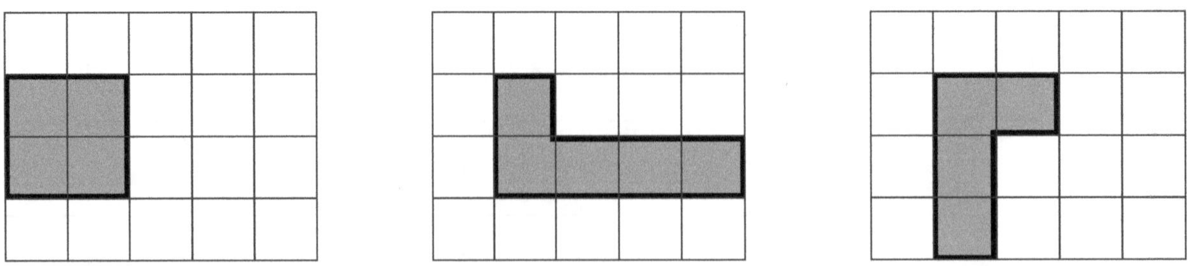

I can compare areas.

Comparing Area (continued)

2 How much larger is the area of Garden 2 than the area of Garden 1?

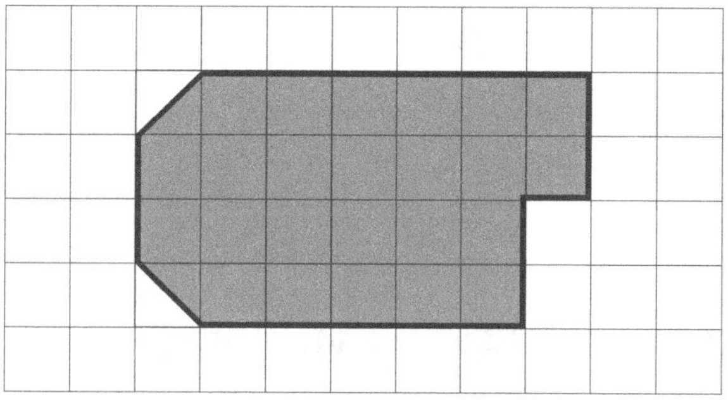

Garden 1

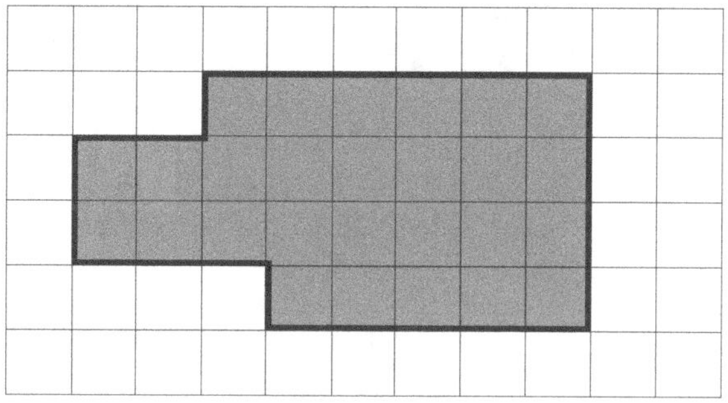

Garden 2

Show your work.

Finding the Area

To find the area of a rectangle, we multiply the length × width.

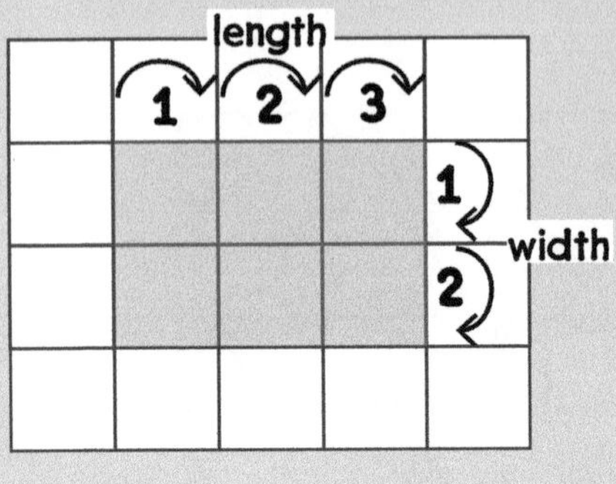

Area = length (l) × width (w)

A = 3 units × 2 units

A = 6 units^2

For measuring area, we use square units (units^2).

1 Calculate the area of the figure.

a

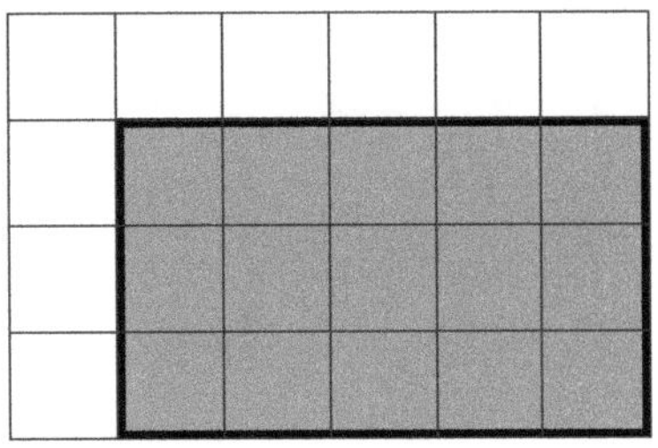

A = ________ units × ________ units

A = ________ units^2

b

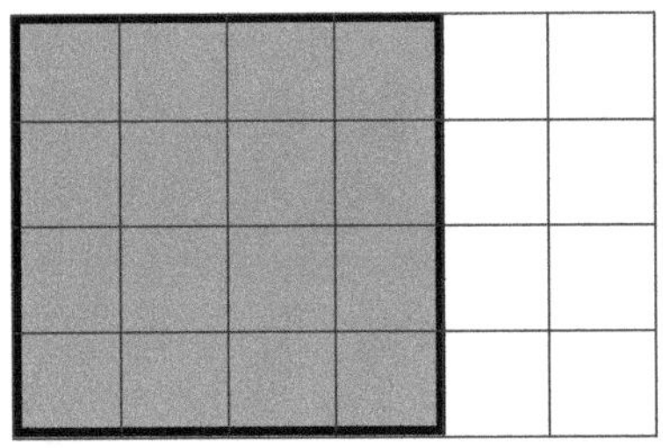

A = ________ units × ________ units

A = ________ units^2

c

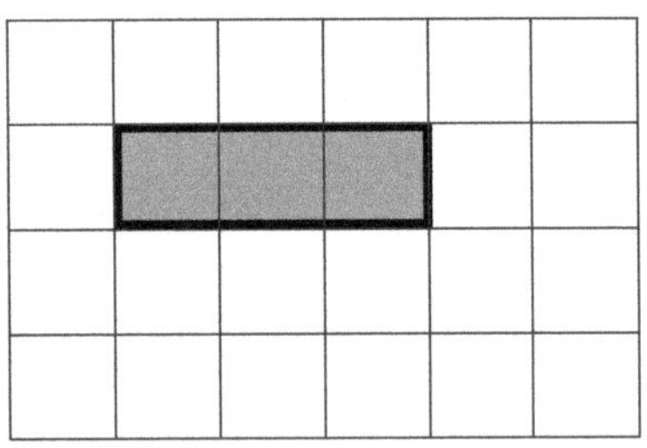

A = ________ units × ________ units

A = ________ units^2

d

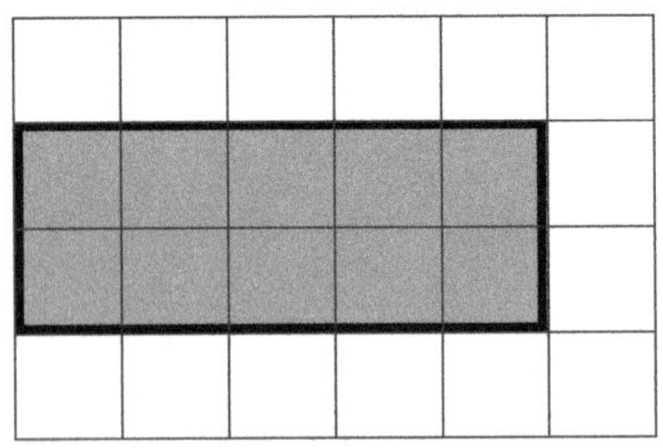

A = ________ units × ________ units

A = ________ units^2

I can calculate area.

Finding the Area (continued)

2 Calculate the area of the figure.

a

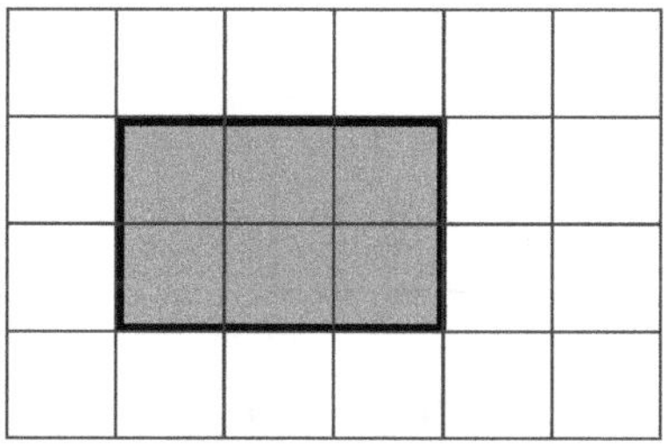

A = ________ units × ________ units

A = ________ $units^2$

b

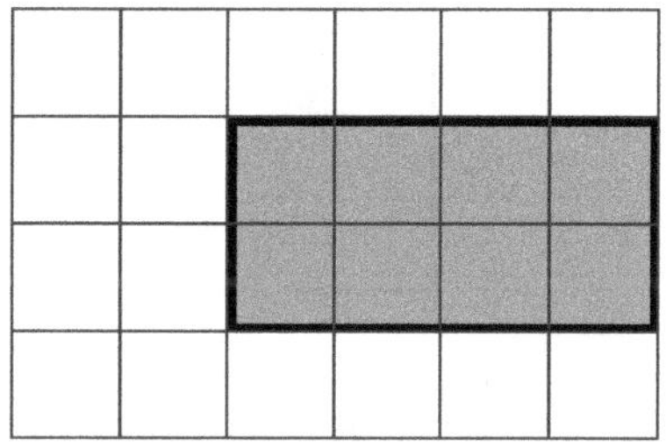

A = ________ units × ________ units

A = ________ $units^2$

c

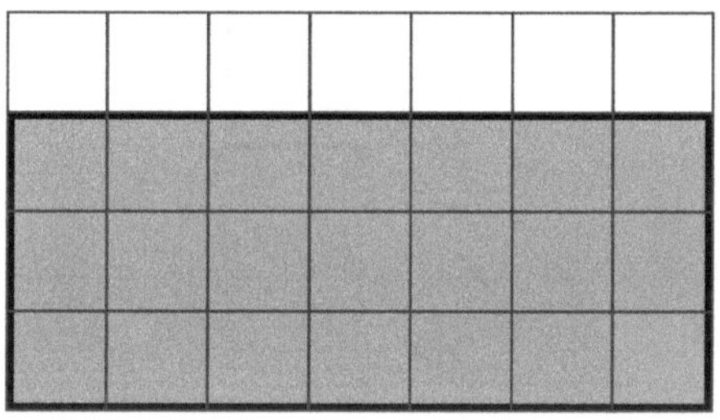

A = ________ units × ________ units

A = ________ $units^2$

d

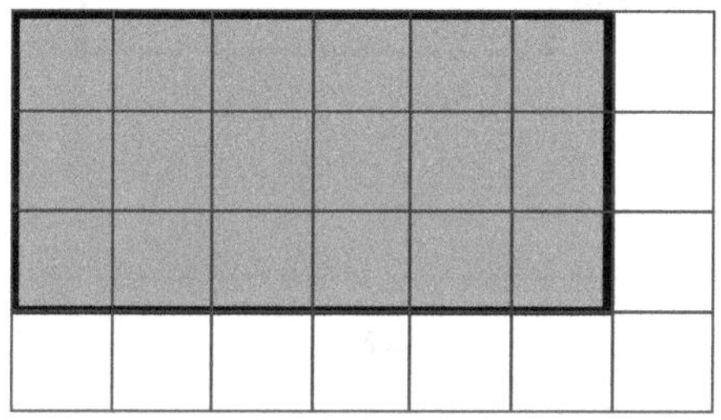

A = ________ units × ________ units

A = ________ $units^2$

e

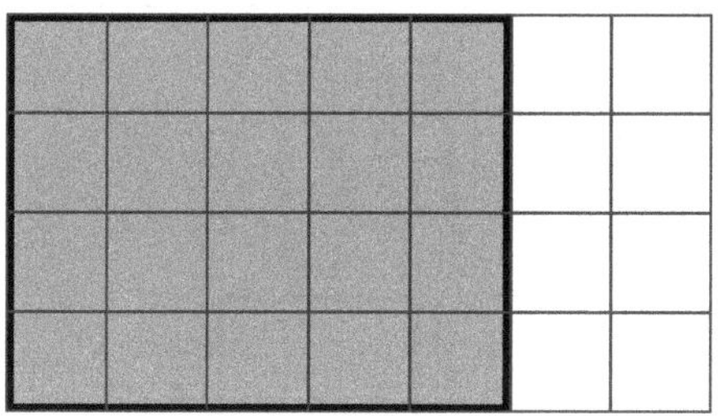

A = ________ units × ________ units

A = ________ $units^2$

f

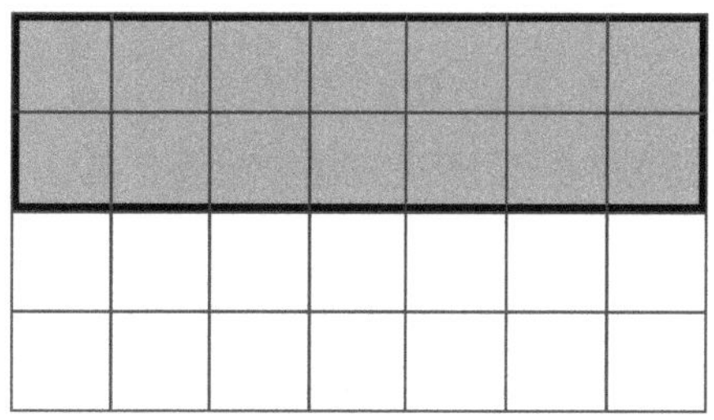

A = ________ units × ________ units

A = ________ $units^2$

I can calculate area.

Finding the Area of Polygons

To find the area of a polygon, multiply the length by the width.

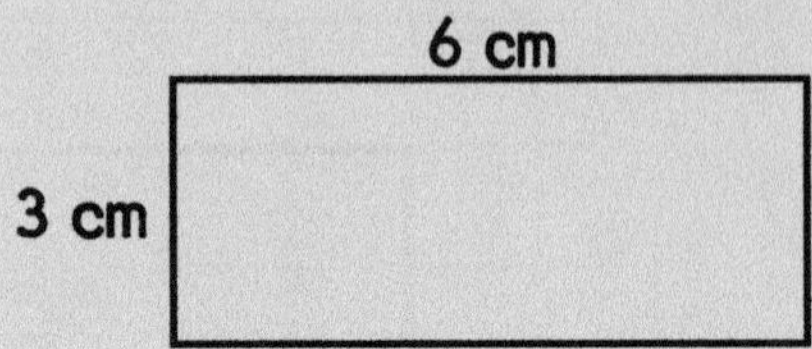

$A = 6\text{ cm} \times 3\text{ cm}$

$= 18\text{ cm}^2$

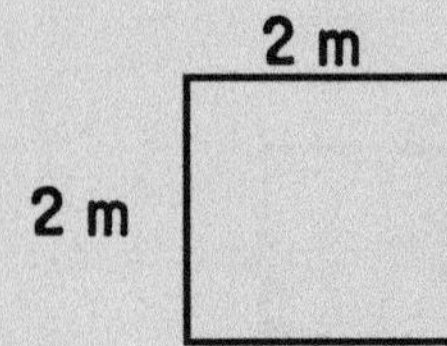

$A = 2\text{ m} \times 2\text{ m}$

$= 4\text{ m}^2$

1 Find the area of the polygon.

a

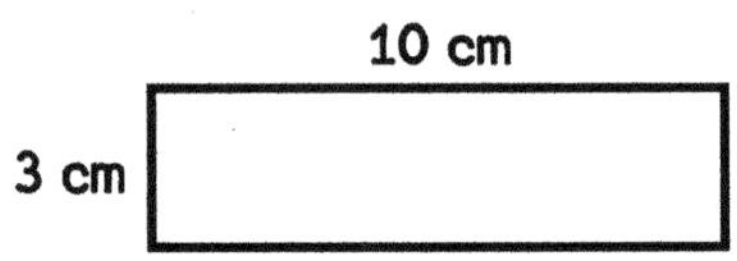

A = ____________________

= __________ cm^2

b

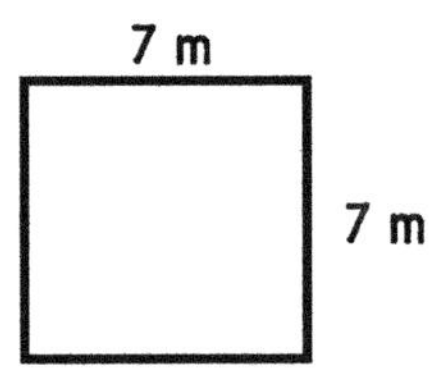

A = ____________________

= __________ m^2

c

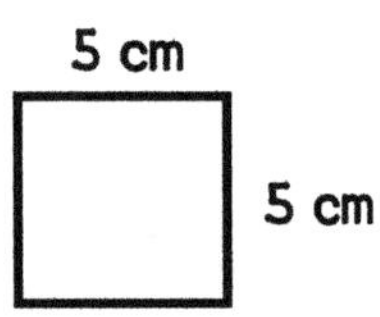

A = ____________________

= __________ cm^2

d

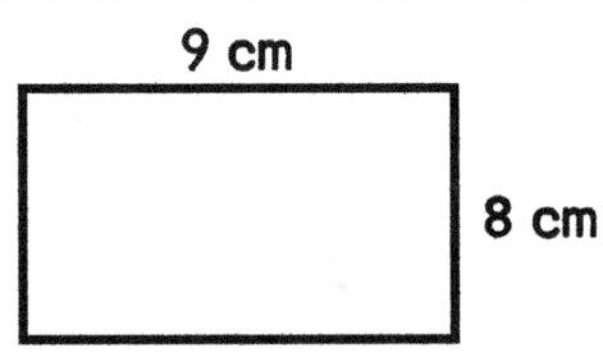

A = ____________________

= __________ cm^2

e

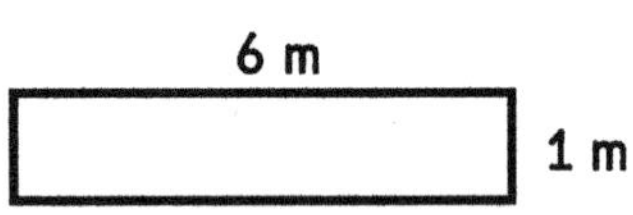

A = ____________________

= __________ m^2

f

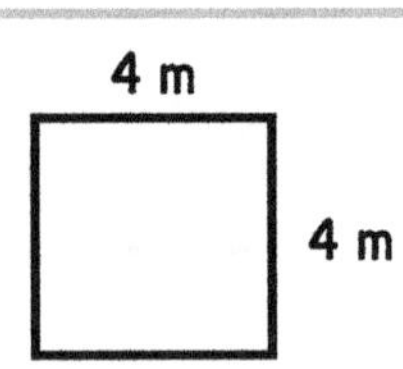

A = ____________________

= __________ m^2

I can calculate area.

Finding the Area of Polygons (continued)

2 Solve.

a Amanda wants to place a rectangular rug in her room. The length of the rug is 5 metres and the width is 3 metres. What is the total area of the rug in square metres? Show your work.

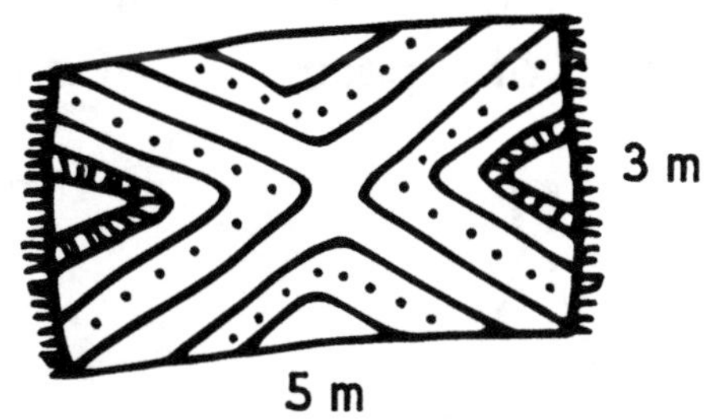

b Pedro has drawn a picture on a sheet of paper. The length of the paper is 9 centimetres and the width is 10 centimetres. What is the total area of the paper in square centimetres? Show your work.

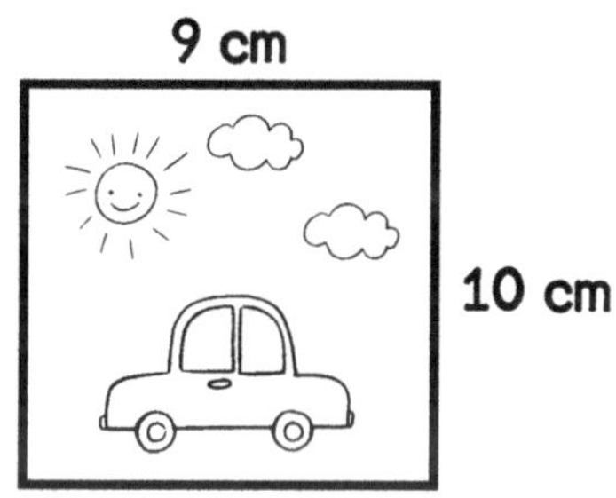

c Thea and Erik are making brownies. The pan Thea uses is 7 centimetres long and 9 centimetres wide. The pan Erik uses is 10 centimetres long and 5 centimetres wide. Whose pan has the bigger area?

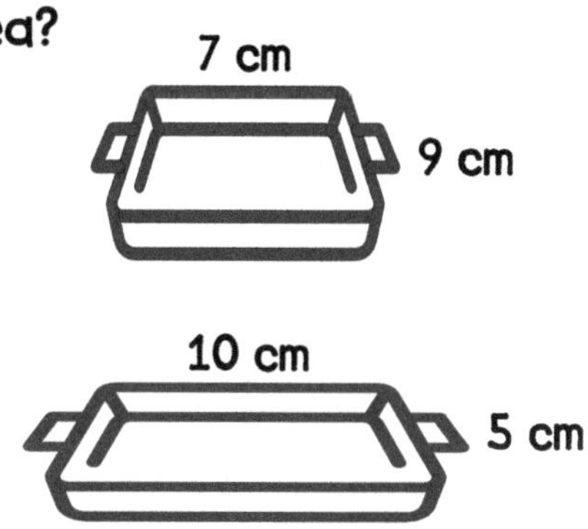

I can solve area problems.

Estimating Units of Length

We use these units to measure **length** or **distance**.

Millimetre (mm)
One millimetre is about the width of the tip of a pencil.

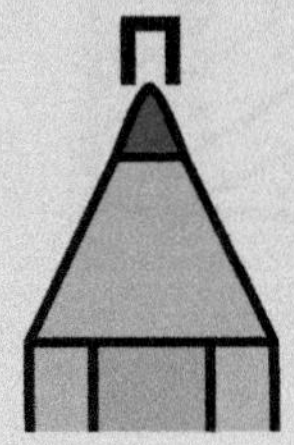

Centimetre (cm)
One centimetre is about the width of a fingernail.

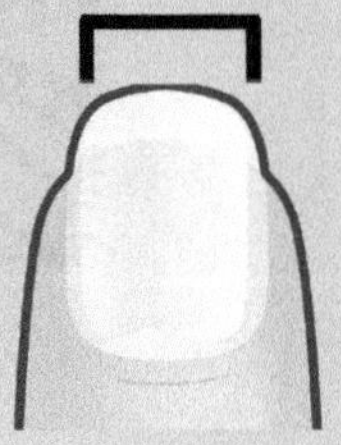

Metre (m)
One metre is about the height of a doorknob.

Kilometre (km)
Use kilometres to measure the distance between two cities.

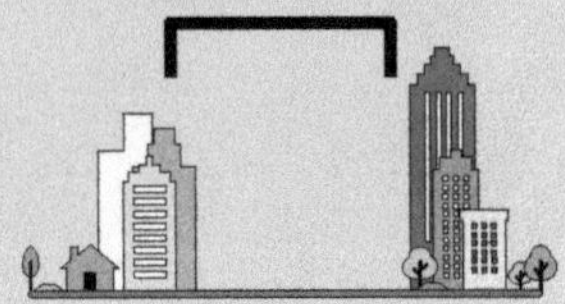

1 metre (m) is equal to **100 centimetres (cm)** or **1000 millimetres (mm)**

1000 metres (m) = 1 kilometre (km)

1 Circle the best unit to use to measure the object.

a

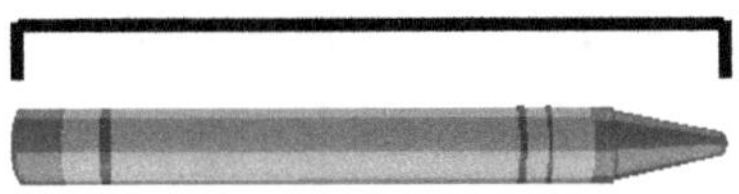

centimetres   metres

b

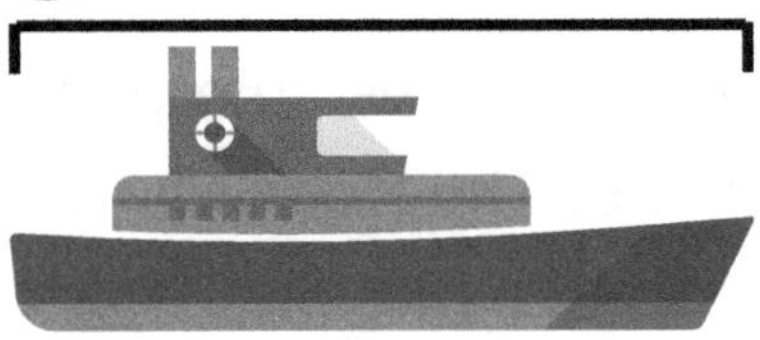

metres   kilometres

c

metres   millimetres

d

kilometres   metres

e

kilometres   centimetres

f

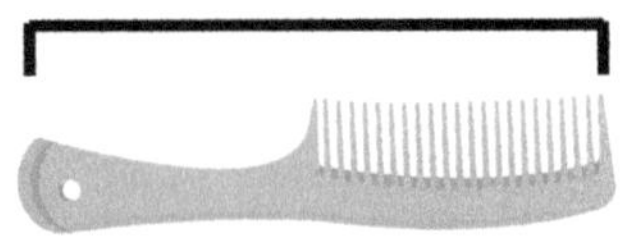

metres   centimetres

I can estimate units of length.

Estimating Units of Length (continued)

2 Circle the most reasonable estimate of the length of the object.

a the length of a peanut

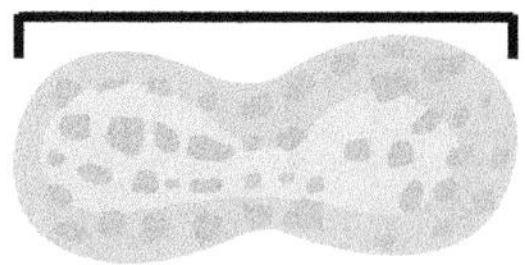

6 centimetres   6 metres

b the height of a mountain

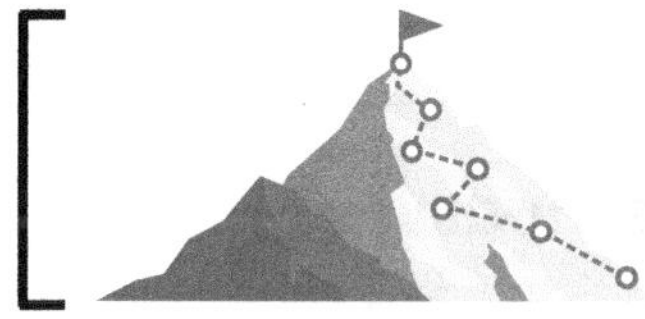

2 metres   2 kilometres

c the length of a corn kernel

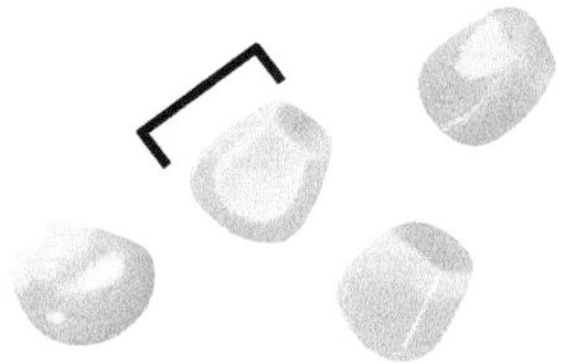

9 millimetres   9 centimetres

d the length of a pen

14 millimetres   14 centimetres

e the distance across a city

6 metres   6 kilometres

f the length of a ladybug

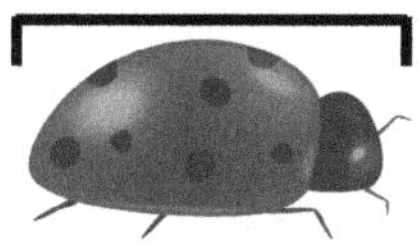

9 millimetres   9 metres

g the length of a key

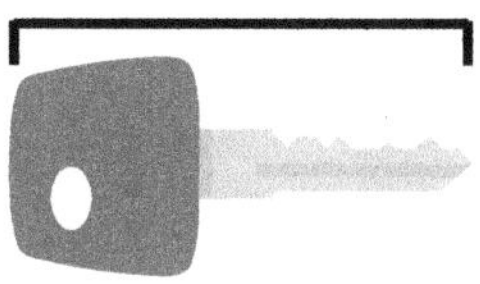

9 millimetres   9 centimetres

h the length of a strawberry

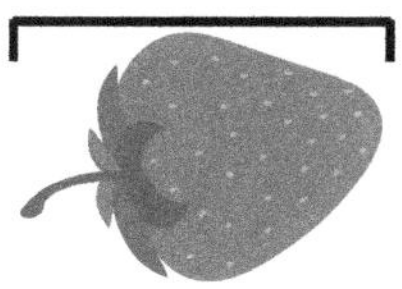

20 millimetres   20 centimetres

Units and Tools for Measurement

1. What would be the best unit of measure for the following?

kilometres | metres | centimetres

Item to Be Measured	Unit of Measure
a length of your leg	
b length of a public bus	
c distance between two towns	
d length of a table	
e length of a living room	
f width of a sticker	

2. Draw a line from the item being measured to the best measurement tool for the job.

amount of flour in a cake recipe	thermometer
weight of 3 bags of apples	measuring cup
temperature on a cold day	ruler
length of a piece of string	scale

I can pick the best unit of measurement.

Measuring with Centimetres and Metres

1 Estimate and measure lengths, heights, and distances using centimetres or metres.

I am measuring the...	I am measuring with...	My estimate	My measurement
length of ____________	______ centimetres	____________ cm	____________ cm
height of ____________	______ centimetres	____________ cm	____________ cm
distance of ____________	______ centimetres	____________ cm	____________ cm
length of ____________	______ metres	____________ m	____________ m
height of ____________	______ metres	____________ m	____________ m
distance of ____________	______ metres	____________ m	____________ m

2 Draw a line that is **6 centimetres** long.

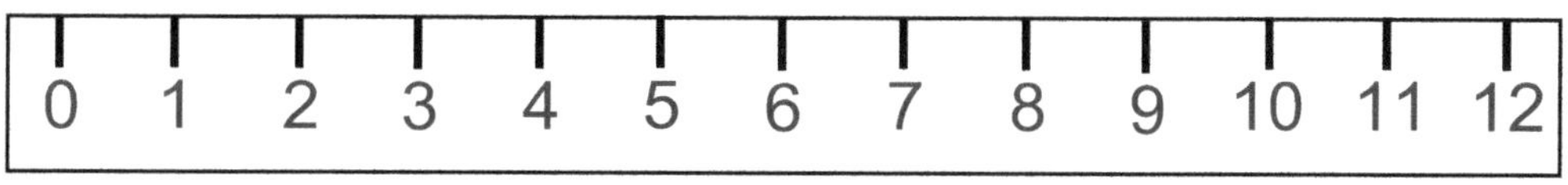

Centimetres

cm

3 Draw a line that is **10 centimetres** long.

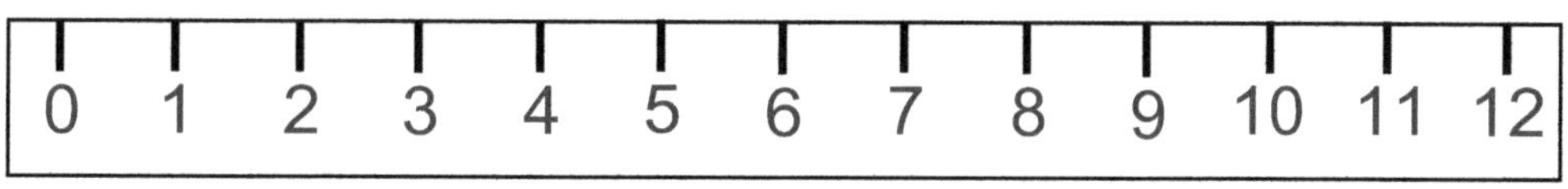

Centimetres

cm

I can measure with centimetres and metres.

Converting Measurements

1 metre (m) = 100 centimetres (cm)

1 centimetre (cm) = 10 millimetres (mm)

1 kilometre (km) = 1000 metres (km)

1 Fill in the table to convert the units.

a mm	cm
10 mm	
	2 cm
	3 cm

b cm	m
	1 m
	2 m
300 cm	

c m	km
1000 m	
	2 km
	3 km

2 Solve.

a Kyle walked 3 km to school. How many metres did he walk?

b Ann's garden is 5 m long. How many centimetres long is her garden?

3 Circle the measurement that is greater in the pair.

a 45 cm or 45 mm

b 600 m or 600 km

4 Trisha needs 6 m of string for an art project. She already has 350 cm of string. What is the length of string Trisha still needs? Show your work.

Trisha needs ____________ more string.

I can convert units of length.

Exploring Various Units of Length

1 metre (m) = 100 centimetres (cm)

1 centimetre (cm) = 10 millimetres (mm)

1 kilometre (km) = 1000 metres (km)

1 Identify what the length of the object is when measured with the given unit.

a **The bed is 200 cm in length.**

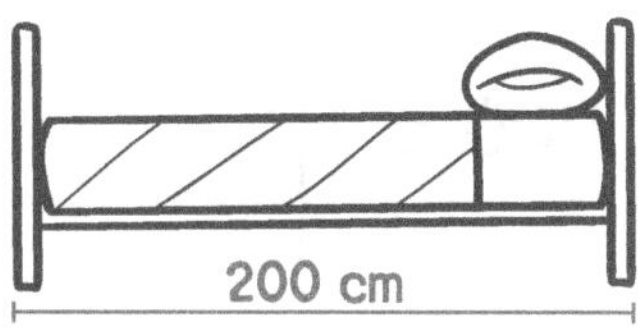

What is the length of the bed in metres? __________ m

b **The card is 90 mm in length.**

What is the length of the card in centimetres? __________ cm

c **The couch is 3 m in length.**

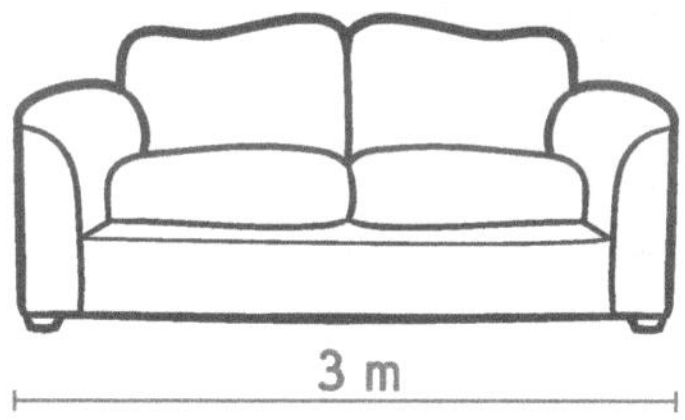

What is the length of the couch in centimetres? __________ cm

d **The key is 4 cm in length.**

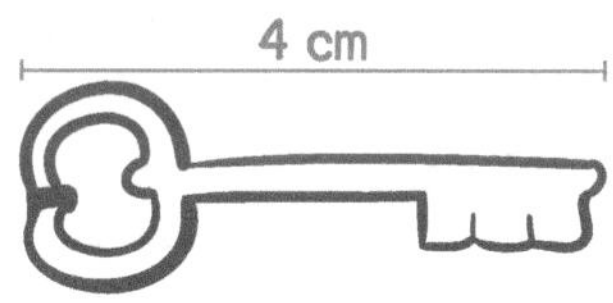

What is the length of the key in millimetres? __________ mm

2 Stacey measures an object that is 5 cm in length. Then, Stacey measures the same object and it is 50 mm in length. Stacey says the object changed in size. Is she correct? Explain.

I can convert units of length.

Exploring Mass

Mass measures how much something weighs.

1 gram (g) = 1000 milligrams (mg)

1 kilogram (kg) = 1000 grams (g)

1. Fill in the table to convert the units.

a

mg	g
	1 g
2000 mg	
	3 g
	4 g
5000 mg	
	6 g
7000 mg	
	8 g
	9 g
10 000 mg	

b

g	kg
1000 g	
	2 kg
3000 g	
	4 kg
	5 kg
6000 g	
7000 g	
	8 kg
9000 g	
	10 kg

2. Solve.

a. Charlie's cat weighs 3 kg. How many grams does his cat weigh?

b. Twyla has 7 g of sugar. How many milligrams of sugar does she have?

c. Bo's book weighs 1000 g. How many kilograms does his book weigh?

 I can convert units of mass.

Exploring Mass (continued)

3 Circle the best estimate for the mass of each object.

a 
130 kg
130 g

b 
100 g
100 kg

c 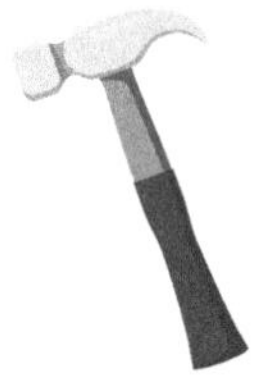
2 g
2 kg

d 
16 kg
16 g

e 
210 g
210 kg

f 
2 g
2 kg

4 Solve.

a Aaron has one orange that weighs 140 g. He has another orange that weighs 135 g. What is the total mass of Aaron's oranges in grams?

b Ramona has one bag of rice that weighs 2000 g. She has a second bag that weighs 3000 g. What is the total mass of both bags of rice in kilograms?

c Audrey has one toy that weighs 700 g. She bought a new toy that weighs 300 g. What is the total mass of both toys in kilograms?

I can solve problems using mass.

Exploring Capacity

Capacity is the amount that something can hold.

1 litre (L) = 1000 millilitres (mL)

1 Fill in the table to convert the units.

mL	L
1000 mL	
	2 L
	3 L
4000 mL	
	5 L
6000 mL	
	7 L
	8 L
9000 mL	
10 000 mL	

2 Solve.

a Wyatt has 2 L of juice. How many millilitres of juice does he have?

b Uma uses 4000 mL of water to wash her dog. How many litres does she use?

c Kevin buys 7 L of water. How many millilitres does he buy?

I can convert units of capacity.

Exploring Capacity (continued)

3. Order the pictures from least capacity to greatest capacity. Label the least as 1, the middle as 2, and the greatest capacity as 3.

a

250 mL

5 mL

10 L

________ ________ ________

b

1 L

15 mL

60 mL

________ ________ ________

4. Circle the best estimate for the capacity of each object.

a

2 mL

2 L

b

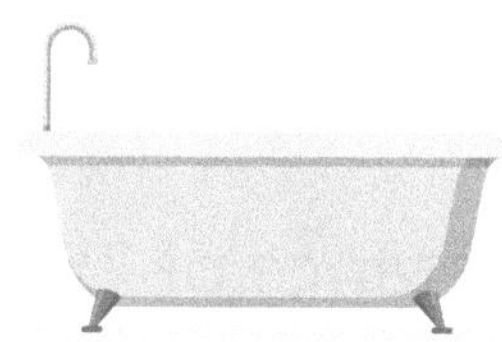

70 mL

70 L

c

200 L

200 mL

d

75 mL

75 L

e

125 L

125 mL

f

2 mL

2 L

I can compare and estimate units of capacity.

Show What You Know!

1 Find the perimeter.

a

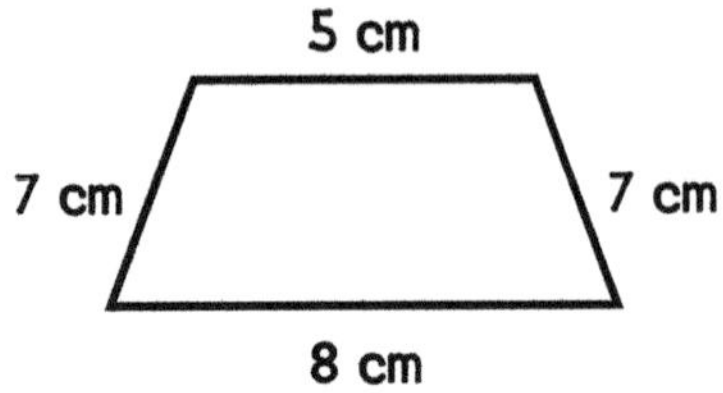

P = ____________________

= __________ cm

b

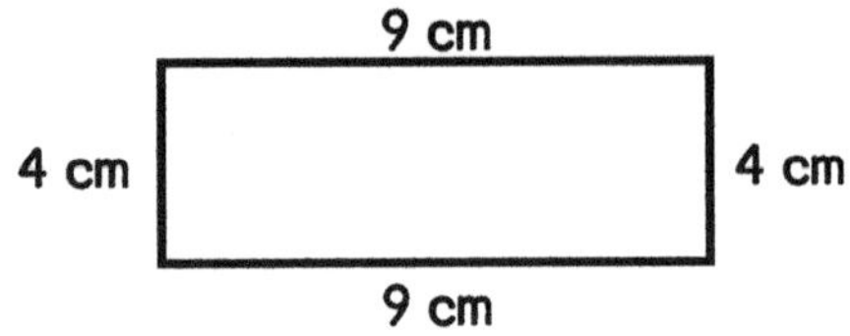

P = ____________________

= __________ cm

2 Find the area.

a

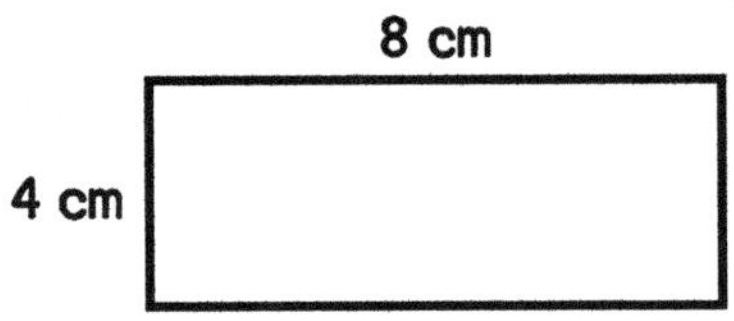

A = ____________________

= __________ cm^2

b

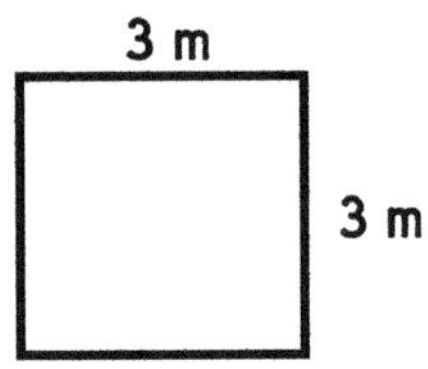

A = ____________________

= __________ m^2

3 A frog jumps a distance of 25 cm on each jump.
If the frog jumps 7 times, how far does it travel?

The frog travels __________ cm.

Show What You Know! (continued)

4 Look at the table below showing the height of 3 students.

Name	Height
Amari	112 cm
Suma	1 m 6 cm
Corey	?

Corey is the tallest of the 3 students by 6 cm.

What is Corey's height?

- **a** 110 cm
- **b** 1 m 18 cm
- **c** 120 cm
- **d** 1 m 12 cm

5 Kabir and Megan each draw a shape.

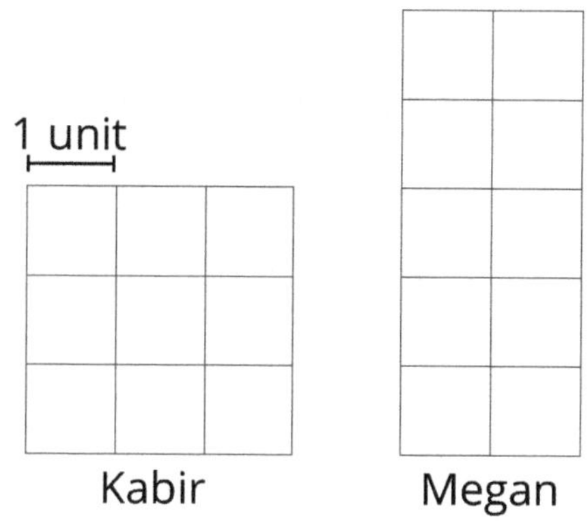

Choose the shape that has the greater perimeter and by how much.

- **a** Kabir's, by 1 unit
- **b** Megan's, by 14 units
- **c** Kabir's, by 10 units
- **d** Megan's, by 2 units

6 Levi has 3000 mL of milk. How much milk does he have in litres?

- **a** 300
- **b** 3
- **c** 30
- **d** 13

7 Choose the list that shows the lengths from shortest to longest.

- **a** 40 cm; 1 m 20 cm; 2 m
- **b** 500 cm; 3 m; 50 cm
- **c** 1 m 50 cm; 25 cm; 2 m
- **d** 3 m; 150 cm; 1 m 50 cm

I Can Checklist:
Time

Use analog and digital clocks and timers to tell time in hours, minutes, and seconds. For example,

- ***I can*** *tell time with clocks with hands (analog) and clocks with numbers (digital).*
- ***I can*** *tell time in hours, minutes, and seconds.*

Telling Time on a Digital Clock

You can tell the time on a digital clock.

Fill in the blanks to tell the time.

1. 

Hour:________ Minutes:________

2. 

Hour:________ Minutes:________

3. 

Hour:________ Minutes:________

4. 

Hour:________ Minutes:________

5. 

Hour:________ Minutes:________

6. 

Hour:________ Minutes:________

7. 

Hour:________ Minutes:________

8. 

Hour:________ Minutes:________

I can tell time on a digital clock.

Writing Time on a Digital Clock

Some digital clocks show the seconds.
Seconds are shown after the second colon.

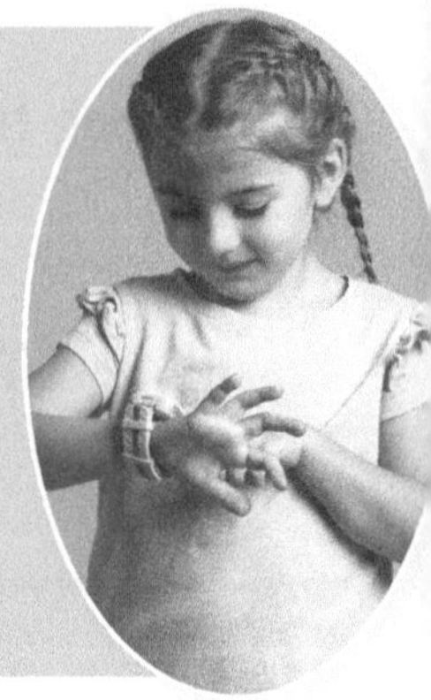

Write the given time for each clock.

1. Hour: 12 Minutes: 20 Seconds: 44
2. Hour: 8 Minutes: 57 Seconds: 01
3. Hour: 3 Minutes: 17 Seconds: 35
4. Hour: 6 Minutes: 9 Seconds: 24
5. Hour: 10 Minutes: 45 Seconds: 11
6. Hour: 1 Minutes: 33 Seconds: 50
7. Hour: 5 Minutes: 10 Seconds: 26
8. Hour: 7 Minutes: 3 Seconds: 42

I can write time on a digital clock.

Measuring the Passage of Time

A clock shows time using numbers and hands.
The face of a clock shows the numbers 1 to 12.
It takes 5 minutes for the long minute hand to move from one number to the next.

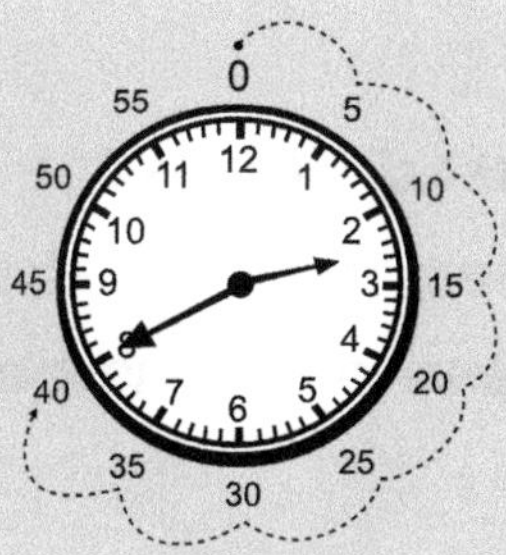

The time is **2:40**.

1 Write the time below the clock.

a

____ : ____

b

____ : ____

c

____ : ____

d

____ : ____

e

____ : ____

f

____ : ____

2 Fill in the correct time. Add a.m. or p.m.

a

This afternoon, Melissa started her homework at this time. What time did she start her homework?

____ : ____ ☐

b

Melissa started her homework at this time and worked for 1 hour and 10 minutes. What time did she finish her homework?

____ : ____ ☐

I can measure the passage of time.

Exploring Elapsed Time

Elapsed time is the amount of time that has passed from the start of a time period to the end of a time period.

Start Time

End Time

25 minutes have elapsed.

Write the start time and the end time. Then figure out how many minutes have passed.

1 Start Time

_____ : _____ p.m.

End Time

_____ : _____ p.m.

What is the elapsed time?

[ ]

minutes have passed

2 Start Time

_____ : _____ p.m.

End Time

_____ : _____ p.m.

What is the elapsed time?

[ ]

minutes have passed

3 Start Time

_____ : _____ p.m.

End Time

_____ : _____ p.m.

What is the elapsed time?

[ ]

minutes have passed

I can measure elapsed time.

Exploring Calendars

Work with a partner to answer the questions.

November						
Sunday	Monday	Tuesday	Wednesday	Thursday	Friday	Saturday
	1	2	3	4	5	6
7	8	9	10	11	12	13
14	15	16	17	18	19	20
21	22	23	24	25	26	27
28	29	30				

1. Mark goes to the store and buys 100 of his favourite candies. If he eats two candies a day starting on November 1, on which day will his bag of candies be half empty? Show your work.

2. Kate's birthday is in November. Her sister Jenn's birthday is in the same month. Kate's birthday is on November 12. Jenn's birthday is exactly two weeks later. On which date and day of the week is Jenn's birthday?

Brain Buster Challenge

How many days in three weeks? ________ How many days in a year? ________

How many months in four years? ________ How many years in a decade? ________

Exploring Temperature

Temperature is a degree of how hot or cold something is and that can be measured using a thermometer.
Temperature is measured in degrees on the **Celsius** scale.

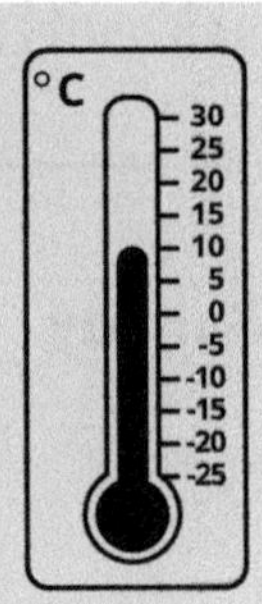

This thermometer shows 10° Celsius or 10°C.

1 Colour the thermometer to the correct temperature.

a

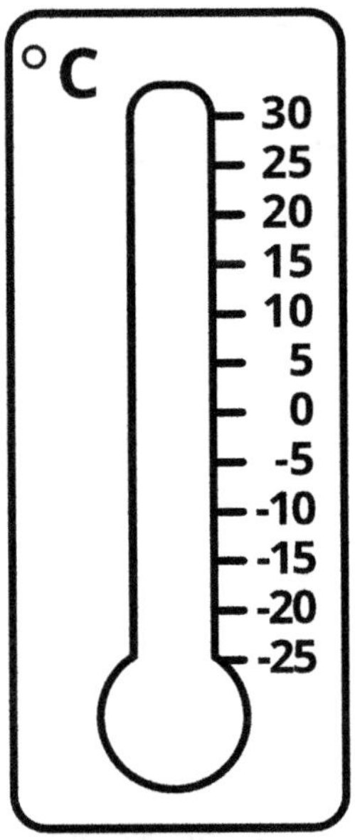

0°C

b

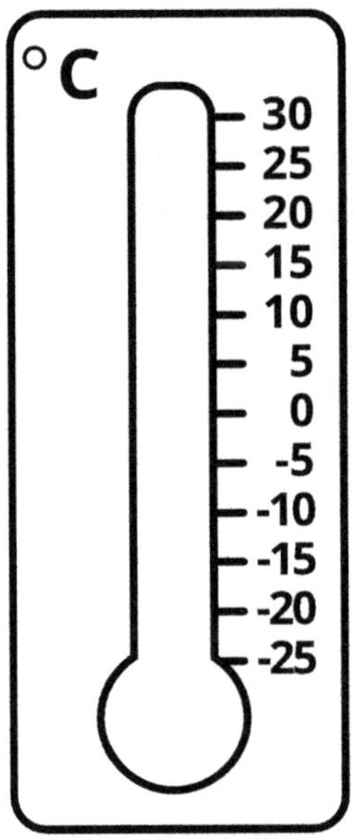

–25°C

c

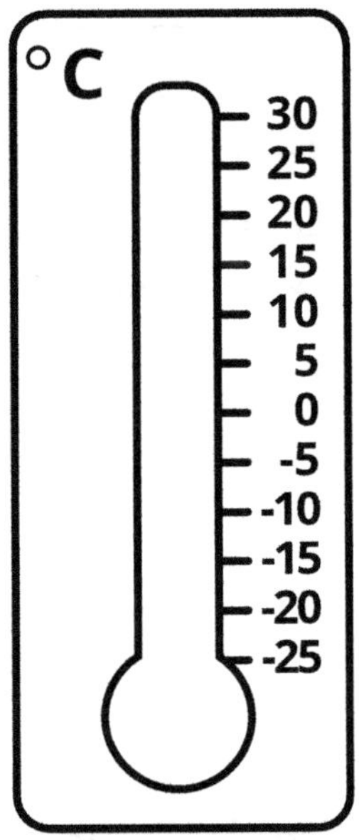

30°C

2 Circle the correct temperature.

a What temperature is it most likely to be in the middle of summer?

18°C

–18°C

b What temperature is it most likely to be in the middle of winter?

–20°C

20°C

I can read temperatures.

Show What You Know!

1 Write the given time on the digital clock.

a Hour: 8 Minutes: 35 Seconds: 23

b Hour: 2 Minutes: 14 Seconds: 12

2 Write the time below the clock.

a

_____ : _____

b

_____ : _____

c

_____ : _____

3 Solve.

a The movie started at 6:20 p.m. and ended at 8:10 p.m. How many minutes long was the movie?

b Emma started baking cookies at 2:00 p.m. The cookies needed to bake for 25 minutes. What time were the cookies done?

c Roger helps his dad in the yard for 2 hours. For how many minutes does Roger help his dad?

I Can Checklist:
Financial Literacy

Estimate and calculate the change required for various simple cash transactions involving whole-dollar amounts and amounts of less than one dollar. For example,

- ***I can*** *guess and figure out how much change I should get back for things that cost whole dollars or less than a dollar.*

5 Dollar Bill

10 Dollar Bill

20 Dollar Bill

50 Dollar Bill

100 Dollar Bill

Dime

Nickel

Quarter

Loonie

Toonie

Methods of Payment

Cash: Cash is money you can touch. You give the right amount of money to the person or store when you buy something.

Credit Card: A special card that you can use instead of cash to buy things. You pay for the items later on.

Debit Card: Another special card that takes money directly from your bank account when you buy something.

Online Payment: Buying things using the Internet with a grown-up's help. They use a credit card or a special online payment service.

Mobile Payment: Paying for things using a smartphone or tablet with a special app. It's like having a digital wallet on your phone!

Read each scenario below and think about the best method of payment to use.

1. You want to buy a toy from a store. ______________________________

2. You are buying a book online. ______________________________

3. Your parent wants to pay for groceries at the store. ____________________

4. You want to buy a new video game from an online store. ________________

5. Your parent wants to pay for a dinner at a restaurant. ________________

I can understand different methods of payment.

Counting Canadian Money

Count the money in each set.
Circle the money that matches the amount on the tag.

1

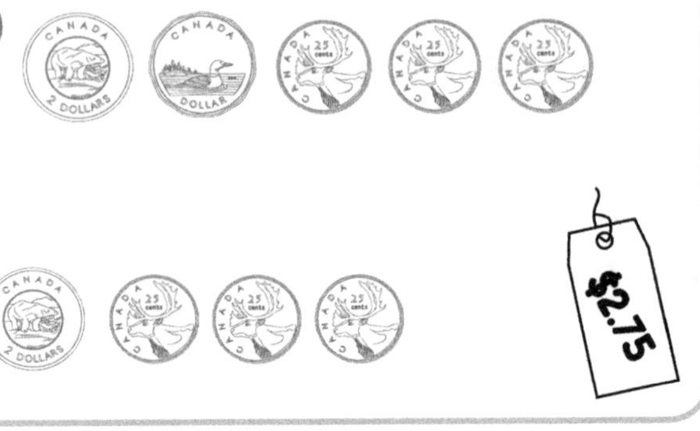

2

3

4

5

6

7

8

I can count money.

Showing Money Amounts in Different Ways

Show two different ways to make the same amount. Draw the money.

First Way	Second Way
1 $3.65	
2 $1.10	
3 $19.90	
4 $6.85	
5 $23	
6 $12.60	

I can show money amounts in different ways.

Matching Money Amounts to Price Tags

Count the bills and coins in each set.
Draw a line from the set of money to the correct price tag.

1 

2 

3 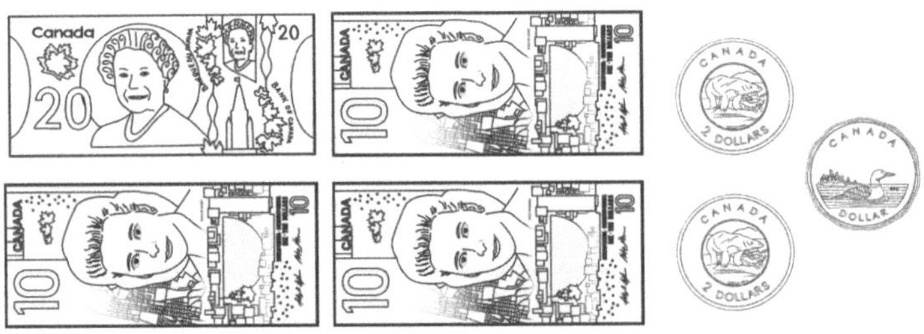

4 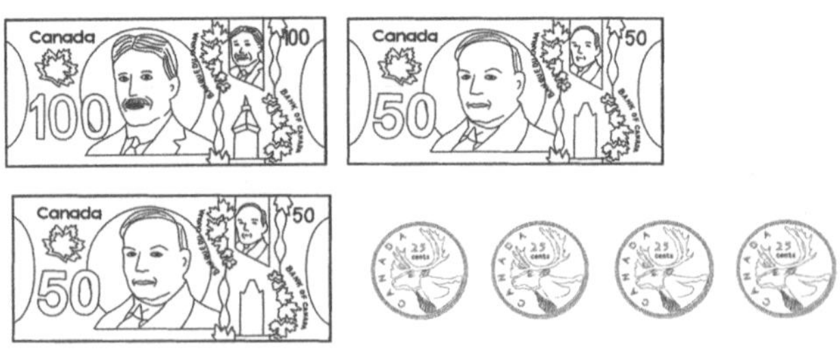

I can match money amounts to price tags.

Exploring Transactions

Look at the movie theatre menu below. Answer the questions.

Tracy's Theatre

Item	Price	Item	Price
Popcorn	$4.50	Smoothie	$6.40
Soda	$2.00	Fruit Tray	$4.00
Chocolate Bar	$1.25	Hot Dog	$3.50
Licorice	$0.75	Nachos	$5.00

1. You have $20 to spend at the movies. What items do you buy?

   How much change do you get back?

2. Amber buys a movie ticket for $7.45.
   How much change should she receive from $10.00?

I can calculate transactions.

Financial Literacy Word Problems

1. Breanne and Lee go to the store to buy hockey cards.

   They bring $4.00 to the store.

   The hockey cards cost $2.35

   They are given $1.55 change.

Do Breanne and Lee get back the correct amount of change?
Show your thinking.

2. Tia and Al go to a craft shop to buy paint and brushes. One bottle of paint costs $4, and 1 brush costs $2. Tia buys 3 bottles of paint and 2 brushes. Al buys 2 bottles of paint and 1 brush. How much more money does Tia spend than Al?

Show your work.

Tia spends ________________ more than Al.

I can solve money word problems.

Financial Literacy Word Problems (continued)

3 Mrs. Andrews buys special markers for her Grade 3 class.
The special markers are sold with 4 in each box.
Mrs. Andrews would like to buy 30 markers.

a How many boxes should Mrs. Andrews buy? Show your thinking.

b One box of special markers costs $2.00, how much money does Mrs. Andrews need to buy the special markers? Show your thinking.

I can solve money word problems.

Show What You Know!

1 Zack receives $5 a week for doing chores. He wants to buy a remote control car that costs $38.

How many weeks will it take him to save enough money to buy the remote control car?

a 5 b 7

c 6 d 8

2 Uma uses the money shown below to buy a fruit smoothie.

She gets back 2 dimes in change. How much does the fruit smoothie cost?

a $3.50 b $3.20

c $3.75 d $3.55

3 On Monday, Jaden earns the coins shown below.

On Tuesday, Jaden earns the same amount of money. How much money does he earn in total over the two days?

a $2.80 b $2.25

c $1.40 d $3.35

4 Cleo buys a magazine with the coins below.

Sarika buys 3 of the same magazine. How much money does Sarika spend?

a $1.80 b $2.50

c $3.60 d $2.70

5 Tyler buys a new backpack for $12.75
How much change should he receive from $20.00?

a $6.50 b $7.25 c $7.75 d $6.25

Show What You Know! (continued)

6 Farah buys a muffin for $1.15 and a smoothie for $3.55.

Circle the set of coins that shows exactly how much Farah needs to buy both items.

a

b

c

d

7 Juan buys the following school supplies.

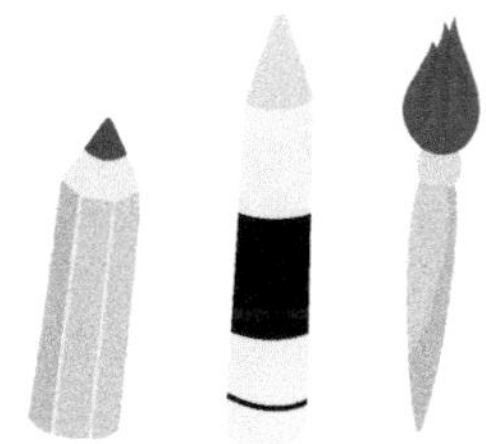

15¢ 25¢ 45¢

If Juan pays with a loonie, how much change should he receive?

a 15¢ b 25¢

c 20¢ d 10¢

8 Elyssa spends the money below to buy a soccer ball and a stuffed bear.

How much money does Elyssa spend on these two items?

a $7.90 b $4.55

c $8.65 d $8.45

Answers

Counting Practice p. 5

1. 765, 767, 769, 771, 773, 775, 777

2. 665, 670, 675, 680, 685, 690, 695

3. 315, 325, 335, 345, 355, 365, 375

4. 400, 425, 450, 475, 500, 525, 550

5. 845, 835, 825, 815, 805, 795, 785

6. 835, 735, 635, 535, 435, 335, 235

7. 120, 100, 80, 60, 40, 20, 0 **8.** a) 420, 415, 410

Ordering Numbers p. 6

1. a) 767 b) 215 c) 554 d) 101

2. a) 899 b) 439 c) 199 d) 789

3. a) 15, 25, 35, 75, 90 b) 89, 95, 178, 196, 202

4. a) 656, 560, 516, 506, 416 b) 83, 75, 74, 67, 61

5. $67, $54, $54, 51, $49, $38

Greater Than, Less Than, and Equal p. 7

1. a) > b) = c) < d) > e) < f) < g) = h) > i) > j) =

2. c) >

Representing Numbers in Written Form p. 8

1. a) forty-four b) twenty-one c) ninety-eight d) seventy-six
e) four hundred fifty-five f) one hundred ninety-four
g) three hundred two

2. five hundred fifty-three **3.** one hundred ninety-eight

Representing Numbers in Different Ways p. 9

1.

Standard Form	Expanded Form	Written Form
1708	***1000+700+8***	one thousand seven hundred eight
637	600+30+7	***six hundred thirty-seven***
893	***800+90+3***	eight hundred ninety-three

2. 400 + 60 + 8 **3.** 942 **4.** seventy

Number Bonds p. 10

1. a) 500, 7 b) 900, 60 c) 300, 40, 6

2. a) 281 b) 543 c) 462

Counting Hundreds, Tens, and Ones p. 11

1. 652 **2.** 287 **3.** 806 **4.** 200 + 90 + 4, two hundred ninety-four

Round Up or Round Down p. 12

1. a) 50 b) 50 c) 770 **2.** a) 400 b) 800 c) 300 d) 200 e) 400 f) 500

3. b) 186

Rounding Numbers Using a Number Line p. 13

1. a) 850 b) 850 **2.** a) 180 b) 200

Show What You Know! pp. 14–15

1. b **2.** c **3.** a **4.** c **5.** b **6.** b **7.** d **8.** 11

Fractions Show Equal Parts p. 17

1. a) 3/7 b) 7/9 c) 1/2 d) 2/4 e) 4/7 f) 3/5

2. Answers will vary.

Types of Fractions p. 18

1. a) improper b) proper c) mixed d) proper e) mixed
f) improper g) mixed h) proper i) improper

2. a) 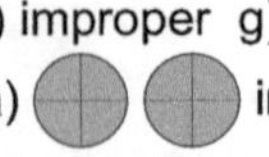 improper b) 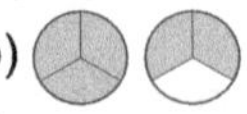 mixed

Exploring Fractions p. 19

1. a) Ensure each quarter is a different colour.
b) Ensure each half is a different colour.
c) 5 triangles should be blue. d) 4 circles should be yellow.

2. a) 4/12 b) 3/7 **3.** circles: 4/8 squares: 4/8

Exploring Fraction Bars pp. 20–21

1. a) 3/6 b) 3/4 c) 2/4 d) 1/2

2. a) 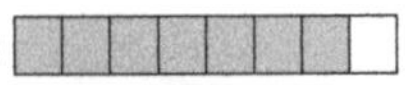 1 b) 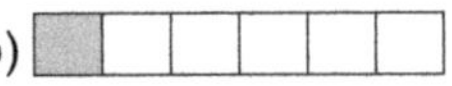 0
c) 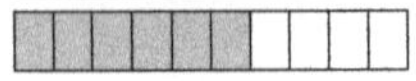 1/2

3. a) one whole b) 1/3 c) one half d) 1/2 **4.** 2 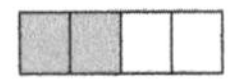

Exploring Equivalent Fractions p. 22

1. not equivalent **2.** equivalent **3.** equivalent **4.** not equivalent

Writing Equivalent Fractions p. 23

1. Answers will vary. Sample answers given.
a) 2/6 b) 4/10 c) 2/5 d) 2/3

2. Each friend gets 2 slices or 2/8 slices.

Comparing Fractions p. 24

1. a) > b) < c) > d) < **2.** a) Max b) Barry **3.** Answers will vary.
Sample answers given. a) 5/6 b) 1/4

Fair Shares p. 25

1. a) 14 b) 7 c) 2 **2.** a) 4 b) 4/40 or 1/10

Fair Shares with Remainders p. 26

1. 11 **2.** 5 each with 1 left over **3.** 3 each with 2 left over

Fraction Word Problems p. 27

1. 6 **2.** 6 **3.** 4/6 or 2/3 **4.** 8

Show What You Know! pp. 28–29

1. a) 12 b) 6 c) 1 d) 5 **2.** a) 5/8 b) 2/5 c) 1/3

3. a) improper b) mixed

4. a) 3 squares should be green b) 4 circles should be blue

5. 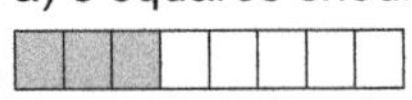 1/2

6. Answers may vary. Sample answers given. a) 1/2 b) 1/3

7. 4/8 or 1/2

Using Estimation to Add and Subtract p. 31

1. a) 20 + 60 = 80 b) 70 + 20 = 90 c) 80 – 20 = 60
d) 50 – 40 = 10 e) 30 + 90 = 120 f) 20 + 80 = 100

2. 300 + 300 = approximately 600 mL

Three-Digit Addition Without Regrouping pp. 32–33

1. a) 685 b) 637 c) 698 d) 897 e) 962 f) 948 g) 685 h) 595

2. 625 + 132 = 757

3. a) 358 b) 469 c) 566 d) 337 e) 359 f) 779 g) 189 h) 467
i) 378 j) 496 l) 699 m) 499 n) 697 o) 538 p) 956 q) 639
r) 464 s) 586 t) 669 u) 243 v) 787 w) 317 x) 492 y) 536

Because he was feeling crummy!

Answers

Three-Digit Addition with Regrouping pp. 34–35

1. a) 821 b) 980 c) 861 d) 840 e) 1022 f) 620 g) 921 h) 830

2. 136 + 178 = 314 pages read

3. a) 707 b) 742 c) 558 d) 518 e) 952 f) 797 g) 420 h) 766 i) 872 j) 725 k) 496 l) 269 m) 564 n) 726 o) 520 p) 460 q) 726 r) 657 s) 473 t) 718 u) 956 v) 553 w) 796 y) 917

A lumpy milkshake!

Three-Digit Subtraction Without Regrouping pp. 38–39

1. a) 313 b) 444 c) 118 d) 222 e) 311 f) 251 g) 450 h) 126

2. 789 − 332 = 457

3. a) 353 b) 131 c) 325 e) 540 f) 220 g) 465 h) 242 i) 173 k) 123 l) 245 o) 812 r) 101 s) 222 t) 311 y) 124

Look for the grey hares!

Three-Digit Subtraction with Regrouping pp. 40–41

1. a) 193 b) 168 c) 161 d) 592 e) 110 f) 537 g) 281 h) 270

2. a) 128 b) 159 c) 91 d) 747 e) 72 g) 107 h) 619 i) 307 j) 129 k) 390 n) 134 r) 229 s) 95 t) 46 w) 264

Searching the web

Show What You Know! pp. 42–43

1. a) 874 − 405 = 469 b) 389 + 475 = 864 c) 285 + 527 = 812 d) 532 − 297 = 235 **2.** a) 358 + 234 = 592 b) 832 − 459 = 373 c) 456 + 274 = 730 d) 725 − 305 = 420

Exploring Arrays p. 45

1. a) 3 × 4 = 12 b) 2 × 7 = 14 **2.** a) 3 × 4 = 12 b) 4 × 4 = 16

3. a)  8 × 3 = 24 b)  7 × 2 = 14

Multiply by 0 and 1 p. 46

1. a) 11 b) 0 c) 0 d) 1 e) 4 f) 0 g) 9 h) 0 i) 2 j) 8 k) 0 l) 3 m) 0 n) 5 o) 6 p) 0 q) 0 r) 12 s) 0 t) 7

Two Times Table p. 47

1. A) 16 E) 10 I) 22 M) 0 N) 24 O) 2 P) 8 S) 20 T) 4 X) 14

An impasta!

2. a) 4 b) 1 c) 9 d) 7 e) 8 f) 11 g) 5 h) 12 **3.** 2 × 8 = 16

Three Times Table p. 48

1. E) 30 I) 21 G) 12 O) 24 P) 6 R) 18 S) 36 T) 27 V) 15 W) 9

It overswept!

2. a) 3 b) 1 c) 2 d) 0 e) 8 f) 9 g) 7 h) 5 **3.** 3 × 4 = 12

Four Times Table p. 49

1. A) 0 B) 12 C) 32 E) 8 G) 48 K) 44 L) 36 R) 24 T) 28 U) 20

A garbage truck!

2. a) 3 b) 2 c) 6 d) 8 e) 4 f) 7 g) 9 h) 11 **3.** 4 × 7 = 28

Five Times Table p. 50

1. A) 30 E) 35 F) 5 H) 20 L) 10 M) 45 O) 15 P) 40 S) 0 T) 25

All of them!

2. a) 3 b) 4 c) 11 d) 2 e) 9 f) 0 g) 8 h) 6 **3.** 5 × 9 = 45

Six Times Table p. 51

1. A) 18 B) 66 E) 48 H) 54 I) 30 K) 12 N) 60 R) 36 T) 72 V) 24

The river bank!

2. a) 11 b) 1 c) 6 d) 8 e) 7 f) 10 g) 0 h) 3 **3.** 6 × 4 = 24

Seven Times Table p. 52

1. A) 35 C) 49 D) 21 E) 70 H) 56 L) 84 M) 28 O) 42 P) 63 S) 77

A shampoodle!

2. a) 2 b) 1 c) 3 d) 8 e) 10 f) 12 g) 6 h) 7 **3.** 7 × 5 = 35

Eight Times Table p. 53

1. A) 64 C) 16 E) 96 H) 72 M) 0 P) 32 R) 80 S) 40 T) 48 W) 56

The mewspaper!

2. a) 4 b) 7 c) 2 d) 12 e) 5 f) 6 g) 1 h) 10 **3.** 8 × 9 = 72

Nine Times Table p. 54

1. A) 108 E) 54 G) 99 I) 72 L) 0 N) 90 P) 9 S) 63 T) 45 W) 36

It wasn't peeling well!

2. a) 2 b) 1 c) 3 d) 6 **3.** 9 × 10 = 90

Ten Times Table p. 55

1. E) 120 F) 40 G) 50 H) 100 I) 0 K) 110 O) 10 R) 60 T) 90 Y) 30

It forgot the key!

2. a) 2 b) 6 c) 11 d) 5 e) 3 f) 7 g) 0 h) 1 **3.** 10 × 4 = 40

Multiplication/Division Table p. 56

Missing numbers from top left to bottom: 0, 1, 9, 6, 0, 21, 16, 10, 45, 0, 36, 35, 70, 16, 36, 10, 90

Exploring Division p. 57

1. 2 groups, 2 **2.** 5 groups, 5 **3.** 4 groups, 4

Relate Multiplication to Division p. 58

1. 8 **2.** 5 **3.** 5 **4.** 3 **5.** 3

Use Related Multiplication Facts to Divide with 0 and 1 p. 59

1. 11 **2.** 1 **3.** 0 **4.** 1 **5.** 0 **6.** 1 **7.** 0 **8.** 0 **9.** 6 **10.** 0 **11.** 9 **12.** 4

Divide by 2 p. 60

1. A) 7 E) 1 F) 5 H) 12 I) 3 J) 0 N) 4 O) 8 S) 11 T) 9 U) 6 W) 2

When it is full!

2. a) 12 b) 16 c) 24 d) 22 **3.** 12 ÷ 2 = 6

Divide by 3 p. 61

1. A) 5 C) 1 E) 8 K) 11 L) 2 M) 7 O) 9 P) 12 R) 10 S) 6 U) 4 Y) 3

You crack me up!

2. a) 27 b) 24 c) 21 d) 9 **3.** 21 ÷ 3 = 7

Divide by 4 p. 62

1. A) 5 D) 12 E) 2 I) 10 L) 4 N) 1 O) 9 R) 3 S) 7 T) 8 U) 11 W) 6

It was run down!

2. a) 28 b) 20 c) 40 d) 4 **3.** 16 ÷ 4 = 4

Divide by 5 p. 63

1. A) 8 B) 2 E) 1 G) 9 I) 7 L) 5 N) 11 P) 4 R) 12 S) 3 T) 6 U) 10

A sunburnt penguin!

Answers

2. a) 60 b) 50 c) 40 d) 15 **3.** 35 ÷ 5 = 7

Divide by 6 p. 64

1. A) 4 E) 8 F) 2 G) 5 H) 3 K) 7 L) 1 O) 9 R) 12 T) 6 W) 10 Y) 11
Take away the letter g!

2. a) 54 b) 48 c) 18 d) 42 **3.** 48 ÷ 6 = 8

Divide by 7 p. 65

1. A) 9 C) 12 D) 6 E) 7 F) 2 L) 3 N) 8 O) 5 R) 11 S) 1 T) 4 U) 10
Tentacles of course!

2. a) 56 b) 35 c) 42 d) 70 **3.** 49 ÷ 7 = 7

Divide by 8 p. 66

1. A) 6 B) 3 C) 5 E) 4 L) 7 M) 9 N) 12 O) 2 P) 10 R) 8 S) 1 U) 11
An umbrella!

2. a) 24 b) 88 c) 64 d) 80 **3.** 64 ÷ 8 = 8

Divide by 9 p. 67

1. A) 5 B) 4 C) 8 D) 11 H) 2 I) 9 O) 6 R) 10 S) 3 T) 7 U) 1 V) 12
It had a virus!

2. a) 36 b) 72 c) 27 d) 45 **3.** 45 ÷ 9 = 5

Divide by 10 p. 68

1. A) 4 E) 8 G) 11 H) 3 I) 12 M) 2 O) 6 P) 1 R) 9 T) 5 U) 7 V) 10
The mooovie theatre!

2. a) 80 b) 30 c) 120 d) 70 **3.** 70 ÷ 10 = 7

Repeated Addition with Fractions p. 69

1. 1/6 + 1/6 + 1/6 + 1/6 = 4/6

2. 1/10 + 1/10 + 1/10 + 1/10 + 1/10 = 5/10

3. 2/8 + 2/8 + 2/8 + 2/8 = 8/8

Stating Ratios p. 70

1. a) 1:3, 1 to 3, 1/3 b) 2:3, 2 to 3, 2/3 c) 4:6, 4 to 6, 4/6 **2.** 5:1

Scaling Ratios p. 71

1. 4:6, 8:12, 2:3 **2.** 2:8, 4:16, 1:4 **3.** 5:10, 10:20, 1:2

Show What You Know! pp. 72–73

1. c **2.** d **3.** d **4.** d **5.** a) 7 b) 32 c) 7 d) 30 e) 24 f) 5 g) 3
h) 8 i) 10 j) 7 k) 24 l) 9 **6.** 1/5 + 1/5 + 1/5 + 1/5 = 4/5

7. a) 3:4, 3 to 4, 3/4 b) 2:5, 2 to 5, 2/5 **8.** 2:4, 4:8, 1:2

Exploring Patterns p. 75

1. a) 5588 b) △ ▽ c) ★ ○ ■

2. a) 5, 8, 11, 14, 17 b) 40, 60, 80, 100, 120 c) 100, 150, 200, 250, 300

Extending Patterns p. 76

1. 34 **2.** ◖◗ **3.** ☆◆ **4.** 50 75 **5.** ○ ■

6. ⇧ ⇩ **7.** 10 30

Translating Patterns p. 77

1. ABCABC clap, quack, stomp, clap, quack, stomp

2. AABAAB clap, clap, quack, clap, clap, quack

3. ABBABB clap, quack, quack, clap, quack, quack

4. AABBAABB clap, clap, quack, quack, clap, clap, quack, quack

Exploring Increasing Number Patterns p. 78

1. a) 20, 25, 30, 35 Start at 5 increase by 5 each time.
b) 37, 47, 57, 67 Start at 7 increase by 10 each time.
c) 250, 255, 260, 265 Start at 235 increase by 5 each time.

2. a) 24 b) 115 **3.** Answers will vary.

Exploring Decreasing Number Patterns p. 79

1. a) 400, 300, 200, 100 Start at 700 decrease by 100 each time.
b) 64, 54, 44, 34 Start at 94 decrease by 10 each time.
c) 225, 200, 175, 150 Start at 300 decrease by 25 each time.

2. a) 45 b) 695 **3.** Answers will vary.

Exploring Growing Patterns p. 80

1. a) ●●●● ●●●● ●●●●● ●●●●● b) Answers will vary **2.** □△ △ △ △ △ **3.** ◇ ◇ ◇ ◇ ◇ ◇☾

Exploring Shrinking Patterns p. 81

1. a) ■■■ ■■■■ ■■■■ b) Answers will vary. **2.** □□□□ □□□□ □□ □□□□

Exploring Pattern Attributes p. 82

1. a) orientation b) size c) orientation, size, colour

2. to 4. Answers will vary.

Input/Output Tables p. 83

1. a) 50, 100, 150, 200 b) 2, 4, 6, 8 c) 5, 10, 15, 20
d) 100, 200, 300, 400 **2.** 4, 8, 12, 16, 20, 24, 28, 32

Solving Pattern Problems pp. 84–85

1. No, she will finish one day after September 30.

2. 86 crayons in total. **3.** 9 weeks in total.

Show What You Know! pp. 86–87

1. 678 **2.** 

3. a) 175, 200, 225, 250. Start at 100 add 25 each time.
b) 84, 82, 80, 78. Start at 90, subtract 2 each time.

4. AABB, clap clap quack quack

5. **a)** 65, 61, 57. b) Start at 81, subtract 4 each time.
c) 40, 36, 32, 28, 24, 20

6. Answers will vary. **7.** a) 10, 20, 30, 40 b) 20, 40, 60, 80

Matching Expressions p. 89

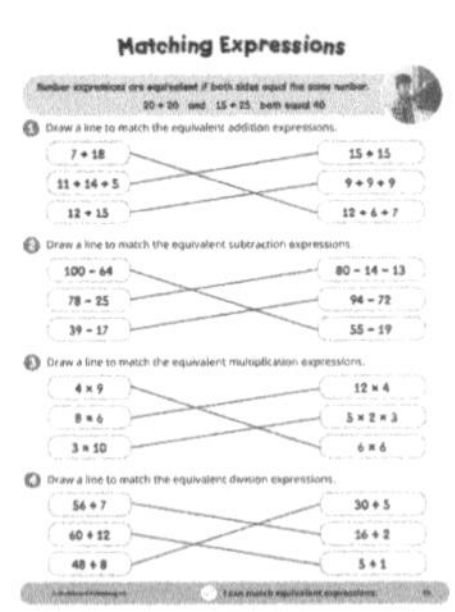

Exploring Variables p. 90

1. a) n b) y c) p **2.** a) $p = 22$ b) $m = 37$ c) $y = 15$

3. a) $30 - n = 18$ b) $n + 14 = 56$

Exploring Balanced Equations p. 91

1. a) ✓ b) ≠ c) ✓ d) ≠ e) ≠ f) ✓ g) ✓ h) ✓ i) ≠

2. a) 19 b) 10 c) 4 d) 8 e) 11 f) 78

Answers

Show What You Know! pp. 92–93

1. 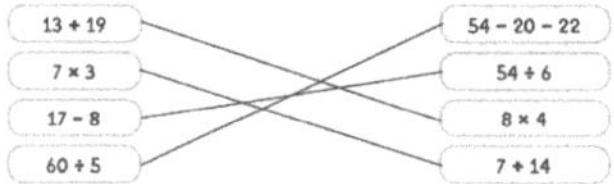

2. a) $m = 12$ b) $r = 13$ c) $n = 4$ d) $k = 12$ e) $p = 33$ f) $h = 27$

3. a) $n + 13 = 36$ b) $27 - n = 11$ **4.** d **5.** d **6.** b **7.** a **8.** c **9.** b

Introduction to Coding p. 95

1. Coloured Items: video game, cellphone, calculator, traffic light

2. and 3. Answers will vary.

Complete the Code p. 96

Answers may vary. Sample answers shown.

1. ↓→→→→ **2.** ←↓←←← **3.** ←←↓

Exploring Writing Code p. 97

Answers may vary. Sample answers shown.

1. Go right 4 spaces, go down 2 spaces, collect chick

2. Go up 2 spaces, go right 3 spaces, collect chick

3. Go left 5 spaces, go down 3 spaces, collect chick

4. Go up 3 spaces, go left 2 spaces, collect chick

Writing Concurrent Code p. 98

1. Girl: Go right 5 spaces, go down 1 space. 6 total spaces
Boy: Go right 3 spaces, go up 2 spaces. 5 total spaces

2. Girl: Go left 3 spaces, go up 3 spaces. 6 total spaces
Boy: Go left 6 spaces, go down 1 space. 7 total spaces

Exploring Loops p. 99

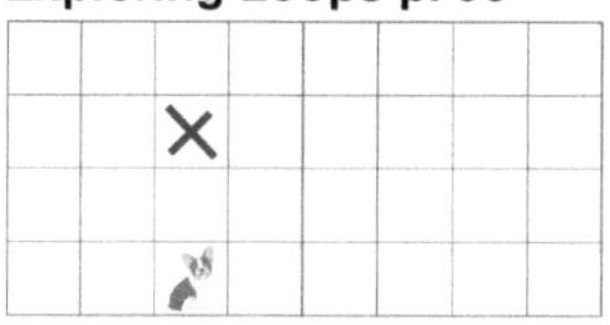

The Same or Different Outcomes p. 100

1. same outcome **2.** same outcome

Altering Code p. 101

1. Line 4: go left 1 space **2.** Line 4: Go up 1 space

Debugging Code pp. 102–103

Answers may vary. Sample answers shown.

1. a) Line 1: Move left 5 spaces b) Line 3: Move right 3 spaces

2. a) 3, 5, 1, 2, 4 or 3, 5, 2, 1, 4 b) 4, 1, 5, 3, 2 c) 2, 1, 4, 5, 3

Show What You Know! pp. 104–105

Answers may vary. Sample answers shown.

1. a) Go right 6 spaces, go down 3 spaces, collect duckling
b) Go up 2 spaces, go left 3 spaces, collect duckling

2. Line 3: go down 1 space

3. 

4. Line 2: move down 3 spaces

Exploring Venn Diagrams p. 107

1. school newspaper, chess, recycling

2. swimming, dance, track and field **3.** band, crafts

Sorting Using a Carroll Diagram pp. 108–109

1. Has more than 2 legs and can fly: bee, ladybug, fly
Has more than 2 legs and cannot fly: cat, lion, bear
Has 2 legs or less and can fly: duck, owl, cockatoo
Has 2 legs or less and cannot fly: fish, penguin, snake

a) 6 b) 3

2. Has 4 sides and is grey: A, G, J
Has 4 sides and is not grey: F, C
Has more than 4 sides and is grey: H, D
Has more than 4 sides and is not grey: B, I, E

a) quadrilaterals b) Students should choose any 3 of the following: star, octagon, pentagon, hexagon, cross. c) 5 d) 10

Exploring Tree Diagrams pp. 110–111

1. a) 8 b) 4 c) jeans, shorts d) sneakers, sandals

2. a) 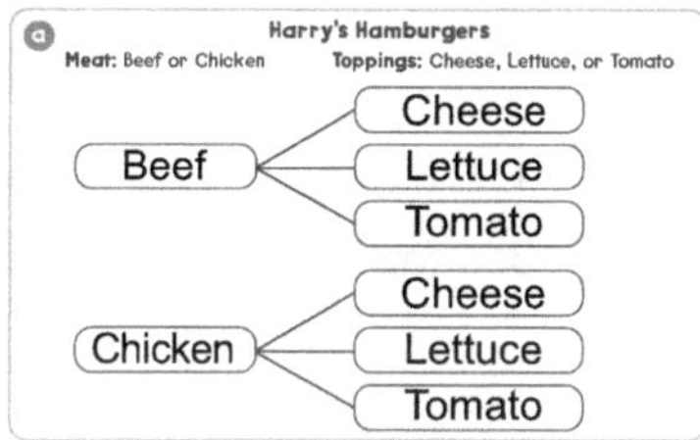

b) 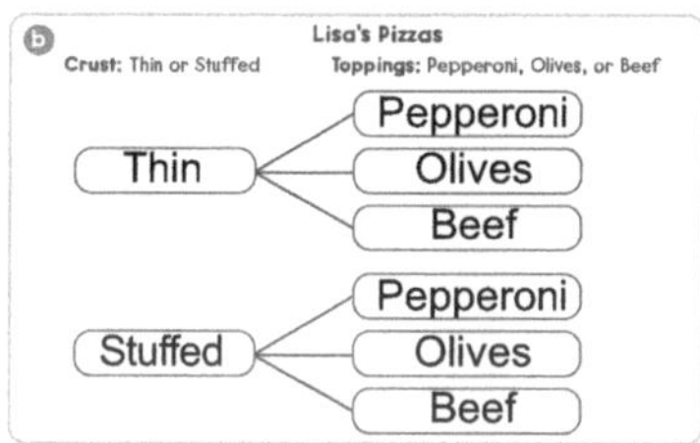

Organizing Data: Frequency Tables pp. 112–113

1. Red: 4 |||| Blue: 3 ||| Green: 7 ~~||||~~ || Purple: 4 ||||

a) green b) blue c) red and purple d) 1 more for red e) 18

2. Apples: 6 ~~||||~~ | Grapes: 3 ||| Pears: 1 | Kiwis: 5 ~~||||~~
Cherries: 5 ~~||||~~

a) apples b) pears c) kiwis and cherries d) 2 less for grapes e) 9

Reading a Pictograph p. 114

1. 2 books **2.** Class 3 **3.** 2 books fewer **4.** 9 books

Exploring Pictographs p. 115

1. Chocolate **2.** Strawberry **3.** 22 **4.** 64 **5.** 58 **6.** 144

Exploring Bar Graphs p. 116

1. Bear **2.** Dog **3.** 40 **4.** 20 fewer **5.** Dinosaur

Reading a Bar Graph p. 117

1. Cherries **2.** Pears **3.** 6 **4.** 4 more **5.** 54 **6.** Oranges

Answers

Making Bar Graphs pp. 118–119

1.

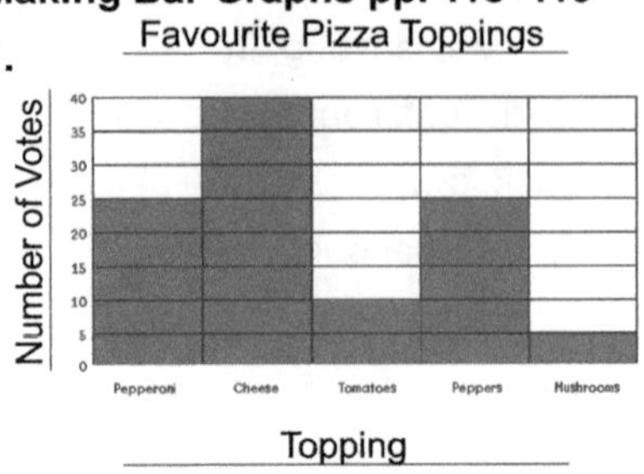

2. Answers will vary.

3. Graphs will vary, ensure students choose an appropriate scale and that data is correct.

Reading a Tally Chart p. 120

Dogs: 9 Cats: 6 Birds: 4 Lizards: 5

1. Dogs **2.** Birds **3.** Cats **4.** 24

Exploring Bar Graphs and Tally Charts p. 121

Nickels: 10 Dimes: 𝍸 𝍸 || Quarters: 9 Loonies: ||||

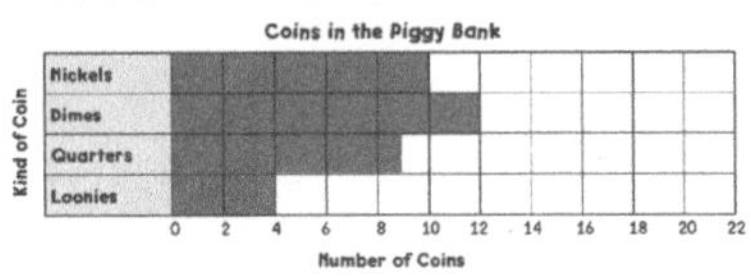

1. Dimes **2.** Loonies

3. 1 fewer **4.** 35

Exploring Mean p. 122

1. 3 **2.** 4 **3.** 7 **4.** 10 **5.** 4 **6.** 6

Exploring Mode p. 123

1. a) 5 b) 7 c) 8 d) 15 **2.** 30

Show What You Know! pp. 124–125

1. b **2.** a) 35 **3.** a) 7 b) 10

4.

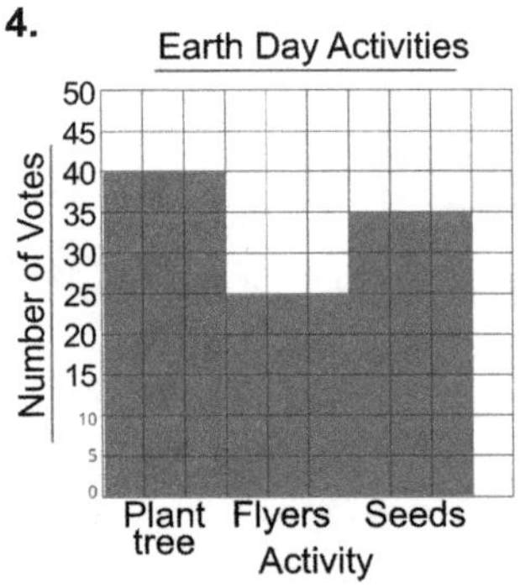

What Is Probability? p. 127

1. a) likely b) unlikely c) certain d) impossible

2. Answers will vary.

What Is the Probability? p. 128

1. a) likely b) likely c) impossible

2. a) unlikely b) impossible

Making Predictions About Likelihood p. 129

1. likely **2.** unlikely **3.** likely **4.** unlikely **5.** likely

Show What You Know! pp. 130–131

1. c **2.** a **3.** b **4.** Spinner 2

Matching Three-Dimensional Objects p. 134

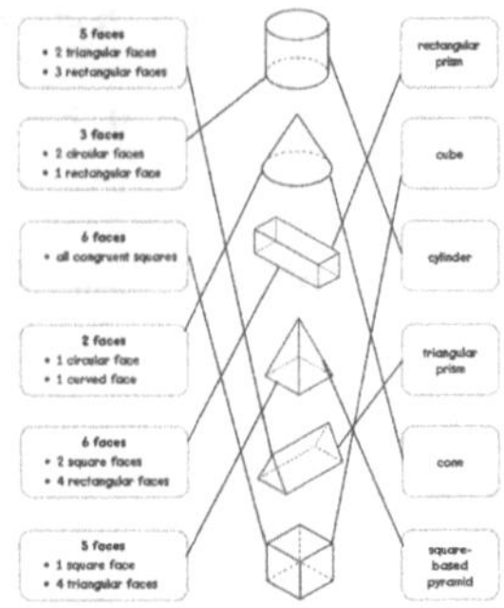

3D Objects: Edges and Vertices p. 135

1. Cube, 12 edges, 8 vertices

2. Triangular prism, 9 edges, 6 vertices

3. Rectangular prism, 12 edges, 8 vertices

4. Cylinder, 0 edges, 0 vertices

5. Cone, 1 edge, 1 vertex

6. Square-based pyramid, 8 edges, 5 vertices

Matching Nets p. 136

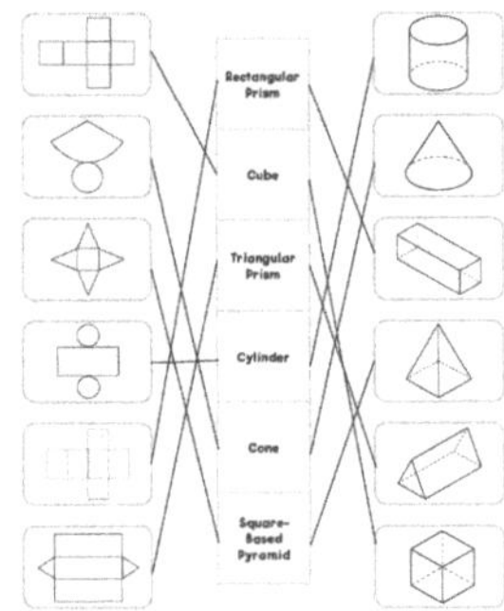

Sorting 2D Shapes and 3D Objects p. 137

2D Shapes: circle, rhombus, rectangle, triangle, square

3D Objects: square-based pyramid, cube, cylinder, cone, rectangular prism

Identifying 3D Objects p. 138

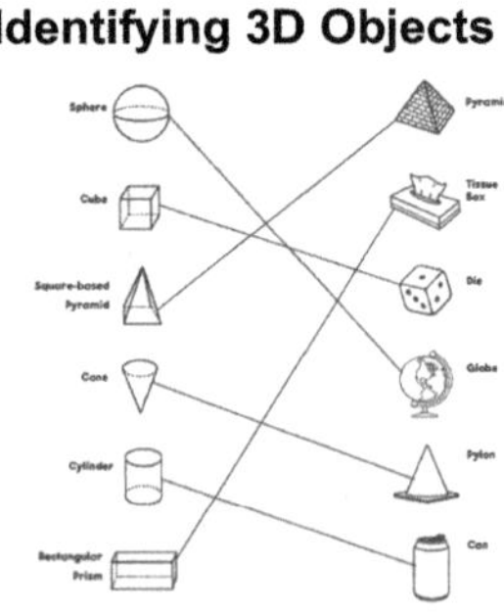

Exploring Polygons pp. 140–141

Triangle, 3 sides, 3 vertices

Square, 4 sides, 4 vertices

Rectangle, 4 sides, 4 vertices

Rhombus, 4 sides, 4 vertices

Parallelogram, 4 sides, 4 vertices

Trapezoid, 4 sides, 4 vertices

Pentagon, 5 sides, 5 vertices

Hexagon, 6 sides, 6 vertices

Octagon, 8 sides, 8 vertices

Answers

1. 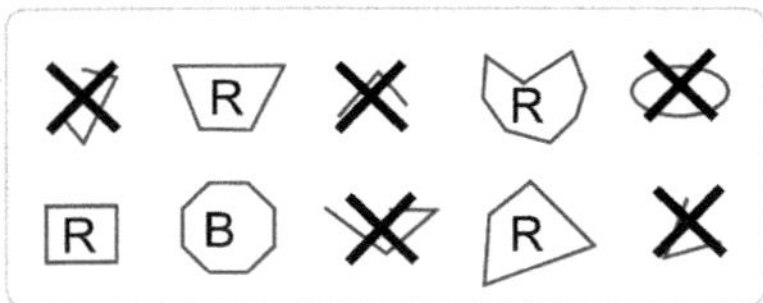

2. 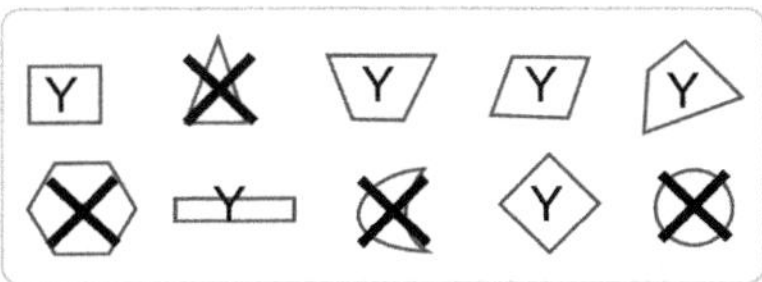

Sorting Polygons p. 142

more than 5 sides: 4, 3 4 vertices: 1, 8, 10, 9, 6

only 3 sides: 5 square corners: 9, 10

more than 1 set of parallel lines: 1, 4, 3, 8, 9, 10

Exploring 3D Figures p. 143

Sphere: 0 faces, 0 edges, 0 vertices

Cube: 6 faces, square, 12 edges, 8 vertices

Square-based pyramid: 5 faces, 1 square 4 triangular, 8 edges, 5 vertices

Cone: 2 faces, 1 circular 1 curved, 1 curved edge, 1 vertex

Cylinder: 3 faces, 2 circular 1 rectangular, 2 curved edges, 0 vertices

Rectangular prism: 6 faces, rectangular, 12 edges, 8 vertices

Exploring Symmetry p. 144

Exploring Congruent Figures p. 145

1. yes **2.** yes **3.** yes **4.** no **5.** no **6.** yes **7.** no **8.** yes **9.** no **10.** no **11.** no **12.** yes

Reflections, Translations, and Rotations pp. 146–147

1. a) translation b) rotation c) reflection d) rotation

2. Answers will vary.

3. a) reflection b) translation c) reflection d) rotation e) translation f) reflection g) rotation h) translation

Transformations in Everyday Objects p. 148

1. rotation **2.** reflection **3.** translation **4.** reflection **5.** rotation **6.** translation **7.** reflection **8.** rotation

Describing Turns p. 149

1. half turn **2.** quarter turn **3.** quarter turn **4.** half turn

Exploring Location and Movement p. 150

1. hedgehog **2.** deer **3.** 2 spaces right, 1 space down

Describing Movement on a Grid p. 151

1. 5 right, 1 up **2.** 3 left, 3 up **3.** 1 left, 2 down **4.** 4 right, 1 down

Describing Movement on a Map p. 152

1. south **2.** west **3.** south **4.** east **5.** north **6.** east

Performing Movement p. 153

1. 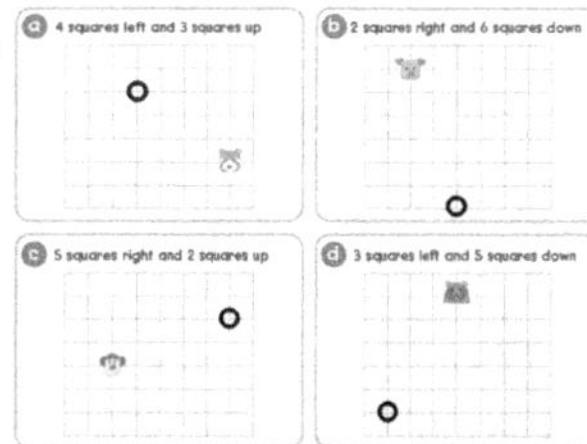

2. Answers will vary.

Show What You Know! pp. 154–155

1. c **2.** c **3.** a) 8 edges, 5 vertices b) 12 edges, 8 vertices

4. 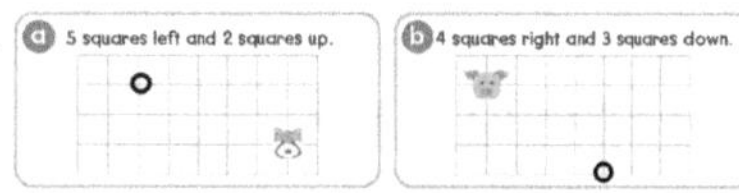

5. H, X

Exploring Perimeter p. 157

1. 12 **2.** 6 **3.** 14 **4.** 8 **5.** 10 **6.** 12

Comparing Perimeter: Polygons p. 158

1. E **2.** B **3.** A **4.** F **5.** E **6.** D

Drawing Perimeter p. 159

Answers will vary, ensure shapes have the correct perimeter.

Exploring Perimeter p. 160

1. 4 + 4 + 4 + 4 = 16 units **2.** 8 + 6 + 5 = 19 units

3. 9 + 6 + 4 + 8 = 27 units

Finding the Perimeter: Polygons p. 161

1. 3 + 3 + 3 + 3 = 12 cm **2.** 8 + 2 + 8 + 2 = 20 cm

3. 4 + 4 + 4 + 4 + 4 = 20 m **4.** 9 + 6 + 7 + 6 = 28 cm

5. 5 + 5 + 5 = 15 cm **6.** 2 + 2 + 2 + 2 = 8 m

Perimeter Word Problems pp. 162–163

1. a) 8 + 5 + 8 + 5 = 26 m b) 12 + 12 + 12 + 12 = 48 m c) 9 + 6 + 12 + 8 = 35 m

2. A = 15 + 7 + 15 + 7 = 44 m

B = 4 + 2 + 4 + 2 + 4 + 2 + 12 + 2 = 32 m

Playground A has the larger perimeter

Exploring Area pp. 164–165

1. a) 10 b) 8 c) 14 d) 8 e) 6 f) 9 **2.** Answers will vary.

Comparing Area pp. 166–167

1. a) shapes 1 and 3 b) shapes 2 and 3 c) shapes 1 and 3

2. Garden 1 = 25 Garden 2 = 27 Garden 2 is 2 units larger.

Finding the Area pp. 168–169

1. a) 5 × 3 = 15 units b) 4 × 4 = 16 units c) 3 × 1 = 3 units d) 5 × 2 = 10 units

2. a) 3 × 2 = 6 units b) 4 × 2 = 8 units c) 7 × 3 = 21 units d) 6 × 3 = 18 units e) 5 × 4 = 20 units f) 7 × 2 = 14 units

Finding the Area of Polygons pp. 170–171

1. a) 3 × 10 = 30 cm^2 b) 7 × 7 = 49 m^2 c) 5 × 5 = 25 cm^2 d) 9 × 8 = 72 cm^2 e) 6 × 1 = 6 m^2 f) 4 × 4 = 16 m^2

Answers

2. a) 5 × 3 = 15 m^2 b) 9 × 10 = 90 cm^2 c) Thea

Estimating Units of Length pp. 172–173

1. a) centimetres b) metres c) millimetres d) metres e) kilometres f) centimetres

2. a) 6 centimetres b) 2 kilometres c) 9 millimetres d) 14 centimetres e) 6 kilometres f) 9 millimetres g) 9 centimetres h) 20 centimetres

Units and Tools for Measurement p. 174

1. a) centimetres b) metres c) kilometres d) metres e) metres f) centimetres

2. flour - measuring cup weight of apples - scale temperature - thermometer length of string - ruler

Measuring with Centimetres and Metres p. 175

1. Answers will vary.

2. 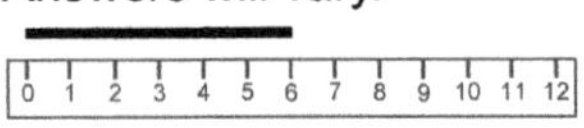

3. 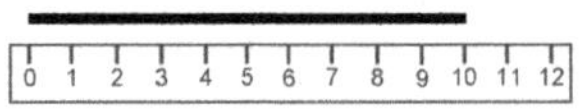

Converting Measurements p. 176

1. a) 1 cm, 20 mm, 30 mm b) 100 cm, 200 cm, 3 m c) 1 km, 2000 m, 3000 m

2. a) 3000 m b) 500 cm **3.** a) 45 cm b) 600 km **4.** 250 cm

Exploring Various Units of Length p. 177

1. a) 2 m b) 9 cm c) 300 cm d) 40 mm **2.** Stacey is not correct.

Exploring Mass pp. 178–179

1. a) mg: 1000 mg, 3000 mg, 4000 mg, 6000 mg, 8000 mg, 9000 mg; g: 2 g, 5 g, 7 g, 10 g
b) g: 2000 g, 4000 g, 5000 g, 8000 g, 10 000 g; kg: 1 kg, 3 kg, 6 kg, 7 kg, 9 kg

2. a) 3000 g b) 7000 mg c) 1 kg

3. a) 130 kg b) 100 g c) 2 kg d) 16 g e) 210 g f) 2 kg

4. a) 275 g b) 5 kg c) 1 kg

Exploring Capacity pp. 180–181

1. mL: 2000 mL, 3000 mL, 5000 mL, 7000 mL, 8000 mL L: 1 L, 4 L, 6L, 9 L, 10 L

2. a) 2000 mL b) 4 L c) 7000 mL

3. a) 2, 1, 3 b) 3, 1, 2

4. a) 2 mL b) 70 L c) 200 mL d) 75 mL e) 125 L f) 2 L

Show What You Know! pp. 182–183

1. a) 5 + 7 + 8 + 7 = 27 cm b) 9 + 4 + 9 + 4 = 26 cm

2. a) 8 × 4 = 32 cm^2 b) 3 × 3 = 9 m^2

3. 25 × 7 = 175 cm **4.** b **5.** d **6.** b **7.** a

Telling Time on a Digital Clock p. 185

1. 7, 18 **2.** 2, 41 **3.** 11, 37 **4.** 9, 05 **5.** 1, 26 **6.** 5, 50 **7.** 10, 09 **8.** 4, 12

Writing Time on a Digital Clock p. 186

1. 12:20:44 **2.** 8:57:01 **3.** 3:17:35 **4.** 6:09:24 **5.** 10:45:11 **6.** 1:33:50 **7.** 5:10:26 **8.** 7:03:42

Measuring the Passage of Time p. 187

1. a) 12:35 b) 8:15 c) 3:20 d) 10:50 e) 5:30 f) 9:30

2. a) 5:40 p.m. b) 4:15 p.m.

Exploring Elapsed Time p. 188

1. 3:35 to 4:35, 60 mins **2.** 12:25 to 1:25, 60 mins **3.** 4:15 to 6:20, 125 mins

Exploring Calendars p. 189

1. November 25 **2.** November 26 **Brain Buster:** 21, 365, 48, 10

Exploring Temperature p. 190

1. 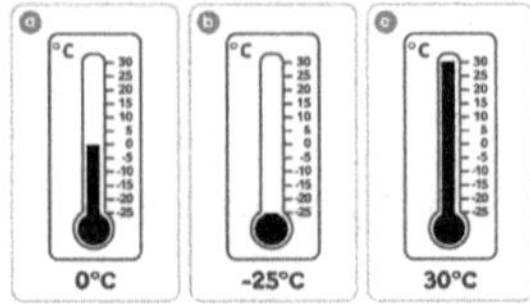

2. a) 18°C b) –20°C

Show What You Know! p. 191

1. a) 8:35:23 b) 2:14:12 **2.** a) 10:50 b) 3:20 c) 12:35

3. a) 110 b) 2:25 c) 120

Methods of Payment p. 193

Answers will vary. Ensure students choose reasonable methods.

Counting Canadian Money p. 194

1. Bottom group **2.** Bottom group **3.** Bottom group **4.** Top group **5.** Bottom group **6.** Bottom group **7.** Top group **8.** Top group

Showing Money Amounts in Different Ways p. 195

Answers will vary. Ensure students show the correct amount.

Matching Bills to Price Tags p. 196

1. $76 **2.** $100 **3.** $55 **4.** $201

Exploring Transactions p. 197

1. Answers will vary. Ensure students don't spend more than $20.

2. $2.55

Financial Literacy Word Problems pp. 198–199

1. No they don't, they should receive $1.65. **2.** Tia spends $6 more. **3.** a) 8 boxes b) $16

Show What You Know! pp. 200–201

1. d **2.** d **3.** a **4.** d **5.** b **6.** b **7.** a **8.** d